Transmedia Television

Transmedia
Television

New trends in network serial production

M. J. CLARKE

B L O O M S B U R Y

NEW YORK • LONDON • NEW DELHI • SYDNEY

Bloomsbury Academic

An imprint of Bloomsbury Publishing Plc

175 Fifth Avenue	50 Bedford Square
New York	London
NY 10010	WC1B 3DP
USA	UK

www.bloomsbury.com

First published 2013

© M. J. Clarke, 2013

Library of Congress Cataloging-in-Publication Data
Clarke, M. J. (Michael Jordan), 1979-
Transmedia television : new trends in network serial production / by M.J. Clarke.
p. cm.
Includes bibliographical references and index.
ISBN 978-1-4411-6552-7 (pbk. : alk. paper) – ISBN 978-1-4411-8300-2
(hardcover : alk. paper) 1. Television series – United States.
2. Television – Social aspects – United States.
3. Convergence (Telecommunication) 4. Mass media. I. Title.
PN1992.8.S4C53 2012
791.450973 – dc23

ISBN: HB: 978-1-4411-8300-2
PB: 978-1-4411-6552-7

Typeset by Newgen Imaging Systems Pvt Ltd, Chennai, India
Printed and bound in the United States of America

For Bam Bam

Contents

Acknowledgments

This book would have been impossible without the guidance and support of countless collaborators. Specifically, this project was formed and drafted through the unflagging assistance of my two mentors: John Caldwell and Denise Mann. Also invaluable was the advice and direction given to me by Steve Mamber, Gabriel Rossman, and Kathleen McHugh.

While composing this book's numerous drafts, I also relied on the support and interest of friends and colleagues: Juli Kang, Sudeep Sharma, Eric Slattery, Casi Slattery, Eric Vanstrom, Alesia Weston, Laurel Westrup, and Heidi Zwicker.

Also I owe a particular debt of gratitude to the media professionals who over the years have taken time out of their schedules to talk to me about their work. It is my hope that the following does justice to the complexity and nuance of their creative lives.

I would also like to thank my parents for their unquestioning support, my two brilliant brothers, Aaron and Chris, for their love and humor, and Ester Dela for being my everything.

A version of Chapter 2 appeared as "The strict maze of media tie-in novels" in *Communication, Culture & Critique* 2(2009): 434–56. And a version of Chapter 5 appeared as "*Lost* and mastermind narration" in *Television and New Media* 11(2): 123–42.

Introduction

Depending on which expert you cite, US network television is either drawing its dying breath or is mutating into something radically different. Regardless of the relative accuracy of either description, change in the everyday organization of work of fictional television programs is evident. Throughout this book, we will examine a recent trend in network television programming, which I call tentpole TV[1] that has, depending upon which narrative one follows, either sought to avoid this premature death or accelerate the medium's evolution by experimenting with alternative organizational and creative forms, aggressively incorporating what Henry Jenkins (2006) has called transmedia, texts that expand entertainment properties across multiple platforms. Through the following chapters, we will investigate both the opportunities and problems associated with this practice for affiliated creatives and the way their resultant transmedia texts find solutions and, further, reflexively comment upon the very institution of expanding television in this transitional phase. To this end, the following will combine an examination of industrial and popular press representing the world of these transmedia workers as well as that of the creative core of fictional television, its writers, with the provisional conclusions from a series of interviews with transmedia professionals. And to this, we will amend brief textual analyses of tentpole TV programs and transmedia texts that, as we shall observe, simultaneously reflect and reflect upon the problems associated with dispersal of managed creativity across multiple platforms.

After establishing the imperiled economic destiny of US network television, this introduction will highlight the business case for one possible mode of production, namely the distribution of branded, creative roles across a number of workers and across a number of platforms, a technique we will call tentpole TV. Addressing the esteemed World Economic Conference in Davos, Switzerland, in 2007, Microsoft chairman and software superbaron Bill Gates predicted that the internet would very soon devour the television stating, "I'm stunned how people aren't seeing that with TV, in five years from now, people will laugh at what we had" (Hirschler 2007). Far from the fevered speculation of an out-there futurist, Gates's opinions joined a chorus of commentators foreseeing great changes in the media landscape, including what will amount to the practical death of US network television.

Near concurrently with Gates's speech, *Television Week* and *Wired* both published their own preemptive obituaries, the former entitled the loaded query "Is Prime Time Past Its Prime?" (Atkinson 2007) and the latter encapsulated with the meager word play, "Youtube vs. Boob Tube"—the winner is self-evident (Garfield 2007). While the stakes and players of such conversations have changed, similar arguments echo earlier stirrings over convergence throughout the 1990s as television executives clamored over digital television and cyber gurus damned television as a Neanderthal art (Caldwell 2000: 9, 15). In fact, the debate has become something of a journalistic perennial recurring in a recent *New Yorker* cover story "Can Youtube kill television?" (Seabrook 2012).

More specifically, both the *Television Week* and *Wired* pieces cite drastic changes in the business of advertising, which historically has been the principal economic engine of network television. Both articles suggest that, due to the increasing nonlinearity of television consumption that both time-shifts with the DVR (digital video recorder) and device shifts through multiple screens, the slowing inflation of television advertising rates, and the growing demand for "smarter," demographically sensitive online spots, this may be changing. The *Wired* piece includes the stronger wording, referring to television advertising as a "vortex of ruin." Blame is squarely rested upon the previously stabilizing institutions of television ratings whose numbers and calculations have traditionally been used to establish on-air value and now have been left chasing the itinerant television watcher who can no longer be relied upon to consume television at a preordained time, at a preordained place, or even through a preordained device, thus avoiding the industry's traditional metrics. In response, the preeminent ratings institution, Nielsen, in the last several years, has employed new methodologies for adding numbers, tracking the habits of college dorm sets (Learmonth 2006), integrating data on DVR consumption along with traditional live viewership (Gough 2007), and purchasing diverse research firms specifically geared toward monitoring media use in other devices, cellular phones in particular. President for media product leadership at Nielsen, James M. O'Hara, described the firm's new aggressive (desperate?) mandate in a recent *The New York Times* article, stating, "I want your TV, I want your Internet, here's a cell phone you're going to use and, by the way, I want to measure your grocery purchases" (Story 2008). What these complications underline is that the business of television, of course, is no longer just about selling viewers to advertisers.

Yet another television doomsayer, *Wired* editor Chris Anderson, acting as the keynote speaker at the 2007 NATPE (National Association of Television Program Executives) conference, solemnly informed the entire television industry that, "you don't have megahits . . . [that] the blockbuster is a diminishing part of the market as demand is distributed on a vast amount of products" (Nordyke 2007). In his speech, Anderson was riffing on his hugely influential business book *The Long Tail* (2006) in which the author discusses a "supply chain revolution" bought by innovations in digital storage and distribution that allows for an infinite amount of shelf space and an infinite range to demand. Anderson suggests that nearly all goods, no matter how obscure, will sell at least a few units when brought to this virtual market and, what's more, they will make money given the streamlined, lean use of e-business strategy. The larger thesis of his book is that the sales of the mass of these nearly infinite niche goods, what Anderson calls the "long tail," outnumbers the volume of sales for mainstream hits. Thus, thousands of blogged video podcasts, taken collectively, do better numbers than *CSI*.

However, I would argue that a certain trend within network television production suggests that the so-called blockbuster is not dying, but may be evolving to meet the challenges cited by those prefiguring the television's death, and in ways not altogether contradicting Anderson's own observations. In fact, just as pundits and commentators such as Anderson split so much ink over television's crumbling edifice, *Variety*'s Ted Johnson (2006), in his review of television's new Fall season, made an ironic discovery with regard to the business of television production; namely that:

> they [that year's new programs] are some of the priciest new dramas in what may be the most expensive TV season in history as studios pull out all the stops with intricate storylines, sweeping scope, large casts and $10 million marketing blitzkriegs, all in a effort to grab viewers' attention . . . their [TV executives'] business is starting to resemble the film industry where studios invest heavily in tentpoles that have one big opening weekend to prove themselves.

In this article, Johnson singles out drastic cost increases in television production as a desperate attempt to hold onto flagging ratings and flat advertising rates, only giving partial credit to his own analogy to the film industry. Just as tentpole film tactics are only in part designed to secure the opening-weekend bonanza, tentpole TV is only partially about ratings. This characterization forgets all the attached media buying and selling that accompanies these blockbusters. In his book, Anderson also describes the vital role of so-called filters that drive demand down the long tail, that is to more and more obscure niche products. The filters mostly addressed are, unsurprisingly, online ones such as user recommendation metrics on long-tail-exploiting internet businesses like Amazon, Netflix, and iTunes. These sellers can use the data of prior transactions to suggest purchase of goods that, all things being equal, are more obscure. What Anderson's online examples ignore is the way in which pre-existing intellectual properties and branded entertainment can too act like a filter and push demand down the tail. Tentpole TV follows just this tactic, exploiting the streamability of content to entice consumers into subsequent transactions. Streamability is a term coined by new media theorist Simone Murray (2005) to describe the way in which entertainment products have increasingly been made to be more replicable and more transferable. I argue that the use of long-tail economics does not eliminate the blockbuster in television, but gives rise to this other trend that, by moving content and affiliated content through multiple channels, allows the filter of the program brand to soak up Anderson's fabled latent demand all the way down the long tail. For example, one can consider the ABC program *Lost*, which hypothetically amasses the largest share of its revenue from its traditional on-air advertising, a little less from DVD sales, a little less from online advertising on affiliated websites, a little less from share of profits from licensed video games, a little less from licensed novels, magazines, and others. It is not unreasonable to suspect that in combining all of these services and products associated with *Lost*, one could construct a model of distribution not dissimilar to the long tail with demand progressively shrinking, but always present all the way down to, for example, the *Lost* candy bar (also known as the Apollo Bar). Thus, while Anderson's argument is essentially about filters expanding the importance of niche products in single industries, tentpole TV, I argue, demonstrates how brand filters can also aggregate demand across a number of niche products revolving around a single textual orbit.

More specifically, tentpole TV producers, through their use of serialized narrative and transmedia extensions, create programs serving as excellent examples of what economists have called beneficial addictive goods. The theory of beneficial addiction was first introduced by Nobel laureates Gary Becker and George Stigler (1977) in their attempt to bring taste within the study of profit-maximizing, that is, economic behavior. In this canonical essay "De gustibus non est disputandum," the authors argue that there is a special set of goods that encourage subsequent usage rather than simply satisfy a need. This phenomenon was explained by what the authors called "consumption capital," which simply means that time spent with a beneficially addictive good—art serves as the authors' example—will enhance subsequent encounters. Therefore, the continued consumption of an addictive good becomes economically rational as continued patronage maximizes the utility of subsequent use. Moshe Adler (1985) elaborated on these theories in his own explanation of the phenomenon of stardom. In this article, Adler extended Becker's and Stigler's claims by insisting that consumption capital is earned by a combination of experiencing, talking about and reading about the addictive good in question. Stardom then develops as consumers maximize their chances of easily finding critical discourse around the good and, thus, maximizing their time investment in it. Tentpole TV replicates this model through its serialized and expanded narratives whereby the more you consume (and, in the process, the more you are either sold to advertisers or the more you pay for additional content), the more you get out of what you watch. All the narrative elements of these programs from character motivation—who is CTU's mole in Season One of *24*—to details of art direction—why is there an ancient Egyptian statue on *Lost*'s mysterious island—are delayed and extended across the episodes and their transmedia manifestations. In an economic sense, the more a viewer invests time and money in these texts, the more consumption capital is accrued and the more valuable are subsequent encounters with the text in all its forms.

In expanding tentpole narratives beyond the confines of the on-air series, producers have used a pricing model similar to that described by economist Walter Oi's (1971) discussion of two-part tariffs. In this essay, Oi examines the two-part tariff system, one in which consumers essentially buy the right to further purchase goods, and suggests, as an example, it would be an ideal model for admission to Disneyland. Briefly, Oi states that consumers should be priced a sliding tax for entry based on their willingness to subsequently pay for individual rides: Those deeply interested in rides would pay a low tax while those not interested in rides would pay a high tax. The obvious problem with such a model is that it is for practical purposes discriminatory. In the tentpole TV adaptation of the model, viewers pay the initial tax through their time investment in the on-air series giving them the necessary knowledge and interest to buy or invest time in subsequent, transmedia manifestations. In essence, audience members self-sort themselves into groups more or less willing to pay for ancillary texts or "invest" in repeat viewings. Tentpole TV consumers then resemble more Oi's secondary description of IBM machine renters who paid a lump sum to rent an IBM machine that gave them permission to use this machine up to a certain amount of time at which point an additional fee activates. The twist in the case of tentpole TV is that while photocopiers have a marginal cost of esentially zero for producers, the cost and difficulty of coordinating and producing transmedia is, as we will see, substantial.

Tentpole TV is not simply the panicked response to a crisis-laden industry but is also clearly a well-considered strategy lying at the vertex of two large-scale shifts in the business of television: one having to do with the evolving nature of television as a mass medium and the other having to do with the place of television within the increasing conglomeration of so-called Big Media. In his important essay, "On Edge," Michael Curtin (1996) describes a fundamental sea change in the work of cultural industries moving from a Fordist to a post-Fordist model. In the former, stability in network television structure, relatively free from outside competition, resulted in programming regularized in national schedules and engineered to maximize audience by utilizing the famous least-objectionable standard of quality. This stasis was challenged, beginning in the 1970s, thanks largely to the development of several domestic entertainment technologies in tandem with the consumer and business practices associated with them, moving from cable and the VCR to the internet and DVRs. Curtin isolates the net result of these innovations as the fragmentation of the mass audience into any number of exclusive or overlapping niches. Responding to and participating in this altered cultural climate, networks and affiliated studios diversified their products, seeking to provide a plentitude of choices. Curtin uses the industrial lingo "edge" to describe the practice of making this more diverse content that, while targeted and positioned toward specific audience groups, has the potential and consequent effect of alienating an audience not preimagined by media makers. The introduction of the Fox Broadcasting Network, a terrestrial broadcaster whose success was initially won by placing a clear "prominence on programming tailored to a young, urban audience," serves as Curtin's most instructive example (189). At the same time of the formation of this new fourth network, the big three (ABC, CBS, and NBC), too, began to experiment more in narrowcasting, engineering programs to appeal directly to upscale audience with high cultural intertextual references and self-referential humor (*Moonlighting* [ABC, 1985–9], *Twin Peaks* [ABC, 1990–1], *Northern Exposure* [CBS, 1990–5]).

More recent thinkers (Johnson 2007, Lotz 2007a) further suggest an additional shift in mode of network television production, moving from a model of mass production to one of niche production to a new era of branding where niche hits are exploited to both establish network identity and generate multiple revenue streams. The theoretical history then moves from a model of a factory of mass production, to a model of an interlocking system of niches, to a model of networks as "program aggregators" (Lotz 2007a: 254) that attempt to amass brands to fill their far-reaching portfolios.

What many critics have referred to as cult television programs, from *Star Trek* to the *X-Files*, have best achieved this textual modularity, that is the ability for texts to be broken down into separate, exploitable narrative elements to be streamed in multiple media channels. However, an exact, useful definition of cult television has been elusive. In his attempt to synthesize the diverging work on the topic, Matt Hills (2004) isolates three interlocking tendencies in definitions of the term: cult TV as a function of texts, cult TV as a function of intertexts, and cult TV as a function of fandom. Similarly, in their own attempt to define the topic, Sara Gwenllian-Jones and Roberta Pearson (2004) discuss this same interaction among texts, intertexts, and fans, stating:

> Seriality, textual density, and, perhaps most especially, the nonlinearity of multiple time frames and settings that create the potentially infinitely large metatext of a cult television text create the space for fans to revel in the development of characters and long, complex narrative arcs both within the commercial texts and their own, non-commercial spin-offs. (xvii)

However, what these scholars ignore is the manner that cult TV is also a mode of production, one that deeply accords with the theoretical history outlined above. Cult TV is, similar to demographic narrowcasting, a way of presorting audience through exploiting exactly the sort of programming expectations laid out by Gwenllian-Jones and Pearson. However, in cult TV, the gamble is not simply, as in Curtin's edge, the sacrifice of the mass audience for a niche audience, but the potential sacrifice of mass audience through textual and genre markers to address a very specific audience, one that is notoriously loyal and dedicated in its fandom, consuming all affiliated, branded media and posing as active brand advocates in peer groups. In their examination of cult TV, Michael Epstein, Jimmie L. Reeves, and Mark C. Rodgers (1996) isolate these enthusiastic fans as the telling feature of form stating, "what distinguishes cult shows from typical fare is that a relatively large percentage of the viewers are avid fans and that these fans have relatively high visibility compared to the avid fans of other shows" (27). The courting of enthusiastic fans is precisely the same impulse driving contemporary tentpole feature film production's preference for preexisting genre material with a grounding in young-skewing, genre material (*Lord of the Rings*, *Spider-man*, *Transformers*, etc.) and their ability to drive active, preexisting, as well as new fans into multiple purchases across presold franchises.

In the wake of the initial success of ABC's *Lost* (2004–10) and NBC's *Heroes* (2005–10), networks aggressively sought the next cult TV hit, perhaps culminating in the 2007 fall season, where *Variety* reported that, "after going dark and moody last year, nets are loading up on fanciful fare, much of it with sci-fi tinges" (Adlain and Schneider 2007). This offhand comment captures an important element to cult TV's appeal, specifically that outside of the markers of seriality, intertextuality, and complex mythology; it is this tinge of something else, frequently drawn from genre traditions, that activates fan enthusiasm, constituting its value as cult. For example, the pilot for *Heroes* was given an early premiere before the fall 2005 airing at that same year's San Diego Comic Con, the world's premiere forum for all things cult. Months before the network premiere of the program, which is essentially an ensemble drama with a sci-fi tinge (they are all superheroes), *Heroes* was shown to a packed hall of 2,000 viewers with hundreds more reportedly turned away (Schneider 2006). These in-person viewers subsequently became online brand advocates helping the series to become an out-of-the-gate success. In this case, the program was engineered for and solicited to a very active audience at their annual gathering and enticed the viewers with a genre tinge, much in the same way that *Lost* flirts with hard science fiction and the supernatural and *Alias* flirts with soft science fiction and the paranormal. In other words, if *Northern Exposure* can be understood as yuppie bait (Caldwell 1995: 251), then tentpole TV series can be understood as "nerd bait," for lack of a better term. Moreover, the courting of cult TV gives networks the brands and filters to drive consumer demand down the long tail. Tentpole TV makers embodying an economic, an organizational, and an aesthetic technique of cultural production, institutionalize the cult TV mode of address by operationalizing many of the fan activities described by Jenkins's *Textual Poachers* (1992) (e.g. webisodes replicate fan videos, official websites replicate fan websites, etc.) as well as the taste for so-called fanciful fare and putting them under the corporate umbrella of Big Media.

Tentpole TV also owes its genesis to larger industrial and regulatory changes in the business of US network television whose mode of production was and continues to be retooled. Lured by a more lax regulatory environment that opened broadcasting to the open market and the luster of ever-increasing advertising rates, Big Media firmly integrated network television operations within its portfolios during the last 25 years. Beginning in 1985, Captial Cities purchased the ABC network for a reported US$3.5 billion (Kleinfield 1985), and the merged company was in 1995 purchased by the Walt Disney Company for US$19 billion (Fabrikant 1995). By the 2004 merger of NBC and Universal Studios, all network television broadcasters were financially affiliated with program producers in large media conglomerates. The synergy of producing studio and broadcasting network was enabled concurrently by the 1995 repeal of the Financial Interest and Syndication Rules (Fin Syn). The Fin Syn rules were designed by the FCC (Federal Communications Commission) in 1970 to protect independent producers and new entrants in the business of television production from monopoly practices of the then three US television networks by preventing the broadcast networks from owning their own programming and thus from benefiting in subsequent syndication deals, deals whose financial terms were directly influenced by a program's ability to remain on network schedules. The terms of the rulings sought to prevent networks from abusing their position as stewards of the television transmissions, which, by law, were only provisionally occupied by the network feed based on the support of the FCC license, and de facto forbade vertical integration in the business of television (Caves 2005: 187). Ironically, it was complaints of barriers to entry that led to the gradual dissolution and eventual repeal of the rule. Early in its inception, Fox Broadcasting featured programming with a strong participation by Fox itself as the producer, arguing that the denial of studio-owned product unduly disadvantaged the ability of a new network to compete with the big three. By 1995, the rules were officially abolished and the effect was almost immediate; by 2001, 35 percent of programs on network television were either fully or partially owned by the airing network (Caves 2005: 197).

Tentpole TV series and their exploitation through transmedia are heirs to this regulatory change and the resultant change in business practice as all the series are owned, or partially owned in the case of *24*, by their home networks and their parent studios. Having cleared ownership allows decision makers to exploit these programs in any number of multiple revenue streams cited by Lotz (2007a) and positions them as uniquely prepared to supply all the stuff of cult TV intertext. How aggressively and how successfully program producers take advantage of these internal synergies with the parent studio varies from case to case, as we will see in subsequent chapters. What is important for our purposes is simply noting the specific regulatory and industrial context that allows for the increased cross-platforming of network-owned properties.

However, using programs to sell more and more stuff down the long tail is not unique to this moment. The history of television is filled with ancillary and spin-off products from *Dragnet: The Board Game* to *The Secret Diary of Laura Palmer* (Lynch 1990). For example, in 1980, the animation firm Hanna-Barbera, working in association with Paramount Television, produced a cartoon series, loosely based on the hit program, *Happy Days*, entitled *The Fonz and the Happy Days Gang*. Voiced by a handful of actors in their original roles and staffed by none of the original program's creative staff, *The Fonz and the Happy Days Gang* told the story of the eponymous characters as they are trapped in a malfunctioning time machine. The series was organizationally, conceptually, and symbolically alienated from the original program; indeed, the principal concept behind the animated show was that the protagonists were struggling, in vain, to get back to the original circumstances, time, and place of the live action series—a goal that is never attained (the show was retooled before this could happen). The same sort of symbolic distancing and spatial alienation occurs in Filmation's animated *Gilligan's Planet* (based on *Gilligan's Island*), which blasts the castaways off into outer space, or Hanna-Barbera's *The Dukes* (based on *The Dukes of Hazard*), which sends the series leads out of Hazard county, globe-trotting through Episode 12, "The Dukes Do Paris," to Episode 18, "The Canadian Caper," and so on. Even a spin-off as fondly remembered as *Star Trek: The Animated Series* (Filmation 1973–4) had a difficult-to-track relationship with the franchise's creative core. Series director Bill Reed recently reported to me that over the course of his work on the series, he had no personal or creative interaction with show maven Gene Roddenberry or even program licensors Paramount Television.

As the result of questionable fidelity to source material as well as suspect actors in the supply chain, such pejoratively termed "knock-offs" have frequently been cast as villains in critical pieces and as the butt of jokes in popular media. In the first case, Eileen Meehan (2005), in her discussion of "transindustrial synergy," blames recycled intellectual properties as clogging up channels that could be better served providing alternative programming and giving voice to marginalized voices rather than simply being a mere celebration of rampant commercialism. At the same time, *The Simpsons*, a fairly reliable cultural barometer, frequently takes shots at the third-rate children's entertainer, *Krusty the Clown*, made to embody the worst aspects of television, celebrity, and this same commercialism. Cardinal among Krusty's many sins is his insatiable appetite for lending his image and his meaningless seal of approval to a series of inferior products, from the Krusty brand home pregnancy test, to the Krusty brand imitation gruel, to the very unappetizing, yet ubiquitous Krusty burger.

However, opinions of television's ancillary, off-hours have significantly softened as the economic fortunes of network television have shifted and a new breed of storytellers, eager to exploit multiple media channels, have been employed in key creative positions. Most importantly, Henry Jenkins's *Convergence Culture* (2006) introduced the critical term of transmedia, legitimating previously dismissed ancillary texts. High-profile network showrunners from *Lost*'s Carlton Cuse and Damon Lindelof as well as *Heroes*' Tim Kring have picked up on this theorization and have used it as justification in their own increased creative presence in everything from *Lost*'s ARG (alternative reality game) to *Heroes*' webcomics. In his examination of the textual universe of *The Matrix*, Jenkins briefly considers the problems of collaborative authorship and the increased complexity of the organization of creative labor, but these problems are largely untested in practice and unexamined in media studies, which has often preferred discussions of potentials rather than labor itself. Recently, NBC-Universal head Jeff Zucker commented upon the growing practice of transmedia in the field of network TV channeling biological metaphor stating, "all of these things have to line up early on in the food chain but not drive the creative" (Wallenstein 2008). Translated from management speak, Zucker is arguing that to be successful, transmedia must originate from the creative core of a series, constituting a 360° shift from the producers' common sense, as emblemized in the animated spin-offs of the past and offering a unique challenge to contemporary producers set on maintaining the prominence of television in a moment of so much doom-speak and handwringing.

In her three-part historiography of network television from mass media to niche media to branded media, Lotz (2007a) considers the current moment as one of creative, organization, and financial experimentation. Uncertain as to the proper economic model to drive television into the future, producers have, according to Lotz, commenced any number of alternative revenue models and financing structures from a return to sharing production costs with advertisers to selling television programs in their first run to consumers. Transmedia, too, is one more of these other revenue streams. In some cases, the products, unlike traditional television texts, are purchased outright. However, in other cases, tentpole producers have sought innovative partnerships with advertisers to fund this expansion. For example, when *Lost* producers created a series of apocryphal documentaries posted on the internet, "Mysteries of the Universe," they relied on the financial support of Kia motors as a sponsor, much in the same way that *24*'s made-for-cellular-phone mobisode *24: Conspiracy* was sponsored by the telecom firm Sprint.

By more closely incorporating these ancillary texts into business plans and story lines, tentpole TV presents several problems in the basic management of televisual labor: Who are your personnel, how is the their work to be coordinated, and the like. Considering just these sort of changes, journalist David Wolf began a recent *Broadcasting & Cable* think piece pondering, "what does the term 'television' mean?'" (2007). In the article, Wolf sees uncertainty in the future of the TV business given the flood of new entrants, from telecoms and new media, and new channels, from HD (high definition) to mobile. Like any number of contemporary business leaders, Wolf concludes by advocating the application of an industrial flexibility among media professionals to take advantage of new opportunities, bought mostly on digital technologies and increased connectivity. This evolution of television is echoed in academic television studies whose recent state-of-the-art work of television studies has posed the medium as existing "after television" (2004), "as digital media" (2011), and as having become "must click TV" (Gillan 2010).

This picture of television with shifting boundaries and an inconsistent set of personnel strongly echoes the observations of a certain strand of contemporary social thinkers who have turned away from the image of a powerful entity of a Society, capital S, built with stable formations that imprint culture on individuals in the manner of orthodox structuralism or functionalism, to examining the much more complicated, fluid arrangements of what we can call loose social bonds. This diverse set of theorists has considered the diminishing power of institutions to guide action (Bauman 2005), has more rigorously isolated the importance of individual practice in reconstituting these, now-fragile institutions (Bourdieu 1977, Giddens 1979), and has studied the consequences of the increasing atemporality and aspatiality of contemporary networked and individualized labor arrangements (Castells 1996). Despite vast theoretical differences and inconsistencies between these and like-minded thinkers, all are in agreement that, in the social science of the past, the solidity of social institutions, their inscribed roles, their stable boundaries, and their solid bonds were all overstated and that, in the words of Bruno Latour,

> [in social observation] it is crucial not to conflate all the agencies overtaking the action into some kind of agency—"society," "culture," "structure," "fields," "individuals," or whatever name they may be given . . . action should remain a surprise, a mediation, an event. (2005: 45)

Tentpole TV, I will argue, with its temporary individualized bonds between per-project creatives, with its unclear boundaries between native and other new media, with its shifting and evolving responsibilities for old and brand new, emerging professions, and with its experimental aesthetic forms that push and pull at the boundaries of a text, becomes a model illustration of just the sort of agglomerations referred to by theorists of loose social bonds and, in the process, a set of provisional responses to David Wolfe's central, open-ended query.

From its inception, television programming has been acknowledged as a writers' medium. Serialized dramas specifically are frequently attributed to writer–producers, known as showrunners (see *The Producers' Medium* 1983 and Wild 1999), who often contribute original story material to their programs and oversee the work of the other staffers employed by the series' writer's room. Not only have these hyphenates, such as J. J. Abrams or Stephen Bocchco, been credited as the creative locus of entire television programs, but they have also increasingly become part of their program's own intertext being profiled in the pages of the popular press in *Entertainment Weekly* features or in one of *Variety*'s perennial showrunner round tables. It is from this forum that tentpole TV showrunners have described both their changing role within television production and how it has been designed to answer to the medium's mounting challenges.

Of course, it is altogether unclear what the trend of tentpole TV ultimately means for the ever-changing, post-digital future of television production, a fact lampooned in a recent satirical *The New York Times* article that begins with a mock job announcement for an television executive who knows how to move content and how to "shovel it onto the Internet in a way that makes money" (Siklos 2006). Echoing and exemplifying the concerns of social theorists of loose bonds, tentpole TV makers have experimented with new job roles, functions, and organizational structures trying to pose solutions to exactly this riddle and, in the process, provide a new model for television production and textuality. Principally, by more actively overseeing the creative integrity of all of a program's off-air manifestations, the job of executive showrunner has evolved to, in the words of *Heroes'* Tim Kring, "managing a brand" (Kushner 2007). What this means is that showrunners hypothetically are not only responsible for just the production of scripts and the editing of episodes, but also for the maintenance of an entire textual world. For example, the *Lost*-themed mobisodes (original content for cellular phones), *Lost Missing Pieces*, were penned by series writers, featuring brief character moments, many implied in the on-air series—literally "missing pieces." What this means is that showrunners must pay increasingly careful attention to these unarticulated gaps and ellipses in the on-air program, textual aporia that can become the source of the next transmedia text. Such work, however, necessitates the existence of a more aggressive breed of creative managers and middlemen to oversee all the expanding manifestations of the core series. For example, *Wired* (Baker 2008) recently profiled the work of Leland Chee, Lucasfilm's "continuity cop," whose job is nothing less than providing "a reference for everyone who was playing in our sandbox," in this case the *Star Wars* universe. Similarly, *Lost* reportedly relies on its accountant-turned-writer Gregg Nations to maintain a ledger on all the minutiae of the intricate series. Showrunner Carlton Cuse described the staff's reliance on Nations's bookkeeping in a recent *The New York Times* article saying, "we quickly realized that we needed some system to keep track of all the details, that we weren't going to be able to do that by memory" (Wyatt 2009). Investigating how exactly tentpole TV showrunners manage all these details in their texts will be a major preoccupation of the remainder of this book.[2]

Traditionally, television studies has been concerned with theories of mass communication and manipulation (beginning with Katz and Lazarsfeld 1955), the humanistic interpretation of programming (popularized by Newcomb 1974), and the cultural studies analysis of television viewers' interaction with texts (inaugurated by Hall 1980 and Morley 1980). However, this book as a whole attempts to add to a new, growing tradition of television studies that has sought to examine the work of television production itself. Critic Horace Newcomb (2007) has recently commented that this other research trend is, in part, a response to the sort of transitions occurring in the business of television stated above, claiming that the increase in studies of television production,

is due in part to a recognition that production practices have never been quite so routine as some would suggest. It also results from the realization that some of these practices are in the process of change altered by developments in technologies, economic factors and the expansion of distribution outlets. (129)

Transmedia Television aims to provide a contribution to the what has recently been called the field of critical media studies (Havens et al. 2009), which "explore[s] the corporate dimensions of the media as a cultural system with its own tacit and explicit, yet contested rules, while connecting these to the actual production and operation of textual forms" (248). More specifically, I am writing in a particular tradition of studies of television production that integrates industrial data in the form of both business strategy and individual practice with textual data through the analysis of programming and suggests the ways in which programming trends replicate, complicate, or anticipate the conditions of production itself.

Several important works of the television studies of the recent past laid the foundations for such an approach. In Feuer, Kerr, and Vahimagi's *MTM: "Quality Television"* (1984), the authors endeavored to construct an industrial theory of collective authorship and, more broadly, attempted to reconcile textual production and the interpretation of meaning with business strategy. In the first case, the authors constructed a picture of a distinct MTM house style attributing repeated thematic and aesthetic elements not to exemplary individuals, but to the producing firm. Ironically, such an operation was achieved through an investigation of the firm's altered relations of production, in this case, in the changing status of the independent production and the showrunner's place in these firms. In the second case, causation for the development of this house style was traced back to a business change in network television which began in the 1970s to court more lucrative demographic-audience groups as opposed to a simple mass, aggregated audience.

John Caldwell's *Televisuality: Style, Crisis and Authority in American Television* (1995), providing another compelling antecedent for critical media studies of television, argues that vast changes in the look of television, understood largely as an increased stylization during the 1980s, were primarily influenced by practioner anxiety thanks to cable- and VCR-born retreats in network audience levels. Caldwell's book does not simply reconnect texts to their conditions of production in a linear fashion, but is an attempt to engage in what the author calls the -emic rather than -etic study of television. By this, Caldwell suggests that television studies should mine media artifacts, be they programs, promos, or technical guides, to reveal their native practitioners' logic, their Geertzian deep structures, rather than simply reapplying preexisting theoretical models. In other words, industry and text, insider information and semiotic analysis merge into one supertext to be mined for its own internal logic.

Interest in the production of television also implies a set of research methodologies, specifically incorporating sociological techniques of data collection about television workers and their practice. These techniques were largely popularized by *Inside Primetime* (1983) in which author Todd Gitlin conducted a series of interviews with television producers, writers, and executives in an attempt to deduce the field of television's latent "common sense." Gitlin was convinced that the actions of decision making, and not simply the texts produced, were the proper site for the analysis of television. However, by the end of his study, his picture of practical consciousness among television workers becomes nearly indistinguishable from a subtractive theory of ideology that limits and constrains expression of practioners, a theory derived from earlier Marxist-influenced television studies. Although Gitlin's results and conclusions are, in a sense, predetermined, his method, involving thin ethnography and interviewing coupled with a reading practice that integrated this empirical data not as offering privileged access to the "truth" of television production, but as indicating deeper structural truths in the manner of anthropological evidence, became highly influential on a tradition of scholarship in television studies that we can term ethnographically informed production studies and on the development of critical media studies of television.

Following in Gitlin's footsteps, Julie D'Acci's *Defining Women: Television and the Case of Cagney and Lacey* (1994), Laura Grindstaff's *The Money Shot* (2002), and Amanda Lotz's "Textual (Im)possibilities in the U.S. Post-network Era" (2007b) all incorporate vast access to production practices and cross-reference their fieldwork with a consideration of the textual possibilities of the medium. D'Acci, in her book, eschews more simple Marxist models of power and production when integrating her fieldwork, but instead, she situates her ethnographic data into narratives of Gramscian negotiation and hegemony between multiple parties arguing at cross-purposes, particularly concerning the representation of women in the series. The author finds that the program's producers voiced a liberal agenda interested in bringing women's issues in an enlightened manner to network television, while network executives were primarily concerned with the new demographically studied market of the single professional woman; however, both are ultimately cast as being subject to the perceived ideological constraints surrounding the proper image of women on television in a television series. In a study of television talk shows, Laura Grindstaff brings to bear her experience as a production staffer and participant observer on several of these daytime programs. Drawing on these observations, Grindstaff assembles a picture of television production as emotional labor where show producers work to prep and solicit bodily performances from their daily guests. The result is outrageous, uncouth displays that reinforce class stereotypes. In the author's words,

> the problem, however, is that producers believe that "those kind of people" [guests] are attracted to "that kind of display," rather than seeing "that kind of display" as partly an expression of the television's industry's assumptions about "those kind of people." (143)

More recently, Amanda Lotz's essay "Textual (Im)possibilities in the US Post-Network Era" was the product of sustained fieldwork around the production of cable net Lifetime's *Any Day Now* and resulted in findings very close to D'Acci's (and Gitlin's). Lotz similarly argues that a negotiated form of ideology is at play in the production of this series, which sought to incorporate tabooed subject matter surrounding issues of race and gender, but was ultimately constrained by the embedded traditions of television production. Despite the liberal–progressive impulse behind the program's production (indeed both D'Acci's and Gitlin's protagonists are equally well intentioned and ultimately misguided), it was, in Lotz's analysis, constrained by residual production values that shied away from the full deployment of "edge," that is niche productions that self-consciously restrict mass audience appeals for specific audience appeals. Each of these authors brings a wealth of sociological data to their projects, but always relates these observations back to texts and, in particular, the representations of class, race, and gender within them.

In both theory and method, these studies of television production echo the claims of sociologists working the production of culture and cultural industries traditions. The former was synthesized as an approach by Richard A. Peterson and N. Anand (2004) in their aptly named essay, "The Production of Culture Perspective." In this canonical work, the authors define their approach as one that "focuses on how the symbolic elements of culture are shaped by the systems within which they are created, distributed, evaluated, taught, and preserved" (311). Production of culture scholars see texts as the result of the intersecting influence of economics, organization, technology, individual careers, and government regulation at play in production. The approach has been fruitfully applied to any number of artistic endeavors from music (Peterson 1997), to literature (Griswold 1981), to painting (Baxandall 1972), to television (Bielby and Bielby 1994), to video games (Deuze and Martin 2007), to newspapers (Gans 1979), to comic books (Kinsella 2000). For example, Peterson's own book *Creating Country Music* (1997) argues that the sound of early country music cultivated by entrepreneurial talent scouts was driven by the need to find a music that sounded "traditional" but could be copyrighted (playing to the needs of economics, government regulation in production) and renewed (playing to the needs of the organization of production) unlike the storehouse of public domain tunes. Furthermore, in Griswold's (1981) essay, the author demonstrates that the so-called American character in US novels of the nineteenth century was more a result of an early copyright regime (again, regulation) that encouraged US publishers to differentiate their product (the demands of the market) from unprotected (and therefore cheaper) works of British authors. Overlapping with this tradition is an affiliated set of researchers who have examined the unique characteristics of so-called creative or cultural industries. These scholars have isolated the unique sociological (Becker 1984 [1982]), economic (Caves 2000), and organizational features (Hirsch 1991, Dimaggio 1977) that distinguish creative work from humdrum (Caves's term) endeavors.

Production of culture scholars provide a level of theoretical grounding as well as a holistic approach to the still young subdiscipline of studying television production and critical media industry studies more generally. However, for the purposes of this book, the school of thought is limited in two distinct aspects. These studies, from the perspective of television studies, are limited in terms of their discussions of texts themselves and they are limited in the types of connections that they establish between texts and their producers. In their seminal essay, "Cycles of Symbol Production" (1975), Richard Peterson and David Berger argued that there is a correlation between the level of industrial concentration in the music production business and the diversity and innovation of its output. It is a compelling analysis, but is hampered by its method of measuring this diversity, which is mostly detected by tracking the number of record firms that had number one hits in one calendar year; the more firms with hits, the more "diverse" the market. Of course, this method completely ignores substantial aesthetic features of the music itself. Such a shortcoming was remarked in Peter Alexander's (1996) own critique that valiantly substitutes the variable of diversity with his own "entropic" measure which granularly graded the musical qualities—their rhythm, their melody, and the like—of hit songs. However, even this vast step forward neglects any number of other qualities of the music that may be tremendously important from lyrical content to instrumentation.

To remedy these shortcomings, my work will synthesize the production of culture approach with the methods borrowed from the textual analysis of film. The consideration of textual form has traditionally been overlooked in television studies, a discipline often more interested in ideology and representation than form and narration. However, the visual and narrative sophistication of tentpole TV in all its manifestations begs this more minute analysis. Indeed, tentpole TV programs often veer into what could be called for lack of a better term formal experimentation. "Blow Back," an episode of *Alias* (Season Three, Episode 14), is constructed with a bisected structure where point of view flips characters halfway through the episode as the plot rewinds and replays all the events from the beginning. "The Constant," an episode of *Lost* (Season Five, Episode Four), features a series of flashbacks and flash-forwards wherein one character is aware of the nondiegetic jumps, in the manner of *Slaughterhouse Five* (Vonnegut 1971 [1968]). "Five Years Gone," an episode of *Heroes* (Season One, Episode 20), takes place in a hypothetical world 5 years ahead in story time that never comes to pass. Through these and any number of examples where these programs include vast temporal breaks of continuity and modernist repetition of events; confusion of the diegetic and non-diegetic events; as well as the inclusion of amotivated and cryptic characters, these programs resemble more art cinema than the three camera sitcom. To properly account for this complexity, I will rely on the work of film analysts (Burch 1973, Heath 1981, Branigan 1984, Bordwell 1985, Bellour 2000) who have examined how film form begets the narrational figures of time, space, and character.

The second danger of the production of culture approach is that the conclusions tend to be one-way in their causality. By this, I mean that, one, the conditions of production are cast as naturally producing the textual results without understanding the textual nuance of the result and, two, the conditions of production are, in a sense, depicted as outside and above the texts produced. What is needed is a measure of reflexivity (again borrowing from Giddens) as a way of understanding of texts not simply as the results of a set of pre-given conditions, but as being in conversation with these conditions, either butting against them or participating within them, but always implicitly commenting upon them. Overtures toward such an approach can be unearthed in Horace Newcomb and Paul Hirsch's (1994) classic essay "Television as Cultural Forum." In this classic piece, the authors advocate an understanding of television's "bardic function" in which the medium serves as a figurative discussion, or metalinguistic event that offers a "way of understanding who we are, how values are adjusted, [and] how meaning shifts" (503). While not primarily about producers, the essay does include a brief section on the makers of television who the authors insist are cultural interpreters. These interpreters produce texts that respond to and comment upon events in social reality, including the context of production itself. *Transmedia Television* shares this same attitude; however, we will constrain the idea's scope. More specifically, I will argue not that producers of tentpole TV are "bards" for the whole of society, but that they are cultural interpreters of their very specific, "native" production culture.

My understanding of industrial reflexivity is informed by the work of the interpretive anthropologist Clifford Geertz. In this author's essay "From the

Native's Point of View," Geertz (1976) argues that the analyst, no matter how deeply immersed she is in the society of her study, can never hope to truly empathize with the subjectivity of her objects of study, thereby debunking the fundamental myth of ethnographic fieldwork. Instead, Geertz contends that it is the anthropologist's task to interpret these subjectivities through a close examination of the subjects' cultural forms. Essentially, this is the task that I set out for myself in examining the industrial, organizational, and aesthetic forms of tentpole TV. By interpreting these interacting domains, one can craft a nuanced explication of a specific logic of practice, or an industrial "subjectivity." Elsewhere, Geertz (2000 [1973]) argued that cultural systems must be understood as both models of society, that is reflecting and reinforcing preexisting social order, as well as models for society, that is generating new and reconfiguring understandings of social order, saying that cultural expressions "both express the world's climate and shape it" (95). I will deploy exactly this theory to amend the shortcomings of the production of culture approach, suggesting that tentpole TV not only embodies the conditions of this difficult, transitional phase of contemporary network television, but also constitutes a running commentary by its producers on exactly this transition and how it should be navigated.

To do this, *Transmedia Television* will take very seriously the frequently dismissed world of ancillary media and its makers. By ancillary, I refer to the use of branded objects, concepts, or characters in artifacts outside a presumed original source. Largely under the radar of conventional television, film, and media studies, these objects have long been essential to the business of culture and, in the last 20 years, have begun to eclipse so-called first-run outlets in terms of economic importance. The centrality of ancillary profits has long been recognized in television, as deficit finance deals, which sink due to short-term losses in the hopes of long-term gains and have historically fuelled television production, and depend precisely upon so-called ancillary sales (see Alvey 1997).

Because the importance of ancillary products and sales is more convincing from the bottom-line perspective of business, texts addressing these objects have primarily drawn on political economic traditions. For example, Eileen Meehan in her essay "Holy Commodity Fetish, Batman" quantifies the vast sea of consumer products associated with the release of Columbia's *Batman* (1989). Meehan ultimately argues that the concept of Batman was bought and sold countless times between media firms and, only in the last instance, was "sold" to consumers. Similarly, Janet Wasko (2001), in her book *Understanding Disney*, investigates the synergistic effort accompanying the eponymous company's roll-out of *Hercules* (1997), which sought to maximize relationships within the Disney corporate umbrella (television stations/networks, radio stations, theme parks, etc.). Furthermore, Justin Wyatt (1994), in his book *High Concept*, provides a causal, historical argument for the rise of ancillary products, explaining that increasing corporate control and saturation releases in feature film distribution, which reduced films to a financial matter or sink or swim, necessitated the increased exploitation of the cross-promotional value of ancillary products. In other words, the use of these ancillary products in all of these studies is primarily understood as a function of changing business policy and organization. The decision to produce these artifacts and the deals fueling their production only in the last instance concern their content. Among these authors, only Wyatt makes the effort to investigate the distinct textual logic of these ancillary forms. However, Wyatt's analysis is essentially dismissive as all such products are primarily concerned with simplifying narrative and selling more stuff. This measured, critical condemnation is easily reconciled with a field (film studies) whose theoretical history is plagued with the so-called problem of the commodification of culture (dismissed in production of culture studies, which sees symbolic production as always implicated in an exchange market).

Conversely, the work of Henry Jenkins, particularly his important book *Convergence Culture*, has made the seemingly heretical claim that ancillary products should be studied as texts and not simply as crass money-making opportunities. In his book, Jenkins does not deny the economic imperative of cross-platformed transmedia, but claims that such a media ecology has equally led to expanded storytelling opportunities and complicated entertainment forms through co-creation, collaborative authorship, and uniquely new media forms. Jenkins finds such an example in the diverse media manifestations of the *The Matrix* phenomenon. To gauge, if not evaluate, such transmedia works, Jenkins introduces the criteria of the "origami unicorn" (a reference to *Blade Runner*)—the way in which an element in an ancillary text can make a consumer rethink the meaning of all other associated texts. In other words, the function of transmedia is expanded production of meaning, not expanded selling/marketing. In his consideration of professional transmedia production, Jenkins largely glosses the problems of creative labor and focuses on transmedia objects that seamlessly manage textual cohesion and singularity through their many manifestations. I agree with Jenkins's passion for opening up the ancillary as a legitimate object of study and his enthusiasm for the new storytelling possibilities of transmedia, but ultimately, this book will be more interested in how occupational, organizational, and industrial circumstances among television and its affiliated producers make Jenkins's elegantly composed multiplatform texts much more messy. More recently, Johnathan Gray (2010), in his own largely text-based consideration of transmedia, singles out this gap in his closing remarks stating, "the production cultures around paratexts [Gray's own term for multiplatforming properties] still need more study" (221).

These two attitudes toward ancillary media artifacts—political economic/textually dismissive and transmedia/textual celebratory—constitute diametrically opposed positions toward their possible object of study. The first sees ancillary artifacts as purely business maneuvers and the second presents the possibility of placing these artifacts in conversation with texts proper. It is my belief that both attitudes are ultimately correct, but need to be combined for a complete understanding of this increasingly important site of media production. Such a contention is skillfully investigated in John Caldwell's (2004) important essay "Convergence Television: Aggregating Form and Repurposing Content in the Culture of Conglomeration" in which the author expounds upon how combined discursive, industrial, and aesthetic changes constitute television's response to and participation in new media. In the case of transmedia, Caldwell discusses the practice of "conglomerating textuality" that includes the discursive deployment of buzz words such as "broadband" and "clutter"; the industrial upgrading of partnerships between television networks and new media dot.com's; and the development of online textual expansions for television programming around such themes as extended backstories, metacritical commentary, and, of course, merchandising opportunities. What remains important for my purposes is the way in which this essay (in discussion of websites associated with network programs) pays attention to both industry and text and to the way(s) that these two fields can be combined in the consideration of transmedia. Another laudable example can be found in Marc Steinberg's (2009) essay "Anytime, Anywhere: Tetsuwan Atomu Stickers and the Emergence of Character Merchandising." In this work, the author draws on Lash and Lury's (2007) understanding of contemporary media culture as a "media of things and a thingification of media" (25) to explain the transmedia work of making the Japanese animation icon, Astro Boy, ubiquitous. Steeped in the historical work of examining exactly how the image of Astro Boy was transformed into a sticker, Steinberg concludes with compelling theoretical arguments about the role that fictional characters play in enabling transmedia and the larger role that emerging transmedia has in mediazation of lived, social environments. In both these multifaceted examples, the authors examine transmedia as both an economic and textual phenomenon, an approach we will attempt to replicate in the following chapters.

The strength of these later approaches lies in their refusal to segregate the spheres of the economics and the aesthetic. Instead, these studies track these layers' complicated interactions in the work of cultural production. In our case of tentpole TV, these factors, in no particular order, interact, as our imperiled industrial model has encouraged a reexamination of the creative potential of off-air television, which in turn has changed the labor relations of television workers and so on. Recently, Jennifer Gillan (2010) also following this implicit approach has closely examined a similar set of network television programs closely considering the integration of transmedia and the dispersal of television texts across multiple media from the perspective of network decision making. It is my hope that this book will more aggressively include the point of view of transmedia workers in the consideration of this televisual sea change and how they interact with the shifting role of the tentpole TV showrunner discussed above who, as a self-stylized executive manager, is often at the problematic vertex of exactly these interlocking organizational and creative changes.

Fundamentally, the thesis offered in this book is one concerned with examining the relationship of industry and textual production. In this book, we will aim to isolate one trend in the production of contemporary network television and investigate it both practically and textually, contending that one can use knowledge of the industry to elucidate texts and that the form of texts can also, in turn, provide insights into the work of producers. As a result, the following methodology seeks to articulate a technique to examine these two domains as well as a justification for their eventual combination. While recent works by Amanda Lotz (2007a) and Richard Caves (2005) give an invaluable and detailed global view of the changes occurring in television, my project is focused on giving a picture of one particular business–stylistic trend situated in this larger context and one that isolates, as best as possible, its dispersed and evolving workplaces and its shifting laborers. Heeding Lash and Lury's (2007) advice (itself echoing Arjun Appadurai) to follow the object through its many instances of production, my case studies demonstrate how the movement of television properties through media (a movement that ultimately resembles Latour's [2005] actor-networks) whose connections are recursively established through acts of rearticulation and coordination. Following a television property closely through its many channels reveals an entirely new set of informant-practioners working on the fringes of the creative core of series and enabling the exploitation of transmedia possible. To achieve this, *Transmedia Television* will draw deeply on trade, popular and industrial press, as well as interviews with professionals affiliated with the tentpole TV.

This leaves only the theoretical problem of determining how on-air texts then interact with production and vice versa. Typically, reflexivity (or, redundantly, self-reflexivity) in film and television studies has referred to a fairly limited set of textual features within television programs that signal when a set of producers want to comment upon their own industry or reflect upon its own recording medium more generally. On the one hand, programs starring diegetic television performers from *The Dick Van Dyke Show* (CBS, 1961–6) to *30 Rock* (NBC, 2006 to present) allow for story lines that lampoon the foibles of the business of television. On the other hand, stylistic techniques such as camera mugging and theatrical asides perpetrated by the likes of Jack Benny or Garry Shandling more implicitly signal an authorial attitude toward either the fictional texts itself or the television industry more largely. Contrary to these designations, I argue that all fictional programming contains trace reflexive elements by virtue of their very construction and it is the analyst's job to pull these traces forward. Observing on-air fictional texts such as Geertzian artifacts, we will consider how programming participates (or not, as the case may be) in the industrial and organizational changes associated with tenpole TV. Specifically, by contrasting our sample of on-air tentpole TV programs with similar programs from television's past and by deploying the meticulous forms of textual analysis pioneered by scholars within traditional film studies, *Transmedia television* will illustrate how these current works' more experimental stylistic elements place them into conversation with the industrial and organizational changes that serve as the programs' context. In the parlance of television studies, we will consider how on-air programming, when closely examined, offers yet another site for "critical industrial practice," Caldwell's (2008: 5–6) term for ritualized forms of self-knowledge in production cultures.

The following then is segregated into two interlocking parts. In Part One, we will examine a series of case studies concerning the production of transmedia associated with tentpole TV in order to investigate the work of streamability. Through each example, we will construct an accurate picture of how these works are produced as well as how these conditions are both reflected and reflected upon in the final texts. Chapter 1 investigates the case of adapted comic books with a particular eye toward the *Heroes* webcomic and the *24* comic book. Chapter 2 examines the work of media tie-in novels, zeroing in on the case of writers of *Alias*-based novels. Chapter 3 describes the business of licensed video games in general and its specific importance to tentpole TV properties. And Chapter 4 more broadly investigates the role of media research in the embrace of convergence and, specifically, the exploitation of mobile TV.

While Part One looks at how tentpole TV series are expanded from the outside, in Part Two, I will take the opposite perspective questioning the modularity of the on-air texts themselves. In this section, we will analyze these series and consider how their unique textual form constitutes a provisional acceptance of tentpole TV and a commentary on the exactly same phenomenon. Tentpole TV programs' experiments in vast time, vast space, and inconsistent characterization constitute both reflections of and reflections on the altered work and business conditions placed upon and participated within by show creative staff. These unique features, I argue, function ultimately to make the programs more amenable to transmedia at the same time that these stylistic innovations also give rise to an entirely new set of aesthetic questions; simply how does one organize these diffuse elements. In Chapter 5, I examine how *Lost* has modeled narrational techniques of reconciling multiple timescapes. In Chapter 6, I investigate the distinct spatial logic of *24* that similarly allows for vast and expanding space. And in Chapter 7, I look at the altered figure of character and motivation itself as it has been reworked in *Alias* and cast it as another example of television makers altering their work to facilitate transmedia expansion and to act as cultural expression of a television in a transitional moment.

PART ONE

1

Tentpole TV: The Comic Book

Ancillary products and branded transmedia texts clearly are not new to the television industry and can be found at least as far back as the Little Ricky Doll sold to young fans of *I Love Lucy* or *Dragnet* board games featuring the deadpan likeness of Jack Webb. Popular live-action television characters and formats have frequently graced the pages of American comic books with results as varied as DC Comics' *Many Loves of Dobie Gillis* (1960–4), Western Publishing's *Twilight Zone* (1962–82), and Now Comics' curious comic-book adaptation of *Married with Children* (1990–4). With few exceptions, these books were crafted exclusively by the comic-book producers with only financial coordination with the intellectual property (IP) owners; famously Western Publishing's Italy-based artist for many of their *Star Trek* adaptations (1967–79), Alberto Giolitti, drafted his issues without ever having seen a single frame of the on-air television program ([Alberto Giolitti biography] n.d.).[1]

According to several pieces of publicity, the executive producers of tentpole TV have sought to more closely integrate the creative efforts of texts managed across media channels, constituting both a new creative-organizational role for these showrunners and a new economic model for exploiting television IP. In the first case, showrunners emphatically insist that the construction of these off-air texts remain close to what we call the creative core of the television serial, namely the writers. In October 2006, *The New York Times* ran a piece subtitled "*Lost*, Inc," in which the author chronicled the extracurricular activities of *Lost* showrunners Damon Lindelof and Carlton Cuse overseeing and creating a flood of products outside the confines of their hit show proper—all of which the producers "in varying degrees, have a say in" (Manly 2006). Similarly, a March 2007 *Wired* article on *Heroes* showrunner Tim Kring quoted the writer-producer as stating, "my job has changed from being in the writing room and editing . . . to managing a brand," again referring to creative work outside the boundaries of the show itself (Kushner 2007).

Near concurrent with this new flood of television-based products, Lindelof (2007) contributed an editorial to the *The New York Times* weighing in on the economic future of network television, beginning with the polemic sentence "television is dying." The article is a defense of the then just beginning WGA (Writers Guild of America) strike that brings to bear the evidence that new media is not simply an experiment for network television to play with, but its inevitable future, a future demanding a new financial logic of production and compensation. Lindelof's think piece also suggests that it is not only creative curiosity on the part of writers—as implied in the two previously cited articles—that has prompted a more aggressive posture toward ancillary products, but it has become an economic imperative for the survival of the "dying" medium. Kring, too, echoed this sentiment in a contemporary *Fast Company* article where the producer claimed that, "in five years the idea of broadcast will be gone" (Kushner 2008). In these articles and others like them, tentpole TV showrunners argue that exactly what constitutes a television program creatively, organizationally, and economically is under transition and is expanding. In these and similar statements, showrunners like Lindelof and Kring subtly position their own use of tentpole TV as a way out of this crisis.

Collectively, all these articles selectively highlight several changes in the production and economic processes of network TV that all point back to the same economic and theoretical motive: to make programming more streamable. Streamability—the ability to move creative products from one platform to another through either repurposing to different recording media or translating intellectual property into new conceptual and/or material objects—in the work of convergence theorist Simone Murray (2005) is cast as the cardinal virtue of contemporary media conglomerates. Murray argues that streamability is linked to the financial need to replace economies of scale, lost with the fragmentation of the homogenous model of the mass audience, with an economy of scope, achieved through clustering products around single brands and allowing products to effortlessly cross-promote one another. The core of Murray's theory echoes the work of Henry Jenkins (2006) on transmedia, Jennifer Gillian on must-click-TV (2010), and James Bennett on television as digital media, all of which insist that contemporary television has evolved precisely in the way in which it has been able to increasingly migrate from the television set. While Murray's theories are compelling, the author's observations lack specificity. Network television producers achieve streamability when they, on the one hand, sell and purchase formats for inexpensive reality programs globally and, on the other, license the image of the hit shows to everyone from print publishers to theme parks. While each is a clear case of streaming in broad terms, the differences between each make such a wide categorization reductive.

In other words, streamability is sought and achieved through any number of strategies. It is my intention in the following to review and analyze two such comparable cases of network television shows streamed into another medium, namely comic books. I will examine how these two productions have attempted to answer the deceptively simple questions: What now constitutes a television show and how is it to be produced? To do this, we will investigate both the production of these comic books and their content as well as how both of these spheres influence one another. If nothing else, the self-proclaimed vigor with which tentpole TV showrunners are embracing unfamiliar ancillary fields implies the importance of meaning managed across different media into products that, as a result, cannot be simply dismissed out of hand as reproductions or derivatives. Ultimately, Lindelof, Kring, and Murray are chronicling the same easy process of translation and content streaming, albeit from vastly different intellectual traditions. It is my hypothesis that Murray's concept of streamability and its public face, constituted in the image of tentpole TV programs projected by these programs' showrunners, cleans up a process that involves the incorporation of work by distant creative professionals and the synchronization of their efforts in terms of both time and meaning, a process fraught with potential complications. More simply, I would like to messy up streamability and to consider the significance of this mess. Cultural products are not metal ingots that can be melted down and cast in a number of forms with little coordination. Each stage of translation is an interaction fraught with negotiation and consequence and these interactions can and should be studied in the course of cultural analysis.

In my own work, I would like to follow up on this complicated relation of producers and their texts through the application of the cultural theory of Clifford Geertz (1973) that will amend the more macroscopic, top-down view with a microscopic gaze interested in the qualitative life of cultural production. In my understanding of Geertz, cultural analysis involves the appreciation of the intrinsic double aspect of culture as both a *model of* the world in which a worldview is coded into symbol or formula in the manner of a chart or formula, and as a *model for* the world in which the symbolic material of culture is transmitted and redeployed in human behavior (95). In adapting this framework to network television, I would state that tentpole programs—that is those which have been used to maximize streamability through multiple articulations—provide both a model for how contemporary and so-called post-network business is to be made and a model of the way that these practices have influenced the work of creatives. A simple example: the work of transmedia producers on these programs rearticulates a certain division of labor through controlled information flows, creating a *model for*, while the use of secondary characters in these ancillary texts expresses and signifies the limitations and constraints of this division of labor, as the texts become a *model of*. This application of Geertz requires two adjustments. First, Geertz's model of/for was originally meant to refer to culture as model of/for the world, in the largest sense of the word. When studying cultural industries, I delimit the "world" to the community of producers while bracketing out the meaning production done by eventual consumers for expediency's sake. Similarly, Geertz's original culture concept was an all-encompassing one universalized across an entire population. Popular culture producers play to a fluid and inconsistent audience. Thus, it makes the most practical sense to center the study on producers and their "world." Ultimately, application of Geertz's cultural theory also reflects the work of Paul Dimaggio's (1977) cultural industries approach that insists that the "core characteristics of 'mass culture' can be seen as attributes of industries, not of societies" (437). In other words, popular culture texts, above all else, can be decoded as artifacts of their native societies, namely cultural producers.

In the following, I will be investigating questions of how streamability is achieved rather than exclusively why it is achieved—a query already handsomely postulated upon by thinkers like Murray—in the practice of network television as ancillary creatives become more central to programming. I have observed and will report on two attempts to use a separate cultural system to reconfigure the practices and routines of television production (model for) and to express and to discuss the inherent issues involved in this very expansion (model of). That is, we will consider the cases of the comic-book translations of two big-budget network TV tentpoles: *Heroes* and *24*. Methodologically, my study was conducted through a combination of primary research through interviews and e-mail correspondences with the creatives involved and a supplementary review of trade literature in both the comics and the television industries as well as formal analyses of the comic books produced. Due to the vastly multi-sited nature of the industry studied, contact has been partial and intermittent. Ultimately, the picture that emerges of transmedia work will be an uneven one with sharp divides separating the creative core from a series of supervisors and freelancers, hired on a per-project basis to assemble a large share of transmedia's extra work in comic books as well as the other media considered in subsequent chapters. Barriers are maintained and contact is minimized between creative nodes of transmedia production. Supervisors use mechanisms such as trust and informal contacts to minimize communication, while freelancers compensate this information blackout with their own fandom as well as ad hoc, improvised artistic choices. In the end, I will argue that this ambivalent division of labor that publicly brings transmedia collaborators closer to the creative core, but internally complicates this abridgement contributes to the dominant thematics at play in the resultant comic-book texts. Specifically, I will draw out the repeating attempts of these comic books to match their on-air antecedents through a near-constant inter-rogation and articulation of character motivation.

At the same time that network TV producers have become interested in expanding the worlds of their programming into the field of comic books, comic-book producers conversely have sought to move their product into new realms as well. While profits connected to physical book production (in both monthly pamphlets and trade collections) have only limited growth potential for comic-book producers, licensing of intellectual property to other media has become a much more significant source of income for comic-book produc-ers. For example, during the first two quarters of 2006, Marvel Comics—the country's largest producer by volume and market share—netted US$73.5 mil-lion and US$48.9 million from their licensing and publishing arms, respectively (Marvel 2007). These figures grew the following year, but at a vastly different clip resulting in US$148.2 million in licensing and US$60.5 in publishing, likely due to the performance of Sony's licensed film *Spider-Man 3* (Marvel 2007a) (see Figure 1.1). Moreover, the most fateful moments in this firm's recent history (the struggle over the company in bankruptcy court and the recent formation of a movie-production arm, Marvel Studios) were resultant from controversies over the management of licensing (the noncompetitive deals over Marvel-licensed toys, the poor profit participation of Marvel in licensed feature films, and their eventual purchase by Disney in 2009) (Raviv 2002, Waxman 2007). Smaller publishers too have sought out increased rents on their IPs, particularly through the courting of feature film adaptations, result-ing in a series of trade articles searching for the "next" Marvel to be mined and exploited in Hollywood (Graser 2007).

Moreover, the producers and supervisors behind *24* and *Heroes* are by no means the only television workers interested in the medium of comic books. Notably, writer Joss Whedon, the former showrunner of *Buffy the Vampire-Slayer* and the writer many credit with innovating the contem-porary action serial, has "continued," with the assistance of many of his staff writers, *Buffy* in a series of books published by Dark Horse Comics, subtitled "Season Eight" and "Season Nine" (*Buffy* concluded on-air in its seventh season) (Purdin 2006). Similarly, the prematurely cancelled serial *Jericho* was extended but not concluded by a comic-book series, produced by both Dynamite and IDW Comics, subtitled "Season Three: Civil War." Both Warner Brothers–produced *Supernatural* and *Chuck* have been adapted for the imprint Wildstorm, a division of DC Comics (also owned by Warner Brothers). IDW also has published adaptations of CBS's *CSI* as well as FOX's *The Shield* and *Angel*.

Beginning in July 2004, comic-book publisher IDW began to produce books based on the FOX-Imagine program *24* and in September 2006,

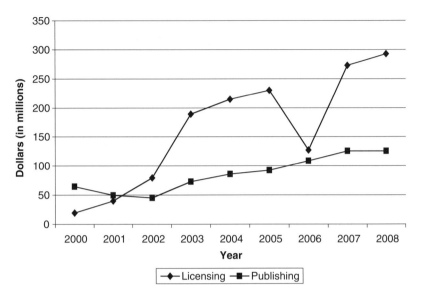

FIGURE 1.1 *Marvel Comic sales.*

publisher Aspen MLT began to produce a series of webcomics for the NBC program *Heroes*. What these two ventures have in common is that they both operate via a combination of freelance creative labor and permanent supervision either closely or loosely affiliated with program producers. In the case of *Heroes*, scripts are drafted by either series writers, staff writing assistants, or freelance writers hired from outside the program staff. Yet, in all these cases, it is the series writers who oversee and determine the content of each issue. The remaining artistic duties on the series (penciling, inking, coloring) are performed by freelance workers on a project-by-project basis that are, in turn, overseen by Aspen's own editors. The production of the comic-book version of *24* is arranged in a slightly different manner. FOX's licensing and merchandising department oversees the project while both the writing and the artwork originate from outside the show proper and outside IDW itself, which, like Aspen, retains very little permanent artistic staff.

Heroes' writer-producer and transmedia advocate Jesse Alexander recently commented upon the *Heroes* staff involvement in its ancillary manifestations stating, "[participation is] critical because if you play in this space, you're opening yourself up to the risk of catastrophe from one small mistake" (Kushner 2008). Yet, despite claims of this sort, actual interaction between supervisors and freelancers in the cases of both the *Heroes* and the *24* comic books is relatively rare. Indeed, the minimization of supervisor contact is a pronounced implicit goal running throughout my observations on the production of each comic-book series. The fact that freelancers are hired short term, per project, facilitates this minimized interaction. I suspect that these efforts could be attributed to several motives. First, minimizing contact is economically rational. Supervisors see no additional fees for reviewing revised content and thus seem less likely to review successive drafts. Minimizing contact also embodies an organizational logic that seeks to free creative resources from being overburdened on single projects, especially when the project is more textually and economically tangential. One writer for *24* comic book recently told me that interaction with licensors is infrequent simply because they "don't want to get bogged down with that kind of detail."[2]

This leaves us with a paradoxical understanding of brand expansion in which supervisors are deeply invested in the work of freelancers—remember that television is dying—but are reluctant to invest themselves entirely. What often stands in for contact, I argue, is the cultivation of trust. Trust, as a theme, has been revisited by several recent social theorists who have noted increasing levels of complexity and uncertainty in contemporary social life that have led not to the submission of actors to the laws of pure rationality and order, but to the use of trust in facilitating social action (Luhmann 1979, Giddens 1991, Sztompka 1999). Anthony Giddens (1991) goes the furthest by suggesting that it is trust in others, derived from infantile experience, which gives an individual a "protective cocoon" that shields the social actor from the pitfalls of rampant existential self-questioning and helps to establish a consistent, reflexive self-identity (36–42). Borrowing on these authors, I use the term trust in our case study in a very specific way. While trust can equally refer to being entrusted, that is to be brought closer to an organizational center through the sharing of resources, I am following Giddens's lead by using the term more in the manner of faith, faith in personnel that assures the party bestowing trust that a task will be met by the trustee without the need for constant interaction. Extrapolating to our case, increasing complexity and uncertainty in the production of television, particularly as it pertains to its porous, transmedia boundaries (an "identity crisis" of sorts), has producers cultivate trust in their freelancers to hold onto their own ontology security, their own sense of the television program as a cohesive, creative act. However, each instance of trust is both a way to eliminate anxiety of uncertainty at the same time that it is a constant reminder of the risk that lies beneath, an observation that could go a long way in explaining the bifurcated behavior of tentpole TV supervisors. Put in more concrete language, television producers are aware of the need to expand the brand beyond the program and invest trust in experienced professionals in other fields to do this, but in each effort, producers risk the possibility of exposing their ignorance of new or other media forms or possible failure. Or, as Erving Goffman (1971) observed (in a vastly different context), "the conditions that allow one to develop trust anew at each contact expose one to all times to sudden cause for doubt" (18). To interject a mundane example: The less I know all the things that could go wrong with my car, the more I can trust it to start every morning. The importance of trust also has a less high-minded place in this equation. Simply put, the more supervisors trust a freelancer, the less they are obligated to maintain contact; the two variables have an inverse relationship.

Outside of speculating on motive, we can examine how this minimization of contact and a simultaneous cultivation of trust are achieved. Supervisors focus interaction with and input for freelancers on the preproduction of texts. This minimizes subsequent interaction by establishing a minimum trust between permanent and temporary workers through the production of preliminary texts such as treatments, thumbnails, or proposals. Supervisors working on these comics seek to dispel the problems of an inconsistent, spatially distant workforce by establishing trust, which, in turn, reduces subsequent anxiety and oversight just as Giddens's concept of a primordial, quasi-psychoanalytic trust seeks to eliminate several existential questions and their consequent anxiety. Put more succinctly, an editor associated with the *24* comic stated in interview that,

> There's usually more scrutinizing at the start because its more a matter of just making everyone feel comfortable with the direction of the story, the look of the artwork. And once they're comfortable with that, they tend to trust you a bit more and don't scrutinize to the same degree.

This technique holds true for both freelance artists and writers. One freelance writer on *Heroes* has stated that, "a majority of the notes come at the outline stage." An artist working on the same series has noted that he was compelled to take additional efforts to clean up his personal thumbnail stage to ensure that his own preproduction would be legible for editorial review by supervisors. Trust here is based on the fruits of prior interaction that are rapidly embedded in preproduction artifacts.

Second, supervisors enact structural measures to ensure a quick, unproblematic hiring process that maximizes trust in the freelancer hired and, consequently, reduces the need for supervisor contact. In both the cases of *Heroes* and *24*, artistic management is farmed out to a series of smaller firms. In the first case, the tasks of drawing and sometimes writing the *Heroes* webcomic was, initially, overseen by Santa Monica–based Aspen, a duty it later shared with another small studio, Invisible College. Aspen is a studio-publisher that was founded by prominent comic book artist Michael Turner that splits its work between creator-owned titles and licensed work for both NBC and other clients such as Marvel Comics. In the second case, both the writing and artistic work on *24* is overseen by San Diego–based IDW Publishing, a comic publisher/design studio that, despite a small permanent staff of 12 employees, is the country's fifth largest comic publisher by volume. Significantly, supervision is further farmed out in smaller ways through the engagement of artistic studios in creative capacities. In the *Heroes* webcomic's first foray into freelance writing, show producers employed workers of "Men of Action Studios," a loose consortium of comic writers. In securing illustrators for the *24* comics, editors at IDW contracted with drafters affiliated with a Brazilian artists' collective, "Impacto Studios." Interestingly, these high-profile television shows have chosen to work with firms that, while highly respected, are decidedly not dominant in their industry, at the same time that clear efforts were taken on the part of those involved to erect a series of supervisory barriers that serve to "run point" on freelance creatives. Most of the artists working on *Heroes*, for example, describe how Aspen served as *middlemen* for NBC fielding any and all questions and creating a de facto shield for those working on the show proper. Moreover, this barrier was mirrored on the NBC side, which also delimited participation by assigning its own middlemen. One Aspen editor described this saying, "it [contact] all funnels through one person at NBC who is my contact." Here trust is established through the construction of supervisor barriers, providing the assurance that someone else is definitively in charge.

Hiring practices, too, work toward the dual goal of minimizing contact and maximizing trust. Specifically, supervisors on both projects employed the work of creative A&R men who tap informal job networks to staff their comic books. In the first case, *Heroes* specifically has relied on experts across the fields to act as go-betweens to secure competent freelancers. The writing staff of the television program, in fact, included prominent comic writers Jeph Loeb and Chuck Kim. Reports have claimed that it was Loeb's past professional and personal relationship with Michael Turner that directly led to the partnership of *Hereos* and Aspen (Tabu 2007). Moreover, Loeb has been instrumental in securing freelance writers, based, again, on his personal contacts. Indeed, one freelance writer at Men of Action described to me that it was through a prior partnership with Loeb (sharing writing duties on DC Comics' *Superman*) that led to his hiring and it was Kim who served as his editorial contact through the production process. More frequently, creatives working on the *Heroes* webcomic describe working with the editorial apparati from within Aspen itself. By facilitating deals between supervisors and freelancers, Loeb and Kim act in a capacity similar to individuals Paul DiMaggio (1977) has called brokers and Paul Hirsch (1991 [1972]) contact men. These

two sociologists found the central organizational dilemma in cultural industries to be the need for constant differentiation and that this difficulty was
met, in part, by employing the work of liminal figures, these brokers or contact men, who could advocate for and to culture-producing firms to tap the
next big thing. This relieves firms from the need to review all aspiring material
at the same time that they give firms orderly access to innovation from the
outside. The case of *Heroes* is slightly different in that the need is not exactly
differentiation but cross-media translation; yet their contact men do provide
a similar service by minimizing the firm's decision making and legitimating a
manageable number of potential freelancers. Moreover, we can suggest that
these contacts serve also to combine the intimate, soft bonds of personal
relations with the frequently alienating aspects of work-for-hire. Aspen and
IDW work in a similar capacity by maintaining long-standing (but temporary)
relations with a "stable" of workers, in particular many of the *Heroes* books
have been drafted by artists who have worked on several other of the firm's
projects.

In lieu of and in addition to these hiring practices, the relations between
supervisors and freelancers in these two comics are typically facilitated by
informal job networks of friendships and acquaintanceships. It is significant
that one freelancer writer in an interview repeatedly referred to the deal
between Aspen and *Heroes* not in terms of a contract, but as a "good relationship." One writer for *24* has reported that he was able to pitch a concept
for the series simply because he knew the "players" at IDW. Similarly, one
artist on *Heroes* informed me that a common way of securing work is hanging
out in bars after comic-book conventions.

In an instructive study, sociologist Brian Uzzi (1997) observed the world
of the New York garment industry to demonstrate the distinct advantage
of so-called embedded relationships—those based on moral bonds—as
opposed to purely market-based relations in cultural industries. Uzzi locates
the advantages in three areas: the cultivation of trust, the rapid transfer of
information, and the mutual solving of problems (36–7). The relationships
active in the production chains in these comic books are in part embedded;
however, I can only detect one of these three hallmarks in action. As I have
stated, the establishment of trust is central to the supervisors' practices and
their efforts to minimize editorial contact. However, I find very little of what
Uzzi calls fine-grained information transfer. Uzzi claims that in style-based
industries (sometimes minute), differentiation often defines competitive
advantage; yet this differentiation is difficult to articulate across collaborating
firms, especially when bonds between companies are formal, market-based,
or even competitive. In contrast, a frequent complaint among freelancers I interviewed (with the notable exception of freelance writers working

on *Heroes*) is the relative paucity of reference material in the form of either images, scripts, style guides, or show bibles. As I argue below, these practices are compensated for and amended by practices associated with fandom among the freelancers.

Freelancers are frequently kept on a distinctly "need to know" basis when it comes to narrative/textual information concerning the on-air program. For example, one artist working on *Heroes* commented retrospectively on his work stating,

> the problem was that the episodes that it [the drawn issue] went out in between hadn't come out yet, so I had no idea of the actual ramifications of it [the webcomic's story] and just how inclusive and important it was to the actual story.

This feeling was echoed in the comments of another penciller working on *Heroes* who stated, "the interesting part about doing these Webcomics is that we really don't get any sneak preview or idea of how the issue connects with the show until it airs." An editor working on *24* similarly stated that licensors "do have story bibles and show bibles, but they're usually reticent to share those with anyone." Former *Star Trek* writer and inventor of the Tribbles, David Gerrold (1973) describes the impossible position of freelance writers in television as paradoxically having to know more about the program than its writers without access to production data. Partially, this can be seen as a consequence of the rapid, weekly schedule of the *Heroes* webcomic— there simply is not enough time to fill in weekly contributors on the series; however, the fact that they are frequently working with the same pool of freelancers and that a significantly less deadline-driven *24* suffers from the same information blackout marks the practice as more global than specific. The practice even extends to information concerning the production of the comic book itself. When I talked with several of the freelancers working on *Heroes*, several were unaware if their issues would be reprinted in a collected trade edition (which they eventually were) and several admitted to being completely unaware of their collaborators, be they writers or artists, until the time when their finished work was published on the NBC website.

After achieving mutual trust, freelancers in my sample (with the exception of *Heroes* writers) are left largely out of the loop. The practice of freelance work is marked by the constant need to get approved, or "signed off," as successive versions and drafts of creative work are sent to supervisors (in the one case by Aspen's editorial staff and *Heroes*' writing staff as well as NBC.com and, in the other, with IDW's editorial staff as well as FOX licensors) followed by a period of waiting and eventual passing of work thus far.

In my interviews, this practice was understated; many interviewed characterized it as a formality rather than an essential component of the creative
process. This presentation may, of course, be skewed by the maintenance
of freelancers' self-image, which depends upon the projection of impec-
cable competence. Regardless, the practice of getting approved is a clear
case demonstrating the many acts of consumption in the assumed singular
act of cultural production. "Pre-consumption" is expertly described in anthropologist Barry Dornfield's work *Producing Public Television, Producing Public
Culture* (1998) in which the author demonstrates how the taste allegiance
of producers guided layers of evaluation in the construction of a single PBS
miniseries. In our case, multiple instances of self-evaluation, according to my
data, did little or nothing and were cast more as inconveniences in often tight
production schedules. Just as little proprietary textual information is shared
with freelancers (again excepting *Heroes*' freelancer writers), little feedback
was given, a blackout that often led freelancers to invent feedback, find it
surreptitiously, or garner it from program fans. Minimizing feedback is accompanied with the minimization of supervisory influence on the project after
the freelancer has turned in his work. This cultural practice of minimal adjustments is commonly referred to as *tweaking* and is marked as nearly insignificant textually and is framed as being more a matter of cleaning up than
anything else. Again this characterization of tweaking must take into account
the reputation maintenance at constant play for freelancers who, as portfolio
workers, are frequently on the hunt for the next job. However, the representation of getting approval and tweaking both point to a perception of if not actual
minimization of supervisory presence in the work of freelancers. Even one
freelance writer for *Heroes*—the most "connected" of freelancer workers in
my study—dismissed supervisory adjustments of his work after the fact as
mere "dialogue tweaks."

Having little or no feedback from supervisors, freelancers use other means
to legitimate and ground their own work. First, many freelancers invent feedback when none exists by construing silence as acceptance. I also found
several cases wherein freelancers went considerably out of their way to contact supervisors, oftentimes after their work had already been completed. For
example, one freelance writer for *24* described to me the "amazing amount
of feedback" that he received from people affiliated with the show only to
subsequently describe how this feedback was transmitted surreptitiously.
The writer described reading notes from FOX licensors which, "I don't know
if we were supposed to see" and talking to staff writers, which "was not
the result of doing the comic or the approval process . . . [but] because I
sought them out." In a situation of minimal feedback, freelancers also often
appeal to third-party sources for legitimation, in particular the response of

fans, who are, if nothing else, notoriously difficult to please. Several artists on *Heroes* have detailed their efforts to play to fans, one by including references to Katsuhiro Otomo's *Akira* in his artwork, and another in his efforts to include so-called easter eggs in his layouts, that is minute references to on-air continuity. This second artist, Jason Badower, went so far in a subsequent interview to suggest the priority of fan response over supervisor judgment when evaluating a collaborator's efforts saying,

> I'm sure that there'll be more opportunities, man. Given the feedback on the boards, which has been great for you. It's some of the best comments I'm getting from people—that it feels like an in-continuity story, about the tone of what you wrote. Hopefully the people in the production office will sit up and pay attention to that. ("Interview: Blackout")

I argue that fandom serves an even greater importance in the production of these comics, and arguably ancillary media in general. Because textual information is meted out on a need-to-know basis, "fannish" knowledge fills in the gaps and allows for the production of meaningful ancillary products, making the consumptive habits of freelance creatives excessively important. In fact, this is an understated principle in creative laborers of all varieties: One must have consumed and internalized certain key works to make contributions to a field.[3] More specifically, I argue that in the case of these comics, fannish knowledge serves in a capacity similar to what sociologist Howard Becker (1984 [1982]) calls *conventions* in his *Art Worlds*. In this work, Becker defines conventions as the shared decisions and techniques buried implicitly and explicitly in a field of expression that make the collective construction and maintenance of an art world possible. This stock of conventional knowledge serves as the common ground for all participants. Becker further argues that any given artwork creates a social "world" that is "in some respects unique, a combination of vast amounts of conventional materials with some that are innovative" (63). This is exactly what happens in the case of branded entertainment forms on a much more microscopic scale where it is not decisions about, for example, notation or instrumentation, but questions of character and theme that are established through convention. Freelancers similarly draw on fannish knowledge as a resource for guiding and facilitating production. Thus, it is no accident that all the freelancers I talked to discussed at least a causal fandom for either *24* or *Heroes* and that, on a more macro-level, it is precisely the TV programs that in some way foster fan participation and/ or speculation, often dubbed cult TV, that can best sustain ancillary manifestations. In other words, fandom not only points to a nascent demand for more on the part of consumers but also to the facilities available for brand expansion. For example, a freelance writer working on *24* described his drafting of a comic story line stating,

> We [he and his co-writer] were extrapolating from a lot of lines of dialogue from the first season . . . it [the story] basically all grew backwards out of dialogue and the scenario of the first season. And a little bit from the third, of course.

Fandom provides the training and instruction that neither supervisors nor freelancers would likely accept and becomes an inexpensive form of professional development on the part of freelancers. However, the same above-quoted writer later demurred from the assignation of a fan subsequently in the interview rhetorically saying,

> I wonder if it is possible to clearly delineate between being an enthusiastic professional who happens to be a fan of the show and people out there doing fan fiction. I'd like to think of myself as a disciplined professional who happens to be just very enthusiastic about this thing.

This author's un-mandated attention to detail is echoed in the comments of one artist for *Heroes* who stated, "as a fan myself, I want to be as accurate as possible."

However, fandom is not simply a body of knowledge lurking behind texts, but is a contested zone fuelled by a distinct form of fan reception characterized by repeated viewings of texts, the insertion of text into social interaction, and the drawing of texts close to lived experience (Jenkins 1992: 53). When media scholar Henry Jenkins (1992) wrote this definition of fannish engagement, he cast these practices as nomadic, claiming that fans fill in the gaps and speculative holes left in programming. It is significant that media producers, in league with freelancers, have mobilized these practices to expand their brands. The filling of these gaps with authoritative texts can be observed in the television programs themselves that increasingly colonize all possible moments of narrative time through serial story forms, through structural experiments in temporality, as in *24*'s "real-time" format or *Heroes*' use of both flashbacks and flash-forwards and through porous spatiality as seen in the expanded spatial scope of *Heroes*' global narratives.

Like the dependence on mechanisms of trust and informal contacts, the importance of fannish knowledge and the performance of fandom suggest the centrality of loose social bonds in the construction of multifaceted television programs. By loose bonds, I am referring to the brand of social theory that avoids the restrictive models and theorems of structuralism and functionalism in favor of a problematization of the social itself, exemplary in the diverse works of thinkers such as Bruno Latour (2005) and Anthony Giddens (1979, 1986). While freelancers are undoubtedly held in economic place with the limits of wages and career opportunities, their confederation is equally maintained by a cultural participation in the series via fandom. In other words, constructing the social form of streamable media, cannot be simply understood as a product of hard bonds and obligations of technological development or rationalized business order, but is in part constructed in and through cultural forms in the manner of Geertzian rituals that constitute and reconstitute social bonds. Indeed, the (hypothetical) social world of tent-pole TV resembles more contemporary social forms (e.g. online social networking) whose shape owes as much to economic stratification as it does to the cultural investment and taste of its denizens.

On the whole, the use of fandom as a resource is, from the supervisors' perspective, similar to the technique endorsed by the recent, popular business strategy book *Wikinomics* (Tapscott and Williams 2006). The authors of this book claim that the future of competitive advantage in business is currently undergoing a paradigm shift wherein the success or failure of firms will be determined not by securing superior human capital or by maintaining strict controls on valued proprietary data, but by having porous boundaries, by sharing intellectual properties and by harnessing the enthusiastic labor of so-called peers. Similarly, the production of both comic books in my study depends squarely on the fannish enthusiasm of its freelancers. The authors of *Wikinomics* insist that this faster, looser, more open firm is essential for capturing elusive innovation. While our comic-book freelancers are emphatically outside the firm, often by several layers as we have seen, the positive shocks that outsiders can allegedly contribute are not always clear. An interesting comparative example can be observed in the Japanese comic book—or manga—industry, which turns a blind eye to massive infringements on character IPs by large groups of otaku amateur artists in the hope that among their ranks, the next prominent, officially sanctioned artist may emerge (Kinsella 2000, Pink 2007). In our case, fan enthusiasm is harnessed, but is through sometimes-strict official all-be-they hands-off channels, which, to an outside observer, can appear stifling. Here I am echoing the thoughts of media critics such as Eileen Meehan (2005) who worry that the expansion of media conglomeration will stifle cultural innovation by flooding all channels with repurposed, rehashed content. While there are certainly conservative influences placed upon freelancers—as we shall see—one would have to discredit their work entirely to fully support Meehan's argument, which despite its elegance does not pay proper respect to either the work of translation or the texts produced from such a process.

Both of our ancillary comic-book projects can be described as *network enterprises*. This is the term that sociologist Manuel Castells (1996) has used to describe the new way of structuring firms centered on maximizing the advantages of new technology—particularly communications technology—and new organizational logics—particularly in flattening hierarchy and making production processes "flexible" and dynamic. These network enterprises are freed from both the temporal and spatial strictures of the shop-floor model; in the first case, innovation, unlike standardization, discourages temporal regularity in favor of flux and immediate feedback and, in the second case, telecommunications help foster interfirm networks that are variable in terms of both size and scope. Freelancers work in an environment where both time and space have become unattached from a centralized firm time clock or office and instead have become "disembedded" or "liquid," depending on which social theorist one turns to. Supervisors' investment in the network enterprise is understood in terms of their interest in *Wikinomics*-infused innovation as well as overall cost reduction; freelance creative labor is cheaper, faster, and, by definition, contains no further obligation on the part of the employer.

The comic-book industry in general is spatially diffuse. In a recent work, geographers Glen Norcliffe and Olivero Rendace (2003) have argued that,

> changes in the labor process [in comic book production] that are linked to the adoption of new production and communication technologies and more flexible modes of production account for the replacement, in the 1980s and 1990s, of an agglomerated bullpen system of mass production located in large comic book publishing houses by a new pattern of geographic separation. (242)

The two further claim that this breakup of industrial formations and the adoption of the network enterprise model have competitively helped comic-book publishers by allowing them quicker response time in exploiting emerging subniches and new technologies. The very existence of smaller publishing firms such as Aspen and IDW owes much to the contemporary communication technology and graphics software alluded to by Norcliffe and Redace, which allow the firms to minimize overhead and still remain in working contact with diffuse creative workers. The geographers, however, do not consider the altered contractual position of artists and the way in which they bear much of the risk associated with these new competitive advantages.

While a system of the geographic isolation of freelancers in comic-book production then predates our cases, supervisors on both *Heroes* and *24* went to great lengths to take ample advantage of it. As stated above, IDW is based in San Diego, but *24*-comics' writers predominantly reside on the east coast of the United States and its artists are mostly located in Brazil. Santa Monica–based Aspen staffs *Heroes* comics with artists from the United States, Canada, and Australia. All this leads to what one artist working on *Heroes* described as "a faceless sort of partnership." This isolation not only keeps freelancers from supervisors (again minimizing contact), but also keeps freelancers from one another. For example, a writer for *24* recently described his abortive attempts to contact his collaborating artists, which failed because of both his inability to master Portuguese and his artist's inability to do the same with the English language. In both of the case of *Hereos* and *24*, I cannot find any of the so-called advantages of flexible work geographies as outlined by Norcliffe and Rendace. In fact, the particular arrangements, as we shall see later, arguably have a more conservative than innovative influence on the finished product. Instead, it seems that the practice of geographic separation is equally accountable to corporate isomorphism, the minimization of contact, and the search for the more exploitable form of creative labor (in the last case, it is significant that many freelancers in these two comics are junior members in their respective fields). In sum, freelance work creates a paradoxical space that, on the one hand, is boundary-less, encompassing the entire globe, but on the other, goes no further than the workspace of the freelancer. As one artist working for IDW put it, "working in the comic book industry means working from home."

The mainstream comic-book industry is deadline driven. Often producers run on month-long production cycles to create 22 pages or more of content. Many workers associated with both the *Heroes* and *24* series claimed in interviews that it is the ability to produce consistently and on time—to be able to live up to the grind—that spells out the ability to succeed as a comic-book freelancer rather than "pure" writing or drawing ability. One artist for *Heroes*, Jason Badower, described a life-changing moment when he, as a young man, met former Marvel Comics editor-in-chief Archie Goodwin who explained to the budding artist that he chose workers based on three categories—how reliable they are, how nice they are, and how talented they are—in that order of importance ("Three heroes podcast . . .").

Without fail, all the artists who worked on *Heroes* described the experience as a very *crunchy*[4] job. Although circumstances seem to shift in individual cases, each artist had to produce five pages, from initial conception to finished art in anywhere from five to eight days. One artist described the process stating,

> the deadlines, I thought, were pretty tough to meet. It usually was about a week between each episode on TV so we had to sync up the Web comic

to the show. We would have to get it drawn and colored and loaded onto the site within five to six days each, I felt pretty stressed.

Artist Badower similarly voiced retrospective regret over the time crunch stating, "I look back at our stuff and think, 'oh, more time! More time!' But there's never more time, so it is what it is" (Interview: Blackout). As referenced in the above quote, rapid deadlines were, in part, justified by making the time frame isomorphic with that of the television program, but, of course, this need not be the case. In fact, statistically fewer of the *Heroes* comics actually contain textual cues that put them in direct conversation with the contemporaneous events unfolding on the series proper. I cannot with any finality claim to understand the preference for rapid schedules, yet several offhand remarks by freelancers working on *Heroes* leads me to believe that the decision is related to, again, the minimization of contact. One artist in an interview remarked on his surprise upon realizing that his work was posted on the NBC website almost immediately after its completion. This late, hurried schedule is important because it essentially precludes the possibility of meaningful interchange between freelancers and supervisors. An editor at Aspen described this state of affairs:

A lot of the troubleshooting doesn't happen on our end . . . a lot of that stuff happens before hand. But what happens is that pushes into the time of us actually receiving because we can't start until its fully approved, because there have been some crazy times where we've started working on one of the *Heroes* graphic novels, one Micah [Gunnell] did a while back, and they wanted all these changes in it, but it was already drawn and it would have been re-drawing the entire thing to get it done, ready for launch on Monday when it was Friday afternoon. It was just impossible. So now they just wait and make sure that the entire thing is done and then give it to us.

In other words, the constraint of time eliminates (or, possibly is used to eliminate) the opportunity of back and forth between collaborating parties. Two artists on the book have also described this relationship between time and contact:

Artist One: "as far as feedback from NBC, they always seemed pretty cool with what we did, so, luckily we didn't have a whole lot of changes or anything like that.
Artist Two: "we'd also finish the day before an episode aired, so I think that they were pretty busy as it was."

Again, the more that creative labor is crunched, the less likely supervisory interaction becomes possible.

Focusing solely on deadlines and rapid production schedules occludes the flipside of the coin in flexible employment schemes, namely, that freelancers can just as frequently be out of work. This harsh fact was underscored in an Aspen panel at a recent comic-book convention, Wizard World Los Angeles 2008, wherein a staff member at the company introduced several "Aspen" artists and writers, all of whom had worked on the *Heroes* comic, as "unemployed." Time, in the case of freelancers, is not simply sped up because of quick deadlines, but becomes what Castells (1996) would call flex-time in which work becomes a situation of feast or famine; "time is managed as a resource not under the linear chronological manner of mass production, but as a differential factor in reference to the temporality of other firms, networks, processes and other products," all or which could be indifferent to the needs (financial or otherwise) of the freelancer (437). However, supervisors working on *Heroes* still adhere to the weekly schedule, a holdover from the mass-production model of broadcast television.

The production of the *24* comic is considerably different in terms of its temporal construction. The license was actively solicited by IDW on the basis of a freelance writer's pitch. There was no effort made to synchronize the book with the contemporaneous events depicted on-air. Furthermore, because of the terms of the licensing deal, it was the publishing firm that was under the constraints of time. The deal, typical in the business of licensing, was one of an advance versus a guarantee. IDW provided FOX licensing with a portion of an agreed-upon lump-sum for the exclusive rights to produce *24* comics (pending approval) for a terminable amount of time with the understanding that the remainder of the initial sum will be paid before the conclusion of the licensing period. Additionally, as IDW produces to complete the guarantee, the firm also agreed to pay royalties on the sale of individual books and issues. Thus, the deadlines, so far as they exist, are mandated by the publisher and not by the show proper as in the case of *Heroes*. These terms affect not so much the timing of the production as much as its space, that is, the size and quantity of issues produced. One writer for *24* claims that his series, *Nightfall*, was initially conceived in seven parts, but lost two issues when five, six, and seven were condensed into one 48-page Issue Five. Because the sales of pamphlets (monthly books) remained consistent regardless of page count and slight changes in cover price, the publisher decided that longer individual issues were more successful than several shorter ones. By reducing the number of issues and increasing the price per unit, IDW reduced the relative royalty cost. Before and after *Nightfall, 24* has been only published intermittently in a series of so-called one-shots, that is single issues, and two multi-issue series. It is small runs in larger format and higher per-unit costs that maximize the terms of their deal—the crunch occurs in a combination of licensing period time and cramped page space. The particular adaptation of the on-air's real-time format in its initial issues symbolizes this crunch, as every two pages were constructed as an hour of time passed, a self-imposed mandate that, by the admission of both writer and editor, subtracted from the clarity and tone of the work. In *Nightfall*, however, 136 pages depict a 24-hour period, as opposed to 48 pages in earlier efforts.

Freelancers, in the roles they construct for themselves, the practices they undertake, and the implicit aesthetic theory that they endorse, negotiate the constraints and conditions of the freelance creative situation indicated in our examples. Working on a "need-to-know" basis with minimal contact, free-lancers often assemble a set of working tactics meant to deal with this challenging creative work. Almost all the freelancers whom I talked to referred to techniques of playing it safe, or practicing a mild form of self-censorship wherein the contributors were loath to embellish their work with any efforts that they pre-assumed to be out of the ordinary. One *Heroes* artist referred to his work as simply "standard comic book layouts," while another claimed that in his drafting, he merely worked "straight from the script." An editor at IDW described the institutionalization of this practice stating, "once you learn what their expectations are and what they'll allow and not allow [it] kind of makes it easier as you go forward just to stay away from that sort of thing." This preemptive self-censorship is equally a response to crunchy schedules that leave no time for subsequent interaction or fixes. This is clearly demonstrated in the comments of another *Heroes* artist who described his work saying, "I really just had to smash it out. There wasn't any time for play on that one. It was just: tell the story." I suspect that playing it safe not only facilitates rapid production, but also works to maintain reputation and reliability on the part of freelancers who prove the ability to work with very little prompting on the part of supervisors as both the program (through fandom) and its producers' standards (through self-censorship) have been internalized.

What little artistic agency claimed by freelancers is party not to any long-reaching artistic goals, but is often based upon ad hoc aesthetic prin-ciples largely developed in the doing or only subsequent to creation. This is altogether unsurprising given the inconsistent, similarly ad hoc character of freelanced comic-book work at large. Freelancers must make do with what assignments come their way in addition while fielding the pressure of using current work as a portfolio for the next possible assignment. The condition of flexible aesthetic standards offers a clear practical example of what sociologist Zygmunt Bauman (2005) has called liquid modernity in which allegiances, social identity, and even conceptions of time and space have given way from solid modernity to liquidity, constantly in flux and under stress. Aesthetic fields, like those occupied by our freelancers, form no clear aesthetic paradigm that could measure all objects leaving the free-lancer locked in a constant cycle of updating and improving their technique while aligning themselves to no clear style in particular. The solution to such a conundrum appears to be ceding responsibility away (as in "playing it safe") and making all decisions temporary ones (through ad hoc aesthet-ics). Thus, many of the most central artistic decisions of freelancers are described away with references to decisions on a case-by-case basis, attri-butions to the "gut" and "instincts." One freelancer writer for *24* explained his creative method by citing an unanswerable rhetorical question, "how do you know what to do when?" —an apt enough definition for freelancers' aesthetic principles.

More concretely, we can observe the relationship between the freelancer's practical situation and his or her creative process through their accumulated practices of saving time and effort. One artist for *Heroes* describes his use of photo collage in this regard:

> I can paste photos here or just leave scratches for a background there and polish it up later, using multilayers of photos and collage and illustration to actually build up my image because some things are faster, a forest, for example, is much faster to actually use a combination of photos and painting over top than actually drawing it in linework.

Another artist discussed a method of tracing to save time: "I actually took freeze frames from the show and fit them into the layout and print them and trace facial features . . . if I did it freehand it would have taken longer to get a better likeness." In either case, I do not mean to imply that freelancers simply cut corners. On the contrary, I would argue that these practices to save time are innovations upon what has already been described as a difficult situation for creative work. Furthermore, we must remember that freelancers are paid on the basis of output, not by the time spent. Thus, there are both strong organizational and economic restraints upon spending too much time on any single project.

The situation of freelance creative labor in our two case studies also tends to encourage the cultivation of several recurring attitudes and roles, many of which have already been tangentially hinted at above. Among freelancers there is a customary deference paid to supervisors, as all of the decision-making is said to occur with them. One artist on *Heroes* underscored this attitude in discussing his rendering of a flashback in his layout, stating, "it really depends on what the editor likes." In a similarly self-deprecating move, a writer for *Heroes* describes the preproduction of his script regarding which super ability would be featured:

> They [staff writers] threw out a power or two which I won't say because they may use it again—and then I threw out a couple. I threw out one that I thought was killer and would have worked perfectly, but then they told me, "oh, we're actually using it" . . . they're going to do a better job with it that I would.

Another writer echoed this deference to the writing staff in describing his work: "they [staff writers] pretty much come up with the stories that they want me to do." Because freelancers stress their inferior position with respect to supervisors, any creative agency that is retained is characterized as *leeway*, that is a matter of finding space either in the script (in the case of artists' layouts) or in editorial mandates (in the case of writers). Freelancers, in their self-directed comments, also often characterize their work as a learning process and position themselves as students. On a very practical level, the flexibility of the job market, which leaves freelancers in a constant search for work and self-development, does in fact leave them in a junior level of employment. Calling themselves students is then, arguably, one way that these creatives can make sense of this instability. Several freelancers working on the comics also voiced a polite deadline resignation. Because of the specific time and supervisory constraints in their work, freelancers occasionally sound a posthumous regret in decision making.

Given what we now know about how supervisors and freelancers act in concert with one another, I would like to make a handful of general conclusions about how this general situation contributes to a loose, implicit aesthetic theory among the freelancers. Considering every element that goes into the construction of television programming from its typical plot threads, its visual style, its thematic preoccupations, its guiding formulas, it is overwhelming through the representation of individual characters that freelancers judge the series and their own contributions to it. This focus on character as the guiding force in modularity and streamability echoes observations on Japanese popular culture's own practice of media-mix. For example, Marc Steinberg (2009) singles out the translation of the image of Astro Boy into the material form of a sticker as the "moment when . . . techniques or modes of media connectivity were developed" (116). Arguably, this character mindedness is institutionally coded in an industry in which the only thing patching together 70 years of *Batman* comic books through its hundreds of contributors is that Bruce Wayne is still trying to avenge the memory of his savagely murdered parents. In other words, characters, their image, and their inscribed mental lives serve as the constant throughout a series' endless differences and derivations. However, beyond this global proposition, specific data show how a character serves our freelancers in their efforts. In general, contributors on *Heroes* webcomic often discuss their work by amending a description with the principal character's name, as in "it's a Ted story." One artist on *Heroes* has commented in an interview that it is precisely the specific visual design of the individual characters with their more or less consistent "uniforms" that serves to bridge the differences in each contributor's style. On the writers' side, one freelancer for the *Heroes* webcomic has explained his script with reference to deep character analysis. In this case, a story about a superpowered energy leech trapped in a hospital "works" for the writer because it demonstrates how series regular Mohinder is "at heart a grass roots guy" (Interview: Blackout). Making the point even clearer, one writer for *24* has claimed that he sees the real-time format as merely the program's "gimmick" and that program appeals to the audience because: "Jack Bauer [the series lead] hits at something basic that's missing from other media. And it's that he's resolute. You know, the stuff he does, the horrible stuff that he does has an impact on the man, but he's resolute about doing it . . . this is a guy who, even when he's wrong, he charges in. And it's sort of a modern interpretation on the John Wayne mythos."

This understanding of the series is echoed by the writer's editor at IDW who claims that the decision to actively solicit the license for *24* comics was based on the fact that, "he [Bauer] just seemed like the kind of character that would translate well into other media." Again, it is the individual character and his or her accumulated attributes that are valued in the translation of the program into comics. This primacy on character on the part of supervisors for the *Heroes* webcomic can be inferred from a subsequent review of supervisor drafted stories, which focus heavily on the articulation of motivation and on the fact that the few moments when program supervisors directly interacted with freelancers were prompted by getting the characters just right. This latter occurrence, to my knowledge, only happened when an actor was cast in a role to be depicted in artwork, but had yet to appear in the on-air series, forcing contact to ensure visual character consistency. However, outside of the particular instances of freelance writers working on *Heroes*, most character analysis on the part of freelancers is based not on supervisor interaction, but on fannish reading practices. This can lead to humorous disagreements between supervisors and freelancers. One comic-book editor reported to me that Paramount licensors insisted that a *Star Trek*–based comic book he was working on was too risqué saying, "they [the licensors] felt like the show kept it a bit more veiled that he [Capt. Kirk] was, you know, screwing with all these different aliens . . . than we did."

Counter to the overall trend of my sample, several freelance writers working on *Heroes* have had uncommon access to on-air staff writers, notably series writers Chuck Kim and Aron Coleite, in the production of their scripts. However, this close access was tempered, I argue, with limitations of subject matter and content placed upon the freelance writers that, once again, eliminated the need for close coordination with the creative core. The first 50 issues of *Heroes* were scripted by a combination of regular staff members (notably Aron Coleite, Joe Pokaski, and Jesse Alexander), junior members of the staff—that is, assistants working for the regular writers— and comic-book professionals brought in as freelancers. The inclusion of outsiders into writing is most likely a concession to WGA rules. Freelanced work first appeared May 28, 2007, in issue 35 and continued until August 21, 2007, Issue 47. These dates coincide more or less with the traditional summer hiatus for network television production. Writers, not technically employed by the series production office, were most likely barred from creatively producing for the comic in this time. Despite their high level of interaction, freelance writers were, in a sense, distanced from the creative core of the program through choice of content. In terms of characters, only two of the freelance-scripted 14 issues dealt with primary and not second- ary characters.[5] Over half of the issues written by show regulars include events that either directly precede, follow, or fall between events depicted on the on-air series, while only two freelance written issues do this, and only as an anterior extension, that is directly following on-air events. Also freelance-written stories are much less likely to include repetitions from the on-air series either in word or image. Additionally, show-writer comic-book scripts depict events that are in the past, present, and future, with respect to on-air narratives, while freelance scripts, with two exceptions that are set contemporaneously with the series, only depict vague stories of the past, in the origin story vein.

Interestingly, these limitations on character and narrative do not extend to the use or reuse of subtext or theme. In reviewing the *Heroes* webcom- ics, I picked out three themes that run through both the on-air series and its comic-book translation: intergenerational/familial conflict, the power of total institutions, and temporal disruption. Of the three themes, freelancers were just as likely to incorporate the first two, but not the last. A possible hypothesis is that while freelance writers are warded off certain elements in a branded universe (characters, continuity), they compensate by focusing on the less-tangible, thematic elements in the series "sand box," themes most likely gathered through the cultivation, again, of fannish knowledge. On the other hand, the fact that freelancers were seemingly disallowed from playing with story time is not surprising—even junior writers, with only one excep- tion, were not allowed to mine this thematic. This theme of the three has the most potential to disrupt show continuity and add contradiction to canon while familial conflict and total institutions can be repetitiously added as story elements without affecting the overall narrative trajectory.

As I have hinted at above, it is the questioning of motivation in narrative, theme, and character that animates much of what occurs in the *Heroes* webcomic. By motivation, I mean simply the explicit and implicit attachment of discursive meaning on action. This preoccupation is clearly encapsulated in a particularly impressive layout (Figure 1.2) appearing in Issue 16 of the series.

In this page, the character Hana Gitelman[6] asks herself, "where did I go wrong?" resulting in a memory-induced collage that depicts, in each of the page's nine panels, a distinct time frame, extending past her own lifetime, with images tracing her maternal ancestors. The layout interrogates causality of the character's action and locates it in the prior actions of one's family and the accumulated weight of these decisions. It is in the character's deep past, stretched through generations, that meaning is sought. This single page synthesizes the webcomics' overarching themes: a preoccupation with intergenerational legacy, an experimental formal attitude toward temporal construction, and most prominently, an investigation of motivation.

This discussion should be amended with the commonsense observation that the goal-oriented, psychologically motivated character is too general an element of fiction to serve as a proper analytic. Indeed, motivated characters are seen as the essential element of Classical Hollywood narrative, which was rooted in the conventions of the realist novel, both of which were certainly borrowed from and continue to be traded on in television drama. However, I would propose a few observations to make a case for the distinction of a particular strand of hyper-motivation present in the *Heroes* webcomics. First, the comics are singularly preoccupied with providing meaning to action to the point of presenting several issues as the elucidation of motivation, rather than its complication, as in classical narrative. In the cases where action is indeed the central feature of the narrative, the meaning of the action is constantly questioned, debated, and rearticulated. While contemporary standards in screenwriting often stress the concealment of exposition and motivation in character action (in service of subtlety), the *Heroes* webcomics are more likely to redundantly depict both. Part of this must be attributed to the formal capacities of the comics themselves. Most issues number five actual pages of content—versus the 90-plus minutes of a feature film or the 300 pages of a novel—and thus, a creator has much less space to investigate character motivation. In other words, perhaps characters are not any "more" motivated, but their motivation is simply more concentrated. Also, this tendency must, in part, be attributed to the institutional legacy of comic books at large and the specific convention of the caption. In the layout of a comic book, a caption is an incredibly fluid thing that can have any temporal (past, present, or future)

FIGURE 1.2 *From "Wireless, Part 4," Joe Pokaski. Aron Eli Coleite [writer] and Micah Gunnell [artist] (page 3).*

or spatial (near, distant) relation to the manifest image and can be sourced to diegetic figures (present or not), to a narrative voice outside of the story, or to an ambiguous source somewhere in between. Commonly, the caption is set in the present tense or looking back from the near future in the voice of a figure either in frame or near off-frame, approximating the filmic use of the voice-over. Captions then are frequently filled with the inner monologue of characters, resulting in an implicit view of the individual that sees herself as constantly aware and self-critical of her own actions at the same time being squarely the master (and narrator) of one's own circumstances. For example, even as the character Gitelman later falls to her death, she surprisingly states in caption, "I suppose in a lot of ways—it's exactly how I expected to die" (Coleite and Badower 2007), giving the character a reflective agency even as it concerns her own violent death. The use of redundancy, condensation, and self-reflective captions all compound into what I term hyper-motivation.

The *Heroes* webcomic series deploys at least four mechanisms in the assignation of the specific meaning of this hyper-motivation:

1 Familial influence: Like the on-air series, the comic is preoccupied with the impact of the decisions of previous generations on their progeny. These influences are reiterated from the on-air series in the case of Mohinder's debt to his deceased father and D. L.'s fidelity to his young family (Issue One and Issue Five, respectively), and in narratives originally concocted for the sake of the comic, as in the case of Hiro's debt to his deceased grandfather (Issue Two), an element of motivation which is never mentioned on-air. The majority of instances of familial motivations are rendered in inner-monologue captions, but they are also depicted structurally, as in juxtaposition of Hana and her ancestors, or even through subtext, as in Issue 21, wherein Hana thwarts a child pornography ring to defend the sanctity of the institution of the family itself.

2 Total institutions: The webcomics, like the on-air television program, also provide redundant motivation to characters by linking them to powerful social formations that we can call, following Erving Goffman (1961), total institutions. This term describes a number of social organizations, such as the military, prisons, cults, and others, which exert a strong, near-constant bureaucratic control over the everyday decision making of its members. For example, Hana Gitelman undergoes her profound moment of self-discovery in the image described above while working at the behest of the secret conspiratorial organization, Primatech Paper. Her suicidal

actions ultimately hinge not just on her familial pride, but also on the insistence of her Primatech commanding officer and father-substitute, Noah Bennett. The issue depicts Gitelman's inundation and adaptation to the orders of a series of total institutions in another montage-like sequence that illustrates, in a series of close-ups, a set of "must" statements give to Hana by her father, her teacher, her military drill sergeant, and Bennett—all figures emblematic of the powerful institutions that inform her actions (Coleite and Badower: 3).

3   Origin stories: The origin story is a time-honored tradition in the field of superhero comic books. Origins (incidentally, the title of a *Heroes* spin-off that was shelved due to the 2007 WGA strike) are Ur-stories that encapsulate everything a reader needs to know about a character, making each subsequent issue potentially superfluous. Classically, they concern traumatic events through which the character finds meaning for the remainder of his or her life (the murder of Bruce Wayne's parents in Crime Alley, the destruction of Krypton, the murder of Peter Parker's Uncle Ben at the hands of an unnamed assailant), and the revelation of the mechanism (often a special ability) through which this meaning will be pursued. In the rare case where origins are withheld, this very absence and ambiguity become a central preoccupation of the character, as seen in the many attempts to shore up the backstory of the extremely popular Marvel character, Wolverine. Arguably, the use of the origin story is influenced by the economic structure of comic books that continues to produce stories over years and decades. By remaining true to origins (which are infrequently modified in substance), readers are allowed to navigate into the series without access to 400-plus back issues. Origins boil motivation and, therefore, character down. The *Heroes* comic, too, often presents origin stories that boil down motivation to a traumatic incident in the past. Isaac's reluctance to use his power of prognostication is attached to the violent vehicular death of a young girl (Issue Eight). Eden's sociopathic behavior is attached to a cruel childhood capped off with matricide (Issue Nine). Linderman's callousness is attached to his banishment from his own family on the pretense of being a heretic (Issue 26). The Haitian's aloofness is explained by his father's attempt on his own life (Issues 35–8). Note how these examples overlap with the familial conflicts addressed above. While origin is a format or formula for understanding motivation, the deployment of familial influence is more an object or source, albeit one that is often plugged into the traumatic frame of an origin.

4 Ethical dilemmas: The webcomics frequently face their characters in difficult ethical decisions whose proper response is debated and weighed, often in interior monologue. For example, Dallas, a solider in the Vietnam War, weighs whether to take the life of a child to forestall further conflict, a variation of a familiar means–ends argument: "you can save a few dozen soldiers or we can save thousands of lives, its up to you" (Issue 26). Similarly, characters are often made to consider and undertake actions of self-sacrifice, usually after much debate over the relative rightness of their action. Issue 34 depicts Hana sabotaging an earth-orbiting satellite by riding into the planet *a la* John Carpenter's *Dark Star* (1974). As she burns up in the atmosphere, Hana's thoughts are rendered in long-winded caption:

> I had to do it. It was the only choice. It was the only way that people like me could be safe. And I didn't want to be a martyr and I wasn't doing it for revenge, or because I had a death wish. I did it because it was the right thing to do. (Coleite and Badower 2007) (see Figure 1.3)

5 Existential problems: While the depiction of ethical dilemmas ends in definitive solution, existential problems, just as frequently depicted in the *Heroes* webcomics, present investigations into motivation that fail to progress out of the stage of questioning—this is motivation in the negative sense. Just as motivation amends meaning to action; amotivation amends meaning to inaction. For example, Issue 12 depicts the fantasy life of a comatose Peter, who, in his dreams, confronts an adversary that is revealed as a doppelganger, invoking self-doubt and confusion of action. And in Issue 18, the secondary character Ted is crippled by self-doubt in the caption while infiltrating a stronghold of a total institution, Primatech Paper, thinking, "I wonder who he is? Does he have a family? Should I leave? Or is he part of this?" (Alexander et al. 2007).

In sum, all of these strategies compound to create a sense of hyper-motivation in the webcomics series that combines a near-constant self-introspection and reflexivity (rendered through the combination of caption and image) and implied self-mastery in which it is the running commentary of personal thought that determines all character action.

This textual pattern can be addressed with the Geertzian model introduced earlier in this chapter. The series' preoccupation with character motivation casts the comic books as a *model for* how ancillary media is to be managed. Given the project's tendencies simultaneously to minimize contact and to highlight the primacy of individual characters, series writers need a mechanism to ensure that characters ring true to audience without the constant supervision of freelanced work. I argue that they achieve this by over-coding, that is, depicting with redundancy and without the concern for explicitness, character motivation. In other words, the comic creators are emphatically underlining their connection to the core series by a near-constant monitoring of a character's mental life.

FIGURE 1.3 *From "The Death of Hana Gitelman, Part 2." Aron Eli Coleite [writer] and Jason Badower [artist] (page 9).*

I argue that this textual preoccupation with motivation suggests how the webcomic provides space to consider the very practices of ancillary media. In the use of redundant, hyper-motivation, creatives use their intimate connection to characters to bridge the gaps between media, but, in their very insistence and repetition, creatives on the series betray a fundamental uncertainty regarding these interfirm translations. In other words, workers on the webcomic series seemingly felt obligated to foreground this connection to character mental life, so much to make it textually auspicious. Moreover, the series' use of hyper-motivation to render character reflects and expresses the production scenario of inconsistent supervisor contact and the use of fandom to fill in these gaps. In some cases, motivation behind character action is a matter of continuity which may be repeated and reexamined (e.g. Bennett's on-air backstory clarifies his dedication to protect Claire, a dedication that is repeated in webcomic Issue 22, which literally depicts Bennett saving Claire as an infant). Here, motivation is a question that can be refilled with a number of answers all reflecting a predetermined response. In other cases, motivation behind action is a matter of simple must-statements to be mimed by transmedia workers (here antagonist Sylar's evolutionary mandate to kill in the absence of a clear origin fits this paradigm nicely [Pokaski and Badower 2007]) who defer subsequent work of the creative core in either case. Here, motivation is a clear mandate whose content is incessantly reiterated. The contrast also serves as a meditation on the textual question—how much are individuals in control of their own actions—a repeated motif of both the on-air and webcomic series. This subtext is refracted through the production circumstances of these webcomics, which also poses the question of freedom of action with regard to how much coordination is made with the creative core and how much leeway (the real-world analog for textual agency) can be pursued by creatives with regard to the translation of character.

Additionally, the webcomics evidence several other patterns that reflect upon the sometimes-difficult circumstances of their production. The series narratives, which are grouped either in single-issue stories or across arcs of two, four, or six issues, exist largely independent of one another. In other words, there is no overarching, developing story line that runs throughout the issues in the manner of the on-air series. At the same time, the majority of the issues have only a vague temporal–spatial relation to the on-air series. As a result, the story information depicted in the series accumulates rather than develops. The practical aspects of this technique of storytelling can be fairly well assumed. Treating material as accumulative facilitates the minimization of contact as each contributor can work on his own piece without being overconcerned with works of prior or subsequent contributors. At the same time, story information can be imagined as a networked grid (without linearity and continuity and containing only tentative connections between stories/nodes), which can be interpreted as a symbol for the networked collaboration of freelancers and supervisors discussed above. As argued earlier, the freelance creative process is a paradoxical one characterized as being spatially both vast and isolated and as being temporally both urgent and empty. This paradoxical treatment of time and space manifests itself in the entire project of accumulative narratives unconnected in time and space, and also in the local treatment of each variable in individual issues that frequently depict large disruptions of continuous time and space. The *Heroes* webcomic is less of an ongoing series than a "networked" one, in terms of narrational style, often only assembled through loose connections of variable characters. The pattern of using a constantly shifting protagonist, inconsistent from issue to issue, is a corollary to this overall technique. The mutability of the protagonist can also be linked to a similar practical need to keep an inconsistent stable of contributors that can be replaced and switched without dire consequences to the overall series.

The five-issue miniseries *24: Nightfall* provides an instructive counterpoint to the *Heroes* webcomic. The comic books follow a covert operation manned by series regular Jack Bauer and then-Senator David Palmer to assassinate a Kosovar war criminal undertaken immediately prior to the events depicted in the on-air Season One. In rendering the narrative, the creators utilized a completely distinct strategy for dealing with character motivation. Captions here are used only to mark the passing of time and, unlike the *Heroes* webcomic, have no special access to characters' inner thoughts or intentions. This blocked access to subjectivity is echoed in the mechanics of the larger story. The series begins *in media res* with Jack and his collaborators already en route to Eastern Europe and never outwardly states the nature or purpose of Bauer's secret mission. The agent's objective is only enunciated on the thirtieth page of the series thanks to the spoken postulations of the intended assassination target, Victor Drazen. In this sense, character motivation is entirely black-boxed, assumed as consistent and not necessitating further explication. This mode of narration reflects the miniseries writer's own philosophy concerning Bauer's characterization; namely, that above all else, the protagonist is "resolute." Furthermore, this black-boxing, which is the preoccupation with a strict and unquestioned consistency with the on-air series' primary characters, extends even to the drawing style of *Nightfall*, which is elaborately photorealistic. Just as the narration refuses to sway from the presumed consistency of the character from the on-air series, the illustration, too, refuses to move away from an absolute (or as much as can be expected) fidelity to the image of the actor/

character. The miniseries' antagonist is also treated to this black-boxing of mental life and image as the comic books, in sum, act as an elaborate explanation as to why Drazen, in the on-air series, spends the entire first season trying to exact revenge upon Bauer and Palmer. In the course of their mission, Bauer and company make a fatal error and end up killing all of Drazen's family and leaving the primary target unscathed and seething. This climax becomes the retrospective seed from which all the events of Season One emanate.

In order to insert surprise and misdirection in the comic books' plotting, the creators juxtapose the black-boxing of primary characters (those who also appear as regulars on the on-air series) with inconsistency, in the form of either unexpected character deaths or rapidly shifting allegiances, on the part of the secondary characters (i.e. those who only appear briefly or not at all on the on-air series). *Nightfall* specifically hinges on the latter as its story depends upon the betrayal of two double agents, one working in the United States and one in Kosovo, who sabotage Bauer's team by blocking access to a surveillance satellite and by supplying Drazen with information about their movement, respectively.

As observed above, the production of *Nightfall* was much less connected to the creative core of the on-air series as compared with the *Heroes* webcomic. Thus, the fact that *Nightfall* is less "connected" to the inner life of the characters is unsurprising. Indeed, I argue that the authors' use of "resolute" characters and a closed narrational style supplemented with the actions of unpredictable double agents is a practical solution to a freelance situation of minimal contact wherein character is the primary element of translation. Series regulars are taken as given and put through a series of steps, via the actions of inconsistent secondary characters, and subsequently act upon their pre-given attributes. This mode of creation obviously depends squarely upon the fandom of the freelancers and their ability to ground primary characters down to an incontestable core. Conversely, the unpredictable movements of secondary characters can be interpreted as symbols of the leeway that freelancers are given to work around pre-given conditions.

While the *Heroes* webcomic translates the series by way of self-questioning, self-doubting characters who continually debate their own actions, *Nightfall* does so through largely silent, "resolute" characters whose very purpose in never clearly enunciated. Certainly, this contrast owes much to the tonal and stylistic differences of the respective on-air series. However, I argue that these differences also owe much to the differing production contexts of each. Through the depiction of the agonized mental life, the *Heroes* webcomic was, in effect, agonizing over demonstrating its exact connection with the on-air series with which it shared some personnel and intellectual resources. However, *Nightfall*, born entirely from freelance labor from pitch to finished comic book, does not investigate character mental life, but leaves Jack Bauer as a known quantity. The *24* freelancers simply did not have the organizational clout to tamper with the character, nor the financial incentive to do so since, one, changes would risk licensor scrutiny over continuity and, two, too radical a change from the on-air series would tamper with the value of the license itself. In other words, there would be little cause to purchase and expensive cross-media license only to radically alter its most recognizable and valuable elements.

Structurally, *Nightfall* plays out through a series of clandestine cell-phone conversations connecting the protagonists back to the United States and the antagonist moles back to Kosovo. This technique of plotting allows the series to occur over a vast distance over the course of only 48 story hours. Yet, in all this elapsed time, the series protagonist, Bauer, and antagonist, Drazen, never interact directly with one another and never share the same rendered space, nor do the series' two central protagonists (Palmer and Bauer). All of the exchanges between these characters are processed through a series of intermediaries. On the whole the comic-book series suggests that, in particular, Palmer's and Bauer's lives were interconnected with one another prior to the events of on-air Season One without either being fully aware. This distanced, networked relation allowed freelancers to connect on-air series regulars without complicating backstory, or tampering with on-air continuity specifically by crafting alternative moments where Bauer "first" met either Drazen or Palmer as opposed to their official on-air meetings. Crafting a plot that affiliated networked characters without direct interaction then serves a clever way of utilizing all the license's characters (the most-valued property in the deal) in what is a very consequential prequel without tampering with on-air story information. Once again, we can also see how the creators used secondary characters, here as the connective tissue in dense interpersonal networks, to assemble resolute characters into a compelling, novel plot. Additionally, these networked layers of connection or interference act as a clear metaphor of the relation of freelancers and supervisors, working together (or against one another?) without direct face-to-face contact.

In this first chapter, we have isolated two illustrative cases of network television transmedia and considered, in depth, both how they are produced how the texts both embody and reflect upon these contexts. These comic books were both created through a series of complicated layers of coordination that both connect and disconnect freelancers to the creative core of each series. In my observations, it was fandom as a practice on the part of creators that filled in for this inconsistent interaction and it was by focusing on character that the connections between texts were ensured. However, the nature of the exact connection of each comic to the creative core greatly influenced how these characters were rendered. In the following section, we will consider a set of transmedia texts, media tie-in novels, whose connection to the creative core is perhaps even more tenuous and whose creators pursue a similar set of compensatory practices and textual strategies to deal with what is ultimately a difficult creative situation. Collectively, both chapters in concert with the later examination of both video-games and mobile-phone content certainly complicate the processes of streamablity and transmedia that are glossed over in prior political- economic, and textual considerations.

2

Tentpole TV: The Tie-in Novel

In conversation, one writer of media tie-in novels recently told me—half in jest—that his novels, in the grand scheme of multi-platform licensing strategies, rank "somewhere beneath the souvenir t-shirt in terms of importance." This perceived low status for tie-in writers and their products is also well demonstrated in the fallout following the *Lost*-integrated novel, *Bad Twin*. The book was positioned as having been written by one of the ill-fated passengers on Oceanic Flight 815, from within the series diegesis. After the book was met with less-than-enthusiastic responses, the *Lost* showrunners attempted to distance themselves from the project, supporting the claim that the book's fictitious author, Gary Troup, was indeed the man flung into the wrecked airliner's engine in the series pilot and that, in the words of co-showrunner Damon Lindelof (in conversation with his writing collaborator [Lindelof and Cuse 2006]), "considering that I have now read *Bad Twin*, Gary Troup got exactly what he deserved."

Yet, this derision is ironic when one considers the larger efforts, briefly outlined in the introduction, of the makers of network tentpole TV programs to extend their reach into other media. As streamability becomes more central to network programming strategies, organizationally, creatively, and economically, the less the contributions of the tie-in novel can be dismissed as tangential to an audience's (or critic's) understanding of any given series. Concomitantly, an examination of any of these television series cannot be complete without considering the creative contributions of these tie-in authors. For example, the tie-in writer Max Allan Collins has drafted six novels based on the fictional world of *CSI* for the publisher Simon & Schuster, another two novels based on the series' spin-off *CSI: Miami*, three comic-book miniseries for IDW Publishing, and two *CSI* videogames, along with another videogame based on *CSI: Miami*. Arguably, Collins has contributed as much to the "world" of *CSI* as many of its on-air producers and writers.

In this chapter, we will specifically examine the work of media tie-in authors, like Collins, primarily through the rubric of one line of books, the so-called APO (Authorized Personnel Only) Series based on the ABC program *Alias*. The ambivalence concerning these projects and their relationship with the on-air programs echoes throughout the process of these books' production and has visible, textual consequences on the finished novels themselves. Drawing again on the production of culture perspective within sociology that "focuses on how the symbolic elements of culture are shaped by the systems within which they are created" (Peterson and Anand 2004: 311), we will specifically consider the organizational structure of tie-in production and demonstrate how this work situation leads to a privileging of a certain set of vernacular aesthetics that provide "solutions" for the difficult creative situation of the tie-in authors.[1] This difficulty largely stems from the ambivalence of participation mentioned above, an ambivalence that we have also detected in the difficult work conducted by transmedia comic-book producers discussed in the previous chapter. By ambivalence, I am simply referring to the fact that the production of these novels is central to the task of achieving streamability—a important strategy of imperilled television networks—while they are, at the same time, distanced from the on-air productions through a number of organizational mechanisms. This distance is observed, for example, in the fact that unlike the production of TV-based comic books, videogames, or websites, where occasionally creative personnel is shared, there is little fluidity between writing talent working on these novels and their television counterparts.[2] Supervisory ambivalence then directly informs a series of paradoxical constraints and restrictions placed upon tie-in writers, which one author described to me as a "strict maze" of "creatively crippling strictures." However, our purpose here is not to decry the creative situation of the tie-in writers, but to demonstrate what strategies and practices they bring to their often-difficult line of work. Following Anthony Giddens's (1979) suggestion that "to study the production of the text is at the same time in a definite sense to study the production of its author," I will ultimately demonstrate how these novels simultaneously reflect and reflect upon the unique circumstances of their production (43). In the very least, this will serve to contribute a modicum of complexity and complication to the theorization of the lived process of transmedia. To achieve this, this chapter will draw on a series of interviews with APO authors along with the comments of supervisors and freelancers working on other similar properties. Lastly, we will amend this consideration of production with a textual overview of the novels themselves. Special attention will be paid to the creative work-arounds utilized and created by media tie-in writers who, like their comic-book counterparts, work in a situation of minimized contact. However,

I begin with a broader consideration of the contemporary publishing industry in general and the importance of media tie-ins.

Like many of the other major cultural industries, print publishing is currently marked by massive upheaval having to do with "the digital" in the broadest sense of the term, that is concerning the threat of potential alternative forms of production, exhibition, and, most importantly, distribution. This anxiety over the changing nature of the business, for example, has indirectly led to the recent replacement of head managers at three of the four top publishers—Random House, Harper Collins, and Simon & Schuster—as firms scrabble to find, like TV's makers—the fabled new business model (Rich 2007, 2008b, Getlin 2008b). Again, the perceived threat to publishing, as to other cultural industries, resides most squarely in disrupting the firms' dominance over mass distribution. Traditionally, major publishers have worked through a system of massive print runs sent to large bookstores and chain retailers, of which 20–40 percent is typically returned to the publisher for destruction (Nias 2008). This system has been profitable for the stores, which are all well-stocked; the printers, who work near capacity; and publishers, who, in the manner described by sociologist Paul Hirsch (1991), overproduce to find and exploit the next "hit." However, this system has been disrupted by the appearance of online distribution, which bypasses both the need for physical retailers and large print runs via the use of print-on-demand manufacturing and direct-to-consumer shipping.

In addition to indirectly leading to the bankruptcy of the United States' #2 book retailer, Borders, these changes have tampered with publishers' ability to market their product. Without the clear-channel conduit of market-dominating bookstores, large publishers are in danger of losing their gate-keeping/agenda-setting role. Within the popular and industrial press, these problems have been answered with a litany of "innovative" firms and entrepreneurs working to embrace new models of business through some of the following strategies.

1 Increased presence on the internet—Trade and popular press reports highlight efforts made by publishers to make their content, as well as web-original content, available online (Senior 2008, Getlin 2008a, Rich 2006). This includes such features as full-text searches of books through publisher websites as well as streamed author interviews.

2 Niche production—Several major publishers have reportedly moved into attempts to capitalize on underutilized markets, particularly through books in Spanish and books focusing on the demographic between "teen" and "middle-age" (18–34 years), who are traditionally understood as light or nonreaders.

3 Nontraditional outlets—Several recent trade articles report on efforts made by publishers to get books in subject matter appropriate, non-book retailers, for example, placing DIY (do it yourself) books in the Home Depot hardware chain or books on upwardly mobile youth in the Urban Outfitters clothing chain ("S&S Turns Ideas into Action" 2006).

4 On-demand printing—Publishers reportedly have also experimented with the idea of on-demand printing, that is limiting book manufacturing to firm orders rather than overproducing, thereby eliminating waste and taking advantage of online consumption habits. Such a scheme has been explored by former Hyperion founder Robert Miller who, for Harper Collins, now heads a division that uses this risk-reduced model and offers potential authors a 50/50 profit-sharing deal, replacing advance payment schemes—the typical method of reimbursement in the era of mass production (Rich 2008a). In other words, on-demand printing allows for new financial schemes whereby publishers profit from the very first book sold instead of waiting for the economies of scale to pay off.

5 E-books—The selling of books digitally in the so-called e-book format has emerged over the last 10 years as a possible alternative to the troubled publishing industry. While beginning slowly, the sales of this format have greatly expanded, assisted through the rapid introduction and adaptation of portable reading devices (most notably the 2010 launch of Apple's Ipad), pushing returns from US$62 million in 2008 to US$863 million in 2010 (Trachtenberg and Peers 2012). How much this quick growth represents new sales rather than siphoned-off losses from the trade cloth (hardcover) business and how digital rights to preexisting works are to be established, the crux of a 2008 antitrust lawsuit against Google's book-retailing arm, are just two of the large questions plaguing the expansion of the e-book business.

6 Cross-promotion—However, for our purposes, the most interesting response to the digital threat in the publishing world involves the use of other media for cross-promotions. Of course, the book business has always relied on other media for exposure (as in excerpts printed in magazines) and content, but the exploitation of properties across media directly addresses the current loss of marketing power, lost in terms of audience attention. Like television producers, book publishers often favor projects that have a multi-platform strategy. Or, in the words of Debbie Olsham, Fox's director of worldwide publishing, "it's such a competitive market, the more you reach out

through many channels to get your property noticed, the better" (Maas 2003b). Perhaps, owing to the fact that publishers infrequently retain any subsidiary rights on their book properties (these, unlike rights to TV properties, are commonly retained by the author) and thus have little economic incentive to do the work of expanding author-born properties, book publishers have achieved this multi-platforming by more aggressively reaching out to partners (frequently in the same Big Media corporate umbrella) in other media forms interested equally in cross-promotion. Licensed book titles have the obvious marketing advantage of having a major film release, a weekly TV series, or some other media event driving its sales. Media tie-ins, in their ability "to tap into a pop lexicon . . . . and sell to a built-in audience," fit squarely within this strategy (Maas 2003a). A new spate of cable serials from *True Blood* (HBO, 2008–present), *Justified* (FX, 2010–present), and *Game of Thrones* (HBO, 2011–present) have leveraged popular book properties into television programs, a practice traditionally more exploited by the film business. Tentpole TV properties have taken the opposite track trying to expand television-born (and television-owned) properties into print.

Film studies scholar Justin Wyatt (1994) finds the roots of cross-promotion, with respect to Hollywood product, in the

conglomeration of the industry, which sought a more financially conservative, less risky approach to filmmaking . . . with saturation releases creating a need for high awareness, the marketing forms— through commercials, music and merchandising—developed to service this requirement. (154)

In other words, Wyatt is describing a more attenuated hit model than DiMaggio that uses ancillary cross-promotion to reduce risk. Such an agenda was arguably advanced as publishing itself became largely an adjunct to media conglomerates themselves. News Corp purchased Harper Collins in 1989 and greatly expanded the publisher with the subsequent purchase of both Avon and William Morrow in 1999. Contemporaneously, Bertelsmann purchased Random House in 1998 and Viacom purchased Simon & Schuster in 1999. Yet more pointedly than even these ownership moves, one can look to the advent of several imprints formed within these larger publishers specifically to exploit entertainment properties, commonly within the same corporate umbrella. For example, on the occasion of the 1998 formation of the imprint Harper Entertainment (HE) within Harper Collins, HE executives announced that the imprint "will offer products related to movies, TV, celebrities and sports" and that "among the first properties to carry the Harper Entertainment logo will be books on the NBA, *The X-Files*, and NASCAR" (Milliot 1998: 10). The later two brands, unsurprisingly, were in heavy rotation on News Corp's own cable and broadcast networks.

More recently, the technique of cross-promotion can be observed in the formation of Simon Spotlight Entertainment (SSE). Founded in 2003 as an imprint under CBS's Simon & Schuster, SSE adopted a mandate to be entirely media-centric; in fact, the firm's very logo is its initials superimposed on a lateral strip of film. In the words of associate publisher Jen Bergstrom, the intention behind the publishing house was to "launch an imprint that would be completely dedicated to taking brands and TV shows and celebrities and issues that are hot in the media and leveraging them into a new format" (Singer 2004). By exploiting the media footprint of exogenous hits, the editors at SSE, and firms like it, have sought to capture more of the coveted 18–34 demographic. Bergstrom further elaborated on the firm's systematic mandate in another interview stating, "We usually know what we want to publish . . . its then a matter of wrapping the right author and spokesperson around it" (Wyatt 2005). Part of SSE's media-centric strategy has been the publishing of traditional tie-ins, that is, novels set within the fictional worlds of preexisting properties. For example, from April 2006 to December 2006, SSE published a series of 13 books based on ABC's *Alias*, subtitled the APO Series.

The production of tie-in novels is by no means unique to the contemporary moment. Indeed, critic Jan Baetens (2007), referencing silent film catalogues as an early variety of textual transcription, has stated that, "roughly speaking novelization is as old as film itself" (228). The same could be said for television with respect to the adaptations of soap opera story lines into magazine digests or the screenplays of Hollywood telefilms into paperbacks. The genealogy of contemporary TV tie-ins could principally be traced back to the exploitation of the original *Star Trek* property that, following industry standards, was first translated into a line of novelizations and eventually into a fully realized line of original-to-print fiction, beginning fitfully with *Mission to Horatius* (1968), which was overseen by Paramount licensors and, according to some, by the *Star Trek* honcho himself, Gene Roddenberry (Ayers 2006). This successful publishing venture, which continues into the present, in many ways set the model of television IP exploitation in print.

However, as I have suggested, there are qualitative differences between these earlier examples and contemporary tie-ins. Economically, the more recent books embody a heightened importance for both the uncertain television and publishing industries. Textually, they also constitute a difference in subject matter. In the past, tie-in writers would typically adapt preexisting materials into a new medium. The APO novels (and other series like them) are "original" novels that expand what critic Matt Hills (2002) has called the hyperdiegesis of the on-air series, that is, the narrative world implied, but not entirely revealed in the original programs. Creative decisions made by current tie-in writers, consequently, have potentially lasting effects on an intellectual property as a whole and, as a result, its financial value. Such an observation goes a long way in explaining the ambivalent supervision to which tie-in writers are subjected in their writing process.

In studying the practices of tie-in production, I have found many areas of overlap with our findings concerning TV-adapted comic books. Specifically, the production of both is marked by an overriding, implicit mandate to minimize contact and interaction among all the participants. To achieve this minimization, all the involved parties—producers (those employed by the producing studio of the on-air series), licensors (those employed by the licensing and merchandising divisions of the parent studio of the on-air series), editors (those employed by the publishing firm that purchased the licensing rights to the series), and the actual novel writers—undergo a series of typical practices that make communication altogether unnecessary, or at least as much as possible. .

Like most ancillary media, the production of tie-in novels is achieved by the combination of supervisory and freelance labor, yet the assignation of either becomes problematic. With respect to the novels' writers, the editors are the supervisors. Editors hire writers on a per-project basis, minimizing a publisher's commitments to the authors, financial and otherwise. Even in cases where authors draft multiple titles for a series, contracts are still frequently based on single assignments. Compensation is typically given in the form of an advance with the possibility of royalties (at the typical rate of between 1% and 3% per unit) to be paid out on the successful accumulation of royalties in excess of the initial advance (*The Business of Novelizations & Tie-ins, Part One: The Deal* n.d.). However, with respect to the licensors, editors are the freelancers. Publishers actively bid for the licensing rights to preexisting properties, entering arrangements that could be based either on the production of a pre-agreed number of books or a preordained amount of time. Ultimately, these licenses lapse and licensors can cultivate deals with multiple publishers over the life of a property. Indeed, such was the case with *Alias*, a program that was featured in a line of Young Adult books published by Bertlesmann-Random House's Bantam Books before SSE acquired the program license. Because these licensors represent the rights holders, they ultimately have the final say in the projects, yet they have no responsibility over the physical manufacturing of the books themselves. One editor-writer has described this common arrangement saying,

> the licensor generally has the "power" in these situations—a writer has to adhere to strict deadlines, while a licensor can drag its heels on approval

and, unless there's a clause in the contract to help you, there's not much you can do—what you can never do is put out material that the licensor has not approved, either specifically or tacitly.

Temporary relationships, the norm for both editors and writers, reduce interaction between all the parties involved in a rationalized approval process. In tie-in writing, interaction between those working on single projects and their supervisors can be characterized as a process of *double approval*. The work of writers is reviewed and critiqued at two levels by both the editor and the licensor—as one APO writer put it, the authors are always "two steps removed" from the actual series—and twice over the course of the project's production.

Often these two separate layers of supervision result in different responsibilities for each. At least one APO writer recounts an instance where licensors were able to spot continuity errors that were ignored by publisher editors (Mata n.d.). Continuity is a term often used by makers of serialized narratives in all media formats. It refers to the accumulated wealth of details and past plot information necessary to create noncontradictory additions to the overall series. This continuity becomes much more difficult to manage in serialized properties wherein each addition potentially contains elements that could alter the subsequent rules of the series. It is then unsurprising that licensors would become the stewards of this continuity given that their relationship with the properties is much more long-term and far-reaching, that is extending over multiple licensing deals and formats. One tie-in writer-editor has suggested that this results in an implicit division of labor whereby "licensors should be concerned with how well the book represents their property, while publishing company editors should be watching for the elements that make a good book, but are not property specific." These multiple layers of supervisor oversight establish a model similar to what Richard Peterson has called the characteristic "decision chains" of cultural industries, wherein projects must be sold and resold within their producing firms before ever being "finished" (Alexander 2003: 94–6). Later, we will consider how this organizational pattern ultimately impacts the novels produced. However, we can now at least point out that editors, as middlemen in the chain, free up the resources of the licensors and minimize their own responsibility in individual projects and, thus, their need for interaction.

The term double approval also refers to the temporal process of tie-in production in which interaction is attenuated into two discrete moments: the review of the outline and the review of manuscript. It is, however, overwhelming during the former that comments, notes, and interactions between the involved parties are most pervasive. Typically, a freelance tie-in writer, in preparation for writing, will produce an outline, varying in length from 10 to

25 pages, which is examined by supervisors. One APO writer described this process saying,

> ABC [the licensor] makes the overwhelming majority of their comments during the proposal stage as opposed to the manuscript stage. It is not unusual to go through several rounds of revisions on a proposal to make sure that its perfect before being given approval to move ahead to the manuscript.

A writer who worked on a tie-in novel based on ABC's *Lost* described an extensive series of steps involved in the preproduction, saying,

> the process was that I had to write five basic plot ideas and then they [the licensors] chose one. And then I had to write a long synopsis for that one . . . they made me write ever increasingly detailed synopses. So, by the time that I got down to actually writing, I'd thought it out pretty clearly.

The practice of focusing on preproduction (i.e. the outline stage) works in a manner similar to that observed in the production of TV-based comic books. Frontloading scrutiny achieves a basic level of trust that reduces the need for subsequent interaction between freelancers and supervisors. I described the previous chapter with reference to Anthony Giddens's social theory that explains that consistency and self-identity are continually rebought through faith and trust in remote others. Similarly, the porous "identity" of tentpole TV programs is won less through extensive scrutiny than through trust in collaborators established by frontloaded interaction. Conversely, the APO writers were typically given very little feedback at the manuscript phase. The same APO author quoted immediately above further stated that, "once I turned in the manuscript, ABC's and my editor's comments were relatively minor." Another APO author described the process of manuscript review as "either serious or minor nitpicks . . . a lot dumb stuff like, let's tone down the violence or there's too much sex for *Star Trek*." In the few instances where these minimal revisions are passed down from licensors to writers, they most frequently dealt again with issues of continuity and the concern of making the novels fit with the property. The focus on continuity at both points of the double-approval process also suggests that it is, ultimately, playing by the rules of the property that is of paramount importance in the production of tie-ins and is, therefore, singled out by both supervisors and freelancers as the essential attribute for tie-in writers. However, there is irony in the fact that both supervisors and freelancers often consider their work in tie-ins as non-canon, that is, not "officially" part of the series continuity. As I will demonstrate later, this attitude greatly affects who is hired to write these novels and how their work is done. But here I suggest only that supervisors often have little to say about manuscripts outside of considering how the novels play into the spirit of the series and, thus, avoid protracted discussion of the more cumbersome elements of novel writing (plot, character, point of view, etc.).

The tie-in novels also frequently employ extremely rapid production cycles and very tight deadlines. This is attributed to both the needs of the licensors/producers who need the novels published either concurrently with a broadcast premiere or hiatus as well as the needs of the publisher because tie-in books are "contracted as needed." One APO writer describes this latter problem saying, "because tie-ins are contracted as needed they [publishers] are less likely to have substitutes available, which would leave a hole in the line and result in lost revenue." The rapid production schedules are exacerbated by the writers' freelance status; occupying the last position in the long decision chain, authors have little temporal control over their assignments. Additionally, there is a fundamental non-isomorphism between the timing of television work and publishing, which frequently forces the latter to speed up to catch the former. Tie-in writers are given anywhere from two-and-a-half weeks to six months to write a novel with three months being the most typical deadline. Writers cope with this organizational constraint by making timeliness the cardinal virtue of their profession. As one APO writer put it, "almost in a weird way, and I don't want to sound derogatory, reliability and dependability is almost more important than sheer talent." Similarly, author Steve Perry has flatly observed that in tie-in production, "the deadline is set-set, and that's it, end of story. If you take the job, best you meet the date. If you don't they tend not to re-hire you" (*The Business of Novelizations & Tie-ins, Part One: The Deal* n.d.). In my own research, I also detected shades of a hot-shot mentality among the writers that takes pride in the breakneck speed and seemingly intellectual precariousness of their work. For example, one prominent tie-in writer, Keith R. A. DeCandido, confessed in a recent article: "I love the looks on people's faces when I tell them that I've written a novel in three weeks with plenty of time" (*The Business of Novelizations & Tie-ins, Part Three: The Deal* n.d.). Making matters more difficult for freelancers is the fact that, typically, any time spent on the outline phase fails to alter the final deadline. When taking a job, tie-in writers must be sure that they can make the deadline regardless of subsequent complications, or as another APO writer put it, "having the confidence to say yes to [the] deadline is an absolute necessity in this business." Again, this limited temporal commitment to the series also works toward the implicit mandate of minimal contact; protracted discussion is simply not possible given the rapid production schedule.

Related to both the mandate of minimizing contact and the practice of rapid deadlines is the rationalization of tie-in work. As in other industries (creative or otherwise), laborers attempt to boil work down to a regularized, machine-like process—or as much as possible. As one tie-in writer-editor put it, "I knew sometimes some very good writers . . . but I would not necessarily hire them for tie-in [work] because that's something that you need to be able to do, churn them out on a regular basis." Regularity is also facilitated by writers' self-stated attempts to mimic the on-air series as closely as possible. In terms of minimizing contact, the close mimicking of the on-air program series serves to reduce the need for communication between the links in the decision chain, as the tie-in's relation to continuity is already emphatically established. This is advantageous to supervisors who can split their attention between projects, but the same could be said of the freelance authors who, given their rapid work style, can turn around in multiple projects. One APO writer stated in an interview, "I try to write six or seven books a year because that's how you make a living . . . If you spend a year writing on an *Alias* book, that's a recipe for bankruptcy."

Just as important as a tie-in freelance writer's familiarity with the on-air series is his or her familiarity with the process of writing tie-ins in general, which is held with as much weight and at least partially determines a writer's ability to have success and secure employment in the field. One APO writer describes the importance of "playing by the rules" in his explanation of the job: "we are playing with somebody's else's ball in their backyard. That means they get to make the rules, we get to stay in the yard. If we don't we're going home." The metaphor here was used to underscore the necessary humility in the tie-in writer, but can just as well be a reference to all the formal and informal "rules" of the production of tie-ins, having to do with both the textual specifics of individual series and the regular practices of the production of the novels in general, that is what is normally allowed and not allowed, how the novels should relate to continuity, and the like.

With respect to the latter issues, supervisors commonly follow a series of hiring practices to maximize trust with freelancers and assure themselves that all the "rules" will be followed in advance. Tie-in editors tend to use and reuse the same stable of freelancers in multiple projects. More so than in other ancillary media, the tie-in labor pool seems even more contracted, as the same writers work on any number of tie-in series based on several different properties. One APO writer describes this practice of what we can call *lateral hiring* saying, "when editors are looking for writers for a specific line, they will often ask other editors for recommendations." The result of such a practice can be seen in the biographies of the APO writers, all of whom (with one exception) have written extensively for other tie-in properties. Greg Cox (author of *Two of a Kind*, *Namesakes*, and *The Road Not Taken*) has written *CSI*, *Star Trek*, as well as several books based on Marvel and DC comic-book properties. Paul Ruditis (author of *Vigilance* and *Mind Games*) has written books based on the TV series *Charmed* and *Sabrina the Teen-aged Witch*. Roger MacBride Allen, a writer of *Star Wars* novels, has bluntly described this practice in an essay entitled "Media Tie-ins: Why They're Nearly Impossible for Beginners to Publish," stating, "ALL of the writers hired to do the *Star Wars* books had written and published books of their own before they were approached. They had track records." Hiring practices for the tie-in novels also differ from those of the tied-in comic books with respect to the fluidity between job roles. In the case of comic books, there has been a movement between those working on the on-air series and the writing tasks of drafting adaptations, seen both in the *Heroes* webcomic as well as recent translations of Warner Brothers' programs *Supernatural* and *Chuck*, FOX's *Fringe*, and CBS's *Jericho*, all of which were drafted by on-air writing staff. There is also a marked fluidity in the tie-in novel decision chain, but it is among editors, licensors, and the freelance writers. Indeed, two APO writers (Emma Harrison and Greg Cox) have spent a considerable amount of time in their careers as editors, handling tie-in projects and one other (Paul Ruditis) began his career in the licensing department of Paramount. These career trajectories again underscore that it is an understanding of the practices and processes of writing tie-in novels that is seen as the most desirable trait in freelancers and most advantageous with respect to the implicit mandate of minimizing their contact with supervisors.

In his recent book, *Media Work*, sociologist Mark Deuze (2007) channels Zygmunt Bauman, illustrating the collapsing boundaries of work, leisure, and rest in contemporary occupations, particularly in the cultural vanguard of media professions. This dissolution of barriers between work and not-work can be observed specifically in the manner in which the skills and products of fandom are deployed in the labor of tie-in novelists. Like their comic-book counterparts, freelance tie-in writers typically espouse a previously existing devotion toward the properties they work on; indeed, all of the APO writers I talked to have discussed an attachment to *Alias* as a consumer prior to getting the assignment to write their novels. A comment by one APO writer sums up his attitude more generally: "I'm a big fan at heart, so I consider myself lucky to be able to do this for a living" (Brady 2007). Sometimes these sentiments are taken even further as another APO writer, in discussing another property stated,

> I was a HUGE fan of *Buffy* and *Angel* and really all things Joss Whedon for many years. Joss is one of the writers that I admire most in the world and

one that I've often prayed to in times of literary need. (Mata n.d.; emphasis in original)

However, this fan's enthusiasm, found in tie-in writers, has more than a theological purpose.

In the condition of minimized contact between freelancers and supervisors, tie-in writers use fandom and non-work viewing habits as an informal source of research. In the previous chapter, I described this in terms of Howard Becker's conventions—social norms that allow for collaboration across an artistic field. Fandom can be characterized as a similar form of social knowledge, facilitating the work of tie-in writers. An intimate connection with the series gives tie-in writers easy access to the minutiae of continuity, already seen to be paramount among the concerns of licensors. For example, one APO writer describes breaking into tie-in novels by virtue of his encyclopedic knowledge of the DC comic-book character, Batman (Brady 2007). This fandom also hypothetically gives the writers easier access to their implied reader, arguably facilitating the conception phase of their work. Or, as another APO writer put it, "it all starts with the fact that I'm usually a fan of these shows myself. So, I always begin with what I want to see in a book like this" (Haag 2004). In addition to tapping their own fandom, tie-in writers also mine the fandom of others, using fan-created artifacts as shortcuts in their own research processes. Quick access to fans on the internet is particularly helpful when, for example, "there's a minor demon that I can't remember the name of," or when you can "drop into an *Alias* chatroom and then ask, 'hey, what kind of car does Sydney drive?'" Another tie-in writer commented on his work on a line of books based on the WB's *Roswell*, stating, "we even communicated with a few uber-fans to see if they knew details of character information that might be helpful" (*Writing a Tie-in* n.d.). These examples again both have to do with the minute details of continuity, yet, as I will demonstrate below, this fan's devotion to continuity has further-reaching effects on the practice of tie-in writing.

Just as often as tie-in novelists insist upon their prior devotion to on-air properties and the advantages of this devotion, the writers also frequently make efforts to distinguish themselves from "hardcore" fans in general. In conversation, one APO writer stated,

now there is a difference between being a fan and being a *fan*. I've never really been a hardcore fan of any show. Never dressed in costume for a convention. Never got into a heated argument about whether Buffy loved Angel or Spike more.

The beginning of this last statement is particularly surprising when one considers that its author has drafted several complete episode guides to a number of the television series. Yet, I would argue that the writer's final statement—having to do with debates over meaning within the show—gets at the heart of the matter and the cause of distancing fandom. Another tie-in writer explains—using a similar example—that,

> there's a serious, hardcore contingent of Angel fans who believe that Buffy is Angel's soulmate and he can never be happy unless he's with her. There's an equally large and vociferous group, though who think the same thing about Angel and Cordelia. The writer can't please both constituencies, so the best thing to do is to present the characters and their relationships at that given moment in the series continuity.

In other words, tie-in writers can use many of the tools of fandom (e.g. minute details won by focused and repeated viewings as well as access to cooperative communities based on the accumulation of series continuity), but must shy away from speculation. Henry Jenkins (1992) describes the former as a fan's mode of reception whereby

> viewers watch television texts with close and undivided attention, with a mixture of emotional proximity and critical distance. They view them multiple times, using videotape players to scrutinize meaningful details to bring more and more of the series under their control. (277–8)

However, in the end, tie-in writers must avoid fan speculation that would, one, fall in error of the principle of playing by the rules of the on-air series and, two, potentially invoke the ire of displeased fans. Avoiding this Scylla and Charybdis means simply avoiding anything that could be construed as interpretation, in the broadest sense of the word.

In his masterful discussion of Quattrocentro Italian painting, art historian Michael Baxandall (1972) goes to great lengths to explain how the important works of that era were deeply in conversation with the broader social context of their creation, going so far as to argue that, "the fifteenth-century experience of a painting was not the painting we see now so much as a marriage between the painting and the beholder's previous visualizing activity on the same matter" (45). In the author's more adventurous moments, Baxandall considers that the paintings were created to be in accordance with the mental peculiarities, or "period eye," of the mercantile patrons of the arts. For example, the author attempts to demonstrate how paintings exploit the visual habits of gauging—that is visually estimating the volume of containers—and setting proportions, two skills essential for the practice of trade and early capitalism among the patrons of early Renaissance paintings. I would argue that tie-in writers, in a clearly different context, also craft their works with the visual attention of their implied readers in mind, in this case fans of the television series. Indeed, I have found that frequently in interviews with tie-in writers and their editors, it is the implied and actual scrutiny of fans that drives their attention to detail. Discussion of this scrutiny even takes on an adversarial tone. One APO writer reports on a catch of a continuity error by a licensor thankfully saying that she was "pleased that someone saw it before we moved forward . . . I know that the fans would have kicked my ass over it" (Mata n.d.). Another APO writer comments upon the particularly exacting standards of series fans upon tie-ins saying, "people will trash a book simply because the author got a character's eye color wrong." The period eye of the implied tie-in reader then is one that dissects the details of the tie-in and gauges them minutely against voluminous knowledge of on-air continuity. The visual skills brought to reading are those won through intensive television spectatorship.

The cultivation of the particular period eye was achieved, in Baxandall's case of gauging and proportionality, by the expansion and propagation of arithmetic education. In our case of *Alias* fans, the period eye is facilitated by the fannish reading practices of incorporating texts into one's social life, repeated viewings, and dissections of individual episodes. The latter practice has been made much more available, if not in practice then in theory, thanks to advances in home entertainment technologies and the exploitation of these advances. Earlier forms of fandom, as outlined by authors like Jenkins, can be described as social formations wherein viewers' textual desires outstripped available products as fans produced their own media artifacts, from dubbed and shared tapes to photocopied fanzines. These practices continue, but, arguably, the poles of desire and availability have been inverted as media accessibility, among a certain strata of consumers, increasingly moves toward complete temporal and spatial ubiquity. Or more simply, in our era of media abundance, one can potentially see anything, anywhere at anytime. In the world of tie-ins, this abundance is a double-edged sword as it facilitates both authors' research as well as deeper scrutiny by fans.

In the case of the former, many tie-in writers discuss an immersive research technique wherein authors use media abundance to become "instant experts" on the canon of the adapted series. In preparation for writing tie-ins, the authors often rewatch any number of on-air episodes, yet, ironically they occupy themselves much less with tie-ins by other authors. Such a practice is described by Max Allan Collins, who outlined his preproduction work on the *CSI* books saying, "I tend to not watch it, but record it and then watch a number of episodes in the days leading up to my starting the book . . . that immersion in the character and style of the show is extremely useful" (*Writing a Tie-in* n.d.). This immersion, in the opinion of at least one APO writer, makes the process much easier, particularly in comparison with "horror stories of people trying to write *Get Smart* novels back in the sixties when they basically had to watch the shows on the air" (Brady 2007). If immersion has to do with volume, that is watching a number of episodes in a concentrated fashion, one can also point to a separate practice among tie-in writers of close reading wherein the authors try to grasp the structure of the on-air series, catalog all its pertinent continuity details, and attempt to understand the property's more ineffable features (tone, mood, theme, etc.). One tie-in writer-editor describes his own, very extensive system of close reading saying, "I make an effort to create my own 'episode guide' . . . noting personality details, background details, location details, etc.—anything that might become important in re-creating the world of the show on paper." Such observations won by focused, repeated viewings give the tie-in writers access to exactly what is neglected in minimized contact with supervisors: the series boiled down to its incontestable core and broken apart into its essential details. It also allows the writers to make pronouncements concerning the nature of the adapted property, such as those of a tie-in writer who described the *Buffy* works by combining the "hero story" with lessons in humor and humility (Mata n.d.). Here we once again arrive at the very fine line distinguishing the tie-in writer from the fan. Immersion and close reading, on the surface, appear to be similar to the devotion paid by a fan and the conclusions won by close readings seem dangerously close to what one could call fan speculation. It seems that the principal distinguishing feature between the two groups is simply the amount of rigor (perceived or actual) applied in their similar practices.

One tie-in writer working on a *Doctor Who* novel described his own practice of immersion saying, "my most recent effort featured the fifth Doctor and one of [the] companions, Nyssa, so I sat [and] watched as many of the TV stories feature these characters as possible, to get the voices of the actors in my head" (*Writing a Tie-in* n.d.). Expanding upon this author's technique, I would argue that more generally immersion and close reading are often in service of achieving character "voice." In my experience, achieving "voice," that is making characters on the written page "sound" like the characters on air, is chief among the accepted virtues of adapting tie-ins and the most telling characteristic in judging the relative success or failure, aesthetic or otherwise, of a project. As one of the APO writers put it, "one of the most flattering comments that I have received is that, in dialogue, my characters tend to sound exactly as they do on TV." Another APO writer, discussing work on a different property, describes her own process of achieving voice saying,

> Sometimes I write a line and then I think, wait a minute! Paige would never say that. That's a Piper line! Then I make the change. I figure that if diehard fans are reading my book they'll pick up on things like that, too. (Haag 2003)

Again it is the implied scrutiny of the fan that drives deeper immersion and consequent fidelity to source material.

Another indirect consequence of media abundance is the importance of making tie-ins value-added. Simply put, the contemporary production of tie-ins is marked by both an editorial mandate and an authorial aesthetic that focuses on giving a reader something more than what is presented in the on-air program itself. Having hypothetical instant access to all the episodes of the series via any number of channels, the implied reader is understood as no longer interested in simple retellings or reworkings of on-air events. Many editors have sought out new methods of attaching tie-in narratives to the series proper outside of mere repetition, particularly through the use of integration, that is giving the book a place in the actual diegetic world of the series, as in our introductory example of *Bad Twin*. At least two problems, however, arise. Integration requires a large amount of coordination between supervisors and freelancers, a form of activity that, as we have seen, is generally in short supply. Moreover, "adding" elements to a series is fundamentally at odds with the other mandate of playing within the rules of a series, making it just one more example of how paradoxical the situation of the freelance tie-in writer can become. The solution to this riddle employed by many tie-in writers is to exploit the "unexplored gems" of the series. In the words of one APO writer: "often times in developing tie-ins, you're looking for that little unexplored gem; something that the original creators never had the time or interest in developing further but something that's worth more thought." Another APO author described a similar process in slightly different terms: "with *Alias*, occasionally I try to find things—filling in the blanks—that they [the producers] don't flesh out too much in the TV show or throwing together different combinations of characters." Tapping the unexplored gem means drawing on elements implied in the on-air series, but not directly addressed. Such a technique can be observed in several of the APO novels. For example, *Namesakes* (Cox 2006) revolves around a revenge plot engineered by an ex-SD-6 agent whose life was ruined when the covert organization was exposed (in Season Two of the on-air series). Here the author is considering the unintended and unexplored consequences of an on-air event. Similarly,

A Touch of Death (York 2006) concerns the reemergence of an SD-6 villain years after the group's above-mentioned neutralization. This book uses the same on-air event and considers that it was not as final as the series protagonists had assumed (however, finality is reachieved with the antagonist's death at the novel's conclusion). While the use of unexplored gems solves the paradox of value-added tie-ins, this practice is predicated precisely upon the forms of intensive, fan-like research mentioned above. In the case of our two above examples from the APO novels, the books' authors needed an understanding of the so-called rebooting of the series its Season Two when the antagonistic organization SD-6 was dismantled. However, the use of unexplored gems further clouds the specific type of fandom that tie-in writers practice; at which point does the drawing out of the implied become interpretation or speculation?

Freelance tie-in writers then practice a very specific form of fandom—writing these novels, in the words of one APO writer, would be torture without this fandom—that marries a devotion to the series with a devotion to the rules of the series surmised through a regiment of strict research. The closest analog that I can find is with academic television studies itself. Both disciplines share a research methodology of minute, concentrated observation, both must find ways of using and managing media abundance, and both must maintain a semblance of fidelity to the on-air series in their own writing. However, the most important distinction between the two camps is that TV studies has largely traded away what little contact tie-in novelists have had with producers for unlimited leeway of approach and subject matter, making us practioners of academic TV studies from a certain perspective, the least tied-in of tie-in writers.

In an article entitled "A Methodological Framework for the Sociology of Culture," Wendy Griswold (1987) introduced what she considered a holistic method for the study of all cultural expression. The first step in this method was the consideration of the "intention" of producers or, "the social agents purpose in light of the constraints imposed on him or her in the production of and incorporation of cultural objects" (5). The construct of intention ("construct" because it could never be fully reconstituted) can be shaped into an intuited contract or "brief" which considers all the influencing factors (both impeding and facilitating) in any given work: social expectations, patron concerns, immediate circumstances, education, physical media, and others. As one brief example, we have already observed how the understanding of the period-eye guides the work of tie-in professionals. This constraint model also echoes the method of study proposed by sociologists Ettema and White (1982) who, in their own examination of mass media work, stated,

> individual work [in mass media organizations] cannot be understood apart
> from its various contexts because it is powerfully shaped and constrained

by them . . . mass communicated creativity can only be effected in a organizational context. (8)

In considering the hypothetical brief concerning the production of the APO novels and tie-in novels more generally, one should first come to terms with the difficulty of translating a property from a visual to a printed one. Specifically, there is the generic expectation in novels to deeply investigate the interior life of characters through omniscient narration, a feature ostensibly absent in television episodes. One APO writer described this distinction stating, "the books are different because we can get 'inside their heads.' In some ways we can be more intimate with the characters than the show can. This can lead to all sorts of difficulties." While those working, for example, on the *Heroes* webcomic frequently use layout decisions and internal monologue to rearticulate motivation (as observed in Chapter 1), APO writers take a slightly different tact. Each of the novels is structured by a diffuse, shifting point of view, punctuated by brief, italicized passages of characters talking to themselves in self-directed asides. Arguably, this device demonstrates how the authors work to "solve" the problem of subjectivity by applying another, previously mentioned aesthetic standard, that of achieving character "voice." These subjective asides are most frequently used to either make passing reference to on-air events or to make explicit links between novel and on-air characters. For example, in Cox's *Namesakes*:

> She [Sydney] figured Rivera's head would explode if she actually gave him the full particulars of her rocky relationship with Michael Vaughn. *Like the time I stabbed him in the ribs and left him bleeding in a ditch, just to maintain my cover. Or the time he married a duplicitous double agent who tried to get us both killed.* (60)

Furthermore, these asides are used to elaborate on echo characters (thus, serving to symbolize the measured, paradoxical connection that tie-in writers have with respect to the on-air series). For example, Sydney draws a parallel between herself and the novel's villain in *Two of a Kind*: "Had Maya led him astray, turning him from harmless stunts to major international espionage? If so she had gotten her alleged fiancé in seriously hot water. *Just like I got Danny killed*" (Cox 2005: 62).

Many APO writers also mention the difficulty of translating the pacing, or distinct temporality of the on-air series into novel form. *Alias*, the television series, frequently featured exceptionally swift story lines incorporating rapid scene shifts and an unusually high number of setups. This caused problems for several of the APO writers, one of whom reported that he had gone two-thirds the way through his original outline, resulting in only 80 finished pages. This author then found a "solution" to this problem by intercutting another subplot involving series regular Nadia Santos. Indeed, all of the authors' subsequent—as well as all the other APO novels—are marked by frequent intercutting between several intertwined plots, or between several perspectives on single events, often motivated by the use of walkie-talkie-like gadgets (an aesthetic device cribbed more or less directly from the on-air series). All of the APO writers use similar techniques to simulate the on-air series' jaunty pace. Several books also make frequent use of what we can call after-the-fact plotting, wherein depicted events occur just after other impor-tant story events that have been elliptically excised. The end result is that the hypothetical pace is quickened by condensing the description of present-tense actions and past-tense together at once. Also several novels make liberal use of repeated events whereby the same action replays multiple times from the perspective of multiple characters. This device functions in an opposite way with respect to after-the-fact plotting, extending rather condensing events, with an arguably similar total effect, that is a sense of juxtaposition and colli-sion. On a more rudimentary level, several of the APO novels employ timed sequences wherein a running clock (often attached to a bomb of some sort) accompanies the actions of the characters. In sum, all these techniques serve to demonstrate that writers must experiment with temporality to achieve a suitable adaptation.

On a more theoretical level, I have found that the brief for tie-in supervi-sors and freelancers can be understood as a combination of two paradoxical mandates that manifest both explicitly and implicitly in the production of the novels. On the one hand, all parties involved are guided by the constraint of non-repetition that disallows anything that too closely resembles the on-air series. In response, tie-in authors ideally attempt to consider ideas/topics/plots in someway addressed, but not elaborated in the on-air series. The vernacular aesthetics of the writers favor what I called unexplored gems to avoid, in advance, supervisors' need to eliminate anything that may overlap with previous or upcoming episodes. One APO writer referred to this con-straint as the "bane of *Star Trek* writers" whereby writers "come up with a brilliant plot and they [supervisors] come back and they say, 'sorry, we're doing that next season, you can't do that.'" On the other hand, because tie-in writing is not, in the words of one tie-in novelist, "a free creative decision," both the supervisors and the freelancers are subject to the constraint of non-contradiction whereby a tie-in novel must never openly contradict the on-air series. We have already seen this in supervisors' (in particular the licensors') attention to continuity and freelancers' tendency to mimic episodes and play by the series' rules. Put in more simple terms, tie-in writers find themselves in a situation where they must not replicate the on-air series while simultane-ously not being able to add anything different to the series. This is precisely the conflict isolated in the previous section wherein authors immerse themselves in the details of a series to find an original angle on the preexisting elements while carefully avoiding anything that could be termed interpretation. Moreover, the predicament returns us to the issue of this chapter's introduction, that tie-in writers are incorporated in the series through repetition of key distinguishing features, but are held at a distance from the series by their limited textual power. These two paradoxical constraints, I argue, are central to the hypothetical contract between freelancers and supervisors and one can understand the resultant novels largely as extended solutions to these problems presented primarily to freelance writers.

These constraints can have—by the accounts of producers and readers—deleterious effects on the novel produced. In conversation, one author recounted to me the difficult process of writing a *Lost* tie-in novel:

> those were my rules to begin with: they [the novel's characters] couldn't do anything that would have any impact on what was actually happening on the series. And the main character had to be a character, one of the other 48 [survivors], one of the sort of background [constraint of non-repetition]. But he could only interact with other people from the show [constraint of non-contradiction]. There couldn't be anyone else on the island. So, in other words, I couldn't use more than one of the background people.

Subject to these two constraints explicitly imposed by supervisors, tie-in writers find themselves in a situation with only a minuscule amount of leeway, a situation that one tie-in author has characterized as a "strict maze."

More generally, freelancers employ a number of strategies to address each of these constraints individually. Noncontradiction, in the case of the APO novels, compels writers to include in their work the familiar elements of the on-air series such as exotic locations, rapid costume changes, and a requisite amount of emotional angst. More abstractly, the APO writers, both in their novels and their discussions of them, work to maintain the status quo of the series. In other words, the APO authors craft their books such that they are hermetically sealed from the larger plot questions of the series. This is particularly ironic and problematic for the tie-in writers given the highly serialized nature of the on-air variant of *Alias*. Isolating their work as stand-alones is preferred by both supervisors and freelancers as a technique of both avoiding the possibility of contradiction and of minimizing the need for coordination and contact. One APO author in conversation recounted his stumbling upon this technique:

> [*Alias*] constantly shook-up who's on whose side, everybody's a triple, double agent who's actually working for this. I really needed to know what was going on and they [supervisors] sent me stacks of scripts and we [the author and

show writer Jesse Alexander] had this long talk on the phone. Even then I discovered that it was probably best to stay away from any of their ongoing arc-plots [and] do a nice stand-alone, beginning-middle-end spy adventure for Sydney that didn't tie into what Sydney's mother was doing this season . . . I would have liked to use characters like Sark and Irina, but they had this tangled continuity that it was better to just invent my own villains and stay away from whatever was the ongoing conspiracy of the season.

The aesthetic impact of maintaining the status quo can be observed in the marked finality of conclusion used in the APO novels themselves. Mostly avoiding the cliffhanging endings that recur throughout the on-air series, *The Road Not Taken* (Cox 2005a), *A Touch of Death*, and *Old Friends* (Hanna 2006) all introduce new archfiends who are emphatically dead—strangely enough, all three plummet to their deaths in the novels—by the narratives' end, prohibiting their subsequent recurrence. Such a repeated device may seem to be obvious given the author's brief; however, I would argue that it displays a fundamental understanding of the rules of the series, which often depicted the death of antagonists, put in the service of noncontradiction. However, in utilizing this finality, tie-in authors arguably run up against noncontradiction in the manner in which the resultant novels neglect the serialized, cliff-hanger structure of the on-air series.

Conversely, APO writers are compelled to abide by the constraint of non-repetition. We have already touched upon this above in the discussion of creating a sense of "value-added," to the experience of the on-air series. Because of this necessary difference in tie-ins, both supervisors and freelancers emphatically insist that their products are not part of the official canon of the series. The relationship between the two is a one-way street characterized by one APO writer who stated, "I always have to explain that, no, my *Star Trek* or *Alias* novels are not going to be turned into episodes of the TV show. That never happens." This isolation between the tie-ins and the series also creates a sense of freedom that one author called a "dead-end alley of continuity" (*The Business of Novelizations & Tie-ins, Part Three: The Deal* n.d.). Because tie-ins never tie back in, their authors can take certain liberties with the series, within reason. Most obviously, one can point to the introduction of new characters in APO novels (a leeway only provisionally granted to the *Lost* writer quoted at length above). Indeed, the plots of many of the APO novels hinge upon the "introduction" of old acquaintances, as in the appearance of Sydney's old college chum in *Old Friends* (Hanna) or Sydney's German terrorist nemesis in *Namesakes* (Cox 2006).

Besides working with respect to one set of constraints or the other, tie-in professionals have also developed a novel set of practices to address both and find a middle ground between.

1   Specifying time frame—Often tie-in writers focus on very specific temporal moments within the life of a property. Indeed, the initial premise of the APO series is to follow the series characters as they worked for the covert organization, APO, something that only happened in the program's Season Four. Working within this fourth season was an explicit editorial mandate handed down to the authors. Even as the on-air program moved into its Season Five, at least one APO writer was told to continue plotting as if it were still the fourth. Moreover, this specification is favored by writers as a way of solving ambiguity within series continuity. Another tie-in writer addressed this stating,

> the best thing to do is to present the characters and their relationships as he or she understands them at that given moment in the series continuity . . . there's usually some moment at which the writer can get a story and say, "here's where the characters were, emotionally, at the moment."

This impulse is taken to its extreme in several APO (*The Road Not Taken* and *Namesakes*) novels that begin with the novel's exact temporal position in the series, between specific on-air episodes. This technique cordons off a space where writers can be certain about the bounds of noncontradiction, but have the leeway of temporally unexplored gem.

2   Seeding the past—To situate themselves within the continuity of the series, the APO novels frequently make references to formative on-air events, usually motivated through the use of character memory. The authors use this same technique to introduce non-canon elements, particularly new characters. Writers seed the past by using flashbacks and recollections to subtly suggest that these new elements (non-repetition) were part of the characters' lives all along (noncontradiction)—a practice known as retroactive continuity, or ret-conning, in the world of comic books. In my analysis, I have found that most of the APO novels contain at least one instance of this practice at work. Both *Two of a Kind* (Cox 2005b) and *Namesakes* (Cox 2006) begin with introductory flashbacks, both prior interactions with characters that then become the narrative's antagonists. More generally, all of the APO novels introduce new characters of whom it is revealed the principal characters already had prior knowledge of. For example, both *Two of a Kind* (Cox 2005b) and *Faina* (Gaborno and Hollier 2005) introduce computer-hacker characters of whom it is revealed that a principal character—in this case series regular and APO technician

Marshall—already knew of their existence. The author of *Touch of Death* freely comments on this technique within the diegesis of the novel itself, omnisciently pointing out that, "it seemed as if ghosts were rising from the past to haunt the APO team" (York 2006: 124).

3   Echo characters—As stated above, the introduction of new characters is an important aspect of tie-in writing. However, to combat the possibly disruptive effects of such inclusions, writers often base these new characters on preexisting ones, making them echo characters. Often this technique has a prudent origin. One APO writer reports that he planned to incorporate a character for the series' first season, a mercenary named Anna Espinosa, but was vetoed by supervisors when it was revealed that the character would be subsequently returning to the on-air series (constraint of non-repetition). To solve the problem, the author simply changed the character's name: "in fact if you're inclined to read that book . . . just basically go in—I can't remember what her name was . . . in the first draft she was Anna Espinosa—my own Anna Espinosa." More generally, many of the APO writers in their work use frequent comparisons to establish new characters. Thus, the eponymous Faina is an extremely gifted young girl, contrasted with Sydney herself. In *Faina*, the protagonist spells out the comparison: "Sydney's fear was forming in her mind as she realized the extent of Faina's skills. *She's even more like me than I imagined*" (Gaborno and Hollier 2005: 137). The antagonist of *A Touch of Death* (York 2006), Gai Dong Jing, is, like series regular Arvin Sloane, an ex-SD-6 member who has managed to elude capture after the criminal organization's dismantling. The character of Sloane points out this mirroring during the course of the novel in describing the antagonist: "he held back something from the Alliance, hiding his assets, hoarding them . . . you wonder how I know that? . . . I know, Jack, because it was precisely what I did" (York 2006: 13). *In the Road Not Taken* (Cox 2005) series regular Michael Vaughn frequently compares an unfaithful wife to his own cheating spouse, Lauren:

> He [Vaughn] watched the blackmail footage play out on the display screen of his cell phone . . . he couldn't help superimposing Sark's and Lauren's faces on the amorous couple in the video . . . *Serves her right, he thought. She made her bed, so to speak.* Just like Lauren had. (Cox 2005: 154–5)

In all these examples, the writers introduce and describe characters that are indisputably new to the series, but can be understood as minor variations on the regular cast.

4 Echo themes—The APO novels also navigate the middle ground between repetition and difference by elaborating on a set of themes borrowed from the on-air series. In particular, a preoccupation with the fragility of social institutions, prominently the permeability of work and family, recurs through both manifestation of the program. The series examines this theme by juxtaposing the covert operations of double agents dismantling secret organizations from the inside with the soap opera developments of Sydney Bristow's broken home. Through this comparison, the series depicts the fluidity between these two overarching institutions—work and family generally—whose barriers have broken down, making one susceptible to the other (much in the manner outlined by Mark Deuze). As astute viewers and scholars of the series, all of the APO writers made efforts to incorporate into their plots narratives of broken families and the "dangerous" combination of work and home. This is most clearly rendered in *Old Friends* (Hanna 2006), in which a character slowly discovers that her husband is a failed secret agent after a series of revelations prompted by instances of domestic abuse. Later, it is revealed that these violent acts were "necessary" to maintain the husband-agent's "cover"; again the dismantling of work and home is depicted as a consequence of their mutual fluidity. Again, family and work collide with disastrous consequences for each: The husband's cover is blown and his wife leaves him. Similarly, *Faina* (Gaborno and Hollier 2005) begins as the home of the eponymous character is raided by political terrorists aiming to use both Faina and her father in their plot to sabotage the world economy. The subsequent story becomes the effort to reunite the family. In both cases, the writers have taken a repeated theme of the on-air series and adopted it to a new set of characters.

Throughout the course of this chapter, we have seen how the recurring ambivalence concerning the advance of tentpole TV has affected the organizational and textual forms it has taken. Ultimately, the streamability that tentpole TV producers covet is bought through the application of a complex and conflicted sociological process that is simultaneously reflected and reflected on the finished tie-in texts. Supervisors seek to maximize trust by preselecting freelancers who know how to "play by the rules" at the same time that freelancers' own financial incentives compel them to follow in kind. Left in a state of minimized contact, authors often turn to particular strand of fandom that combines an attention to continuity detail with a refusal to speculate. The result often emerges in the use of what I have called unexplored gems. This textual strategy, as well as the other solutions described above, contain critical self-understandings of the position of ancillary creators who must transform, extrapolate, and isolate on-air events and characters without being given the license to alter continuity. This delicate dance, or "strict maze," underscores the overriding ambivalence that characterizes television makers' response to tie-in novels that expand revenue potential, but risk continuity and, therefore, long-term brand value. In the following chapter, we will examine another cross-industry alliance, here between television and video-game producers, where this ambivalence is shared by both television workers and by their new media counterparts, who often chaff at the designation of ancillary media.

3

Tentpole TV: The Video Game

In one particularly acidic video-game review, *Los Angeles Times* reporter Pete Metzger (2008) begins with a hypothetical dialogue explaining the underwhelming nature of games adapted from other media:

Q: What comes along with the release of every film targeted to either fanboys or kids?

A: The movie tie-in game, that's what.

Q: And what, with few exceptions, do all movie tie-in games have in common?

A: They are all products created specifically to satiate the appetite of fans of the flick who crave more of the film. They usually lack originality and excitement and are thrown together as quickly as possible to go on sale as the film hits theaters.

Q: And how do these games usually turn out?

A: Rushed and horrible.

Indeed, it has become something of a platitude that licensed digital games, that is, games based on intellectual properties from other, often old media, are uniformly bad and that the cultures of old and new media clash with poor results, evidenced in Big Media's inability to gain a financial foothold in this sector. However, critical opinions like those of Metzger, which find licensed games to be obligatory, uninventive, and financially opportunistic, fail to consider the context of these games' production (i.e. outside the fact that they seem "rushed"). Furthermore, reviews of this genre ignore the fact that video-game publishers, like their old media counterparts, also have vastly mixed feelings toward the practice of licensing games.

In the following chapter, we will examine more closely the production of licensed games, with a particular eye toward those based on television properties and specifically those based specifically on tentpole TV properties (*Alias* [Acclaim, 2004], *24: The Game* [2K Games, 2006], and *Lost: Via Domus* [*LVD*] [Ubisoft, 2008]). I will argue, macroscopically, that licensed titles have a contentious position with regard to video-game publishers' own industrial business strategy and, microscopically, that differing production and organizational standards across media platforms make the transition from small screen to video game all the more difficult. Ultimately, I will suggest, borrowing again from the production of culture school of sociology, that these complications go a long way in explaining what has been considered the questionable quality of these licensed games. Extending the analysis further, we will briefly look at our sample of tentpole TV games in an attempt to put their textual elements in conversation with their complicated production processes. Here our observations and conclusions will be based on a small set of interviews with video-game professionals, supplemented with a thorough review of accompanying trade literature, with a particular eye toward interviews with creative and administrative workers associated with licensed games.

Simultaneously, this consideration of the problems and textual consequences associated with licensing games will be held up as a way out of the blue sky mentality of transmedia thinkers and to take popular conceptions of streamability and media convergence out of the realm of futurism and into a sociological examination of the workplace and interfirm relations. In this spirit, we can begin by contrasting Henry Jenkins's (2006) consideration of the video game *Enter the Matrix* (ETM) (Atari 2003) with the more recent translation of *Lost* into the realm of a digital game. Jenkins identifies *The Matrix* franchise, including a feature-film trilogy, a console video game, a massively multiplayer online game, as well as a number of other connected texts, as a near-ideal transmedia narrative, one that "unfolds across multiple media platforms, with each new text making a distinctive, valuable contribution to the whole" (95–6). These valuable contributions run the gamut from small, wink–wink easter eggs to intimate narrative connections. In the case of the former, Jenkins points to the appearance of ETM cheat codes in the background details of art direction in *The Matrix: Reloaded* (2003) (99). In the case of the latter, Jenkins discusses how the appearance of the character Niobe, in the same film, is preceded by instances of prolonged gameplay. In the ETM, Niobe, an avatar for game players, rushes to reach a rendezvous to rescue film protagonists, Morpheus and Neo. The subsequent rescue is depicted not in the game, but in the feature film itself. In another instance, the Niobe-player destroys a power plant, a consequential event referred to in the accompanying film, but left significantly offscreen. In both cases, the game narrative is firmly couched in the larger causal chain of *The Matrix* brand narrative as a whole.

In stark contrast, *LVD* depicts actions of a character-avatar entirely absent from the on-air series, or any other transmedia manifestation; refuses to share information that would inflect back on the larger mythology of the series; and contains, by its conclusion, an ultimately ambiguous and confounding connection to the overall *Lost* narrative. In an interview, *LVD* producer Gadi Pollack cast the refusal to offer valuable contributions to the brand narrative as a technique of producing a game that offered an "added experience" stating, "the main goal was not to answer any questions related to the show, but really give everyone the experience of being in the show and on the island" (Peckman 2008). It was precisely this ontology-based gameplay that was singled out in a particularly damning review of the game that noted, "immersing the players in the world of *Lost* is one thing, but finding something compelling for them to do is a different matter" (Fritz 2008). Perhaps, the progression of the game narrative itself best characterizes its seemingly inconsequential character. The game begins, like the on-air series before it, with the protagonist-avatar on the airliner Oceanic 815 moments before its crash. Subsequently, the protagonist finds himself stranded, along with the other survivors, on the series' mysterious island, struggling to find a way back home. In the game's solitary conclusion, a conclusion reportedly conceived by series showrunner Damon Lindelof (Peckman 2008), the protagonist finds a boat to escape the island, but before he can set sail, the player-character is interrupted by the image of another plane crash in the distance. Immediately, the screen blacks out and the player-character reawakens again on the island, presumably moments after the game's initial plane crash, and is greeted by a female non-player character (NPC) who was presumed dead during the game's series of in-play flashbacks. In other words, the game's ending implies that every event and action in the course of gameplay has an ambiguous status as textual reality. Whether one interprets the series of concluding cut scenes to mean that the game previously played was just a fevered dream of the player-character or some sort of alternative reality is irrelevant to the larger implication that the twist ending makes the diegetic reality of the licensed game absolutely irreconcilable with the diegesis of the on-air series. Unlike *The Matrix*'s transmedia protagonist who actively contributes to the overall series narrative propelling the story forward, *LVD*'s protagonist can only *be* in the narrative world of the series, but by the game's end, even this mere *being* is made suspect. It will be the business of the remainder of this chapter to consider, in turn, both the industrial and the organizational dilemmas facing makers of licensed video games as well as how the forces and relations behind these productions may encourage less of the former example and more of the latter.

In his exhaustive examination of the contemporary digital games industry, Aphra Kerr (2006) cites two key trends at play in the industry during the last 10 years of increasing competition and climbing financial risk: one, firm consolidation through mergers and acquisitions to take advantage of economies of scale and scope and, two, the exploitation of licensed media properties. Yet, contradictorily, any number of video-game trade articles in this same time frame continually cite a falling interest, on the part of video-game publishers, to take part in this later strategy. In a 2006 *Variety* piece, Jeff Karp, a vice president of marketing at a leading third-party publisher Electronic Arts stated, "video games now have a more mainstream audience, so we don't need to rely on other people to do our content creation" (Fritz 2006). However, these comments must be read with a grain of salt given the firm's reliance on perennial sports franchises (*Madden*, *NHL*, etc.), all licensed from the accompanying professional sports organization. Similarly, in a 2009 interview, Ubisoft Chief Executive Officer Yves Guillemot discussed corporate strategy stating, "the goal is to reduce investment in licenses, and put more emphasis on making our own brands bigger [and appear] more often, with very high quality" (Remo 2010). However, again, the conviction behind the statement is difficult to gauge given that Guillemot's firm had released a high-profile adaptation of James Cameron's *Avatar* (2009) a mere few weeks before the appearance of the article. This complication makes licensed video games unique in my sample of transmedia texts; while IP holders are uniformly ambivalent toward their attachments to ancillary creatives, the context of licensed games is the only one observed where this two-sidedness is reciprocal. Below, we will attempt to delineate the contextual factors contributing to this ambivalence that allows video-game producers, unlike the more conciliatory, affiliated transmedia makers, at least more vocally opposed to their positioning as simply an ancillary medium.

In an attempt to better understand video-game makers' contradictory eager acceptance and active denial of using licensed properties, we must consider the myriad disadvantages and advantages that weigh on the decision to make a licensed game, as indicated by trade data and personal interviews. Beginning with the former, licensed titles, most notoriously, are often held to unrealistic time frames that shorten production schedules from the industry typical 18–24 months to a breakneck speed of 12–18 months (Behind-the-scenes 2007). Such rapid time lines are often the result of both asynchronous production cycles wherein video-game work is made to conform with the pace of old media production and the (mis-)management of intellectual properties where video-game work is commissioned at the end of eventual decision chains, eating away at possible lead time on the part of video-game producers. The former was cited by one video-game executive in conversation who stated,

> The real timing issue with games is—it is absolutely horrific—is when you have to finish a game to come out at the same time that a movie

launches and that has caused more problems in our business for a brand than anything.

Time crunch, the increasing work schedules as deadlines approach, is often cited as the major quality-of-life issue in the game industry at large (Quality of life in the game industry 2004). Arguably, this pressure is absent from television licenses that lack the single release date of feature films. However, I would contend that TV-based games, too, feel the time crunch as matter of production because game producers are continually chasing a moving target; the longer the production takes, the more video-game producers risk being out of sync with program narratives (or popularity, given that programs could be cancelled in the meantime). For example, *24: The Game*, initially conceived while the on-air series was conceptualizing Season Three, narratively deals with the ellipsis between Seasons Two and Three, but was only released after the premiere of Season Five (Bramwell 2006).

Video-game makers could also be dissuaded from pursuing licensed games given these titles' relative high cost and likelihood for low reward. Working in a manner similar to other ancillary texts, IP owners frequently sell the rights to their brands on a guarantee/advance scheme in which rights owners are guaranteed a certain dollar amount regardless of the performance of the ancillary text(s) and are given a significant sizeable portion of that guarantee (the advance) upon commencement of the initial deal. One recent commentator noted that licensors ideally prefer to capture 10 percent of the wholesale price of games sold with a quarter of this amount acting as the initial guarantee (Rogers 2005). These terms seem all the more daunting when one considers that publishers/developers typically retain only 40 percent of the retail price for their efforts (Johns 2006: 163). Of course, the stronger the performance of the brand, the more favorable deal the rights holders can command in negotiations. For example, the giant publisher Electronic Arts reportedly paid US$34 million for the interactive rights to Warners' *Harry Potter* (Rogers 2005). To put this figure in perspective, one should remember that total production budgets for console games typically range from US$10 million to 20 million. When coupled with rising development costs, excessive licensing fees may in fact be unsustainable for video-game producers. In conversation, one video-game licensing executive cast suspicion on the strategy saying:

> we're finding that the whole deal, the model doesn't work anymore because you're worried that you could get a license before and then make a $10 million game on the PS2 [Playstation Two console] and Xbox—now if you get a license, if you're doing anything on the consoles, you're talking about a $20 million investment. The numbers are having a hard time synching up.

So, honestly, we do less of that stuff and anything that we paid recently, the licensing numbers are much lower.

Steep fees for licenses would be a moot issue if licensed games brought back larger rewards to compensate, but this is infrequently the case. It is rare for a licensed game, TV-based or otherwise, to rarely sell over one million units—often the threshold for success in video-game production (King 2008). In fact, in a contemporary review of the 100 most-successful console games, 70 of these games were based on IP original to the video-game publishers (Rogers 2005).

One recent, gloomy appraisal of licensed game production opined, "get used to hearing 'I'll get back to you by Wednesday on that'—especially on Thursday" (Nixon 2006). Although makers of licensed games typically purchase the exclusive interactive rights of the IP used, they, like all transmedia producers, are still beholden for getting approval from licensors during several steps in their own production process, most likely a frustrating process given that, as outlined above, licensees shoulder all of the financial risk in licensed games. The process of getting approval, which positions video-game makers at the end of long decision chains, is cast by video-game makers both as time consuming and creatively crippling. Because protecting IP is of unparalleled importance, licensing can hugely restrict the creative freedom and control developers have over games. In other words, the rights-sharing deals that go along with licensed games are often seen from the perspective of video-game makers as unduly restrictive.

Several other factors come into play against the decision to license properties. When video-game producers make a licensed game, they are ultimately, despite their effort and investment, at the mercy of the performance of a creative good that is entirely out of their hands. As one video-game executive aptly put it to me: "you may sign a deal and you may create a great game, but if the movie blows, you're fucked." Furthermore, while licensed games are typically popular with so-called casual gamers, they are often reviled by the more-established gamer community, as evidenced in the particularly aggressive review quoted at length above. Each decision to license a game flirts with taking on this massive ill will with regard to a publisher's own brand. Additionally, licensed games also have a high, often unremarked opportunity cost. Each expenditure of capital (financial, creative, or otherwise) toward licensed games is a redirection of money and effort from potential original IP projects that, in the last 15 years, have been the major financial hits (*Grand Theft Auto* [Take Two Interactive], *HALO* [Microsoft], and *Gears of War* [Microsoft]) for video-game publishers and valuable franchises in their own right that have, in turn, been exploited in their own transmedia themselves. This last drawback also forms a political economic argument against licensed titles: The preponderance of branded entertainment stifles internal diversity and concomitant innovation within the gaming industry. Deuze and Martin (2007) implicitly suggest this argument in their examination of so-called independent game developers stating that, "like any creative industry, [the video game industry] thrives on new titles to become the next franchise or hits . . . yet, simultaneously, they are choking off their supply of new games available by favoring investments in 'proven' titles" (284).

A consideration of all these daunting drawbacks then begs the question: precisely why does the video-game industry bother with licensed games? In their examination of the video-game business, authors Kline, Dyer-Witheford, and de Peuter (2003) described the industry as one that couples great flexibility and precariousness in organizational structure with a volatile and crisis-ridden market. Like other creative industries, video-game producers are plagued with great uncertainty, but, coupled with the chronic technological and personnel change indicative of the new economy, this uncertainty devolves into a state of chaos, in the words of Kline et al. The stability of work, the awareness of consumer and demand, and the predictable, if not spectacular, economic performance of licensed titles are largely strategies to mitigate this so-called chaos. While this diagnosis is theoretically compelling, it lacks in concreteness. Recent economic data suggest another motivation in turning to licensing and the dangers inherent in the strategy. An IBISWorld 2010 industry report stated that,

> game budgets regularly approach $100 million[1] today and are constantly growing. As such the industry's revenue model is beginning to resemble the Hollywood film industry, whereby a small number of blockbuster releases subsidize smaller art house features that operate at a loss. (34)

Here the reports' authors are channeling Paul Hirsch's (1991) hit-driven model of creative industries. The report further suggests a vicious circle whereby "increasing reliance on franchises and sequels create a more guaranteed line of sales, [and] developers, pressed to put together the next big thing are seeing their costs blow out and their profits fall precipitously" (39). In other words, rising costs for individual projects make each much more risky at the same time that the mitigation of this risk eats away at decreasing margins.

In this schema, licenses are economically and psychologically valuable in their perceived ability to reduce risk by returning on investment (at the same time that they, ironically, raise risk by adding cost). This strategy is clear in a number of trade reports that claim that cross-branding "might get even stronger with increasing development costs: big studios and publishers are likely to continue banking on solid brands and licenses, thus minimizing risk" (Le Dour 2007). Specifically, licensed titles reduce risk in at least three distinct ways. Licenses give their games an automatic awareness with consumers and the ability to ride the coattails of studio marketing and advertising campaigns. Concomitantly, all these games have a built-in audience and, thus, can largely be relied upon to perform at least a certain threshold of success. Furthermore, despite the rising cost and the diminished reward associated with licensed games, these products are often sure modest money makers, provided that budgets are controlled, because of fan/casual gamer sales. Consequently, the rights of many TV-based games are purchased by publishers and then farmed out to smaller, independent developers (*X-Files: Resist or Serve* [2004] was published by Vivendi Universal Games and developed by Black Ops Entertainment; *The Sopranos: Road to Respect* [2006] was published by THQ and was developed by 7 Studios; and *CSI: Hard Evidence* [2007] was published by Ubisoft and was developed by Telltale Studios) who frequently bid and petition for the licensed project on the basis of a financial plan, among other factors. Lastly, licensed titles potentially lower risk through the stability they give to developers and publishers who can continue to work and refine IP-based games through multiple iterations, giving stability to a production slate, a valuable consideration given the so-called chaos of video-game production.

Choosing to produce a licensed title then is best understood as a complex gamble between raising costs and lowering risk. It is a gamble that is equally embraced and bemoaned throughout most segments of the industry. However, outside of simply recounting the two-sidedness on the topic that recurs throughout the trade press, one can look directly at the financial records of video-game publishers (specifically their annual 10-K stock reports with the Securities and Exchange Commission) to gain a picture of the economic footprint of licenses. Table 3.1 charts the costs of making licensed games for four of the largest American video-game developers: Santa Monica–based Activision, Redwood City–based Electronic Arts, New York–based Take Two Interactive, and Calabasas-based THQ. Each company itemizes the cost of licensor fees through a slightly different accounting methodology, listed below the firm name on the chart. The trend in the expenditures is one of slightly increasing over the course of the last 10 years, despite the rhetoric in trade and popular press to the contrary. What these numbers also indicate is that licensing payments encompass a large part of doing business in the video-game sector, especially when one contrasts the annual fees versus the typical total budget of games in general. These fees typically range from 5 to 10 percent of the total revenue from game sales and in extreme cases cost as much as US$100 million in a year.

Table 3.1 Licensing and Royalty Fees for Major Video Game Publishers (Percentage Values Represent the License Fees Proportional to the Total Revenue of Game Sales; X Denotes Information Unavailable.)

Year	Take Two	Activision	THQ	Electronic Arts
	(listed as "prepaid royalties") (US$)	(listed as "intellectual property licenses") (US$)	(listed as "license amortization and royalties") (US$)	(listed as "prepaid royalties") (US$)
2009	X	X	83,066,000	X
2008	56,546,000 (4.6%)	X	99,524,000	X
2007	58,569,000 (8.5%)	110,551,000 (4%)	99,533,000	X
2006	52,700,000	46,125,000 (3%)	80,508,000	X
2005	X	57,666,000 (4%)	85,926,000	X
2004	38,220,000	31,862,000 (3%)	71,132,000	51,000,000
2003	26,418,000	45,002,000 (5%)	84,916,000	63,000,000
2002	33,149,000	40,960,000 (5%)	40,476,000	39,900,000
2001	24,718,000	39,838, 000 (6%)	33,144,000 (8.7%)	65,484,000
2000	X	X	34,675,000 (10.0%)	46,264,000

Source: Activision: 2000, 2001, 2004, 2005, 2006, 2007, 2008, 2009; Electronic Arts: 2001, 2002, 2003, 2004, 2005; Take Two Interactive: 2003, 2004, 2006, 2007, 2008; THQ: 2001, 2002, 2003, 2004, 2005, 2006, 2007, 2008, 2009.

In an effort to understand the interaction of video-game and television production cultures, we must also more closely observe the world of the less-understood former. In examining the distinct pressures and opportunities of video-game production, we will better grasp the conflicts that occur as they collaborate across media and how these conflicts are simultaneously reflected and reflected upon in resultant video-game texts. The processes of video-game production involve delicate operations of mirrored engineering and testing that necessitate a vast series of tests and fixes, renders, and reviews, both major and minor that encourage loose work hierarchies, allowing for the flexibility of change and the accumulation of spare intellectual resources, which may be vital for the next version of the project (or subsequent projects) to blossom. Indeed, both the preproduction and production of licensed games are perhaps best grasped as a series of constant modifications, tweaks, and adaptations. Discussing his own work on *LVD*, video-game producer Gadi Pollack described his work in just these terms stating that, "making games is an iterative process. You put [an idea] on paper, you design, you implement, you try, and then that happens all over again" (Boyes 2008). Moreover, video-game makers not only practice an iterative working model in single projects, but further use this principle across titles, using the format of the last big hit and even portions of accumulated technology and code from one game to the next to build successive products.

The recursive aspect of creative work is frequently commented upon in the studies of cultural preproduction, but is infrequently examined at length. In his account of art worlds, sociologist Howard Becker (1984) discussed his eponymous subject matter as a social unit that produces a "knowledge of professional culture [that] defines a group of practicing professionals, who use certain conventions to go about their artistic business" (63). These conventions, building on previous art practice, define the very rules, resources, and practices used by contemporary artists to continue their own work and advance a field. Thus, art practice itself can, in part, be understood as recursive, as being built upon novel recombinations of preestablished and evolving conventions. Recombination and replication also loom large in descriptions of creative industries in general and of television in particular. In his analysis of network television creative decision making, Todd Gitlin (1983) isolated the simple principle "nothing succeeds like success," as justifying the production of most television programming. The consequent result, for Gitlin, was a television schedule filled with spin-offs, copies, and recombinants and the assessment that "much of what passes for creativity in Hollywood is additive" (75). This observation was echoed by the work of a contemporary, sociologist Robert Perkurny (1982), who described at length network decision makers' reliance mechanism of proven track record and established formula to mitigate risk,

leading to a high degree of repetition. Similar conclusions were also drawn by sociologists William and Denise Bielby (1994) who, after examining the pilot process of one network television season and the decisions that accompanied it, found that the presence of a star from a previous successful project was the key variable in determining whether a program is picked up by a network buyer.

Video-game makers, too, rely squarely on the work, performance, and design of previous games to give shape and meaning to their current projects. In fact, video-game developers (generally understood as the creative locus of video-game production) sometimes rely on previous games to sell current concepts through a process of demo-ing. One development executive described this process of demo-ing similar games for licensors/ investors saying,

> they [licensors] invariably want to take a look at other games that you've done in that genre. You might have to go and do a demo of one of your own previous games. You might have to do a demo of another game that's like the one you want to make so that they can visualize what you have in mind.

Video-game makers, like all producers of consumer culture, also recursively rely on strict genre conventions that delimit decision making and presort eventual audiences based largely on a number of elements from visual design to game mechanics, the latter understood as the inscribed game rules that allow a player to compete and complete in a game, encompassing everything from the mechanical interface and avatar responsiveness. Thus, while our sample of tentpole TV licensed games all originate in old media in terms of visual design and narrative details, they all fit, in terms of game mechanics within preexisting gaming genres; *24: The Game* is a third-person shooter, punctuated with brief minigames; *Alias* is a third-person stealth game; and *LVD* is a third-person survival game. This grounding in previous genres is exemplified in the fact that *Alias* itself was grafted onto a preexisting concept of a clone of *Metal Gear Solid* (Konami 1998), generally credited with being the first sneak-and-kill game. In an interview, game producer Patrik McCormack stated "when we [Acclaim] discovered *Alias* [the on-air series], we were already in an early prototype phase for a stealth combat game that utilized hand-to-hand combat, spy gadgets and elements of stealth," and that the license was only subsequently grafted onto this accumulated genre-recursive work (Berardini 2004).

The presence of recursive techniques of preproduction even appears down to the level of discourse for video-game producers where a repertoire and understanding of previous games are vital for the communication of both novel and commonplace game ideas. Descriptions of the process of preproduction in old media have made note of techniques of pitching and high concept (Wyatt 1994, Caldwell 2006) that boil down potential projects into novel recombinations of the familiar (its *48 Hours* meets *Enter the Dragon*). Drawing on extensive ethnographic fieldwork in two development studios, sociologist Casey O'Donnell (2008) claims that examples from previous games "provide discursive resources for developers trying to describe abstract concepts, like game mechanics" (42). For example, O'Donnell describes a multi-hour impasse in a design meeting that was only resolved when one of the participants offered the comparison, "its like *Spy v. Spy* [Beyond Challenging Software 1984]," to explain a continuous split-screen display.

All this recursive work in the preproduction of video games also suggests a natural preference for licensed and franchised games that are more amenable to the slight adaptation and gradual revision through multiple versions and sequels. Such a system of incremental adaptation was described to me by one developer working on *CSI* licensed games who commented,

> we were lucky in that they [the publisher] had already done a couple of games like it. So, what it entailed for me was studying the previous games, discarding what I wanted to see improved and also listening to what the producers [of the on-air series] wanted to see improved.

Video-game makers also practice a high recursivity by reworking and redeploying tools and techniques earned from work on previous games in current projects. Of course, all fields of artistic production achieve advances through a sort of cannibalization of creative resources; remember Becker's claim that each artwork is necessarily a reconstitution of the object's entire field of practice. Video-game production, however, seems unique in that this reuse goes down to the level of code itself.[2] Contemporary game makers frequently use either proprietary or purchased game engines to help facilitate complex production and forgo the resource-intensive work of everything from virtual game physics to artificial intelligence to the construction of digital foliage, the last of which is made possible by IDV's SpeedTree, a tool made exclusively for the quick creation of digital trees and plants (Rise of Middleware 2007). The use of these production shortcuts, dubbed middleware, and sold by both specialist and development firms, has risen dramatically in the last 10 years. In 2009, gaming-industry reporter Mark DeLoura conducted an informal survey of video-game makers and found that 55 percent of creatives were using middleware in the current project and of this percentage, 39 percent were using the developer Epic's extremely popular Unreal Engine, the software used for the creation of the *Gears of War* franchise. Licensed games are not excempt from this growing rule. *LVD* was produced using Ubisoft's own proprietary engine, YETI, which was originally created to produce games from the firm's Tom Clancy–licensed *Ghost Recon* franchise (Totilo 2008). The producers of *24: The Game* leased the use of the Havok physics engine to create in-game collisions, explosions, and the like (Havok available games).

The ideal–typical development process and accompanying organization structure of video-game production acknowledge that its innate recursivity leaves time and space for constant iteration, modification, and collaboration throughout the life of a project. To understand this, one must consider gaming's unique workflow, which complicates the typical preproduction–production–postproduction schema common in old media. Video-game developers typically work through conceptualization and planning in a preproduction phase that concludes with a working, playable demo or prototype of all the significant elements of gameplay and game mechanics, sometimes called a vertical slice (Van Slyke 2008). After completion of a prototype, the project moves into production proper where tasks are split among groups of animators, level designers, and engineers. Beginning typically halfway through production, finished elements are tested in quality assurance, constituting a virtual feedback loop between what could be considered postproduction and production proper. As game scholars have put it, development becomes an iterative cycle of building-playing, building-playing, and so on, as projects move through initial finished alpha versions to more polished beta versions (Salen and Zimmerman 2006). It is this iteration, this melding of traditional postproduction and production that complicates the already technically difficult process of game production. As one video-game executive put it to me:

> When you're talking about movie making, they've been doing that stuff for one hundred years, so they know exactly [what to do], people have specific roles and do that just because that's the way that its set up. With games, its code. Apple misses games, Microsoft misses games because its very complex. When you're talking about millions of lines of something—fix one thing, another thing breaks down.

Based on extensive fieldwork at Ubisoft Montreal (the development studio that produced *LVD*), sociologists Patrick Cohendet and Laurent Simon (2007) found this firm's unique competitive advantage in the way in which its management cultivates not a hierarchy, but a system of communities where specialists are encouraged to share and develop knowledge across departments, in informal arrangements, oftentimes without even clear rational purpose, producing what the authors call "creative slack." In the authors' words, "sources of creativity as well as efficiency at [Ubisoft] rely on a subtle alchemy among communities" (591). Indeed, looser hierarchy and information sharing are frequently proffered as a solution to the complexity of iterative software production, allowing creatives to share and synchronize efforts and minimize conflicts across departments through the inevitable sequences of fixes and modifications. Loosening hierarchy to facilitate iteration and deal with complexity is characterized as wasteful, but necessary in the game developer Valve's use of its own so-called Cabal system of management:

> Just about everything in *Half-Life* [Sierra, 1998] was designed by a Cabal. This at first seemed to add a bit of overhead to everything, but it had the important characteristic of getting everyone involved in the creation process and personally invested in the design. Once everyone becomes invested in the design process as a whole, it stops being separate pieces owned by a single person and instead the entire game design becomes ours. (Birdwell 2006 [1999])

Ideally, looser management structures and information sharing are commonly isolated as solutions to the problems associated with iterative production practices. The question then becomes whether the case of licensed games allows for such a unique organizational structure.

Similar to the ancillary texts studied in Chapters 1 and 2, the production of licensed video games has its own set of internal reviews and checks. Much in the same way that comic-book and traditional print-book editors are responsible for managing the work of freelancers, video-game publishers oversee the creative work of game developers. Publishers, acting in a capacity similar to Hollywood studios, typically secure financing, manufacturing, and marketing for games created by development firms that are internally owned by the publisher, by another publisher, or by an independent entity. *LVD*, for example, was published by the French/Canadian firm Ubisoft and was developed in-house by the firm's own Montreal-based development wing. *24: The Game* was published by 2K Games, a division of New York–based Take Two Interactive, but was developed by a Sony-owned development firm, Sony Cambridge. And the game *CSI: Hard Evidence* was also published by Ubisoft, but was produced by the independent development firm Telltale Studios (itself a spun-off company from Lucasarts), a job that Telltale actively petitioned Ubisoft, the owner of the interactive rights to the CBS program, to obtain. Among the supervisory responsibilities of publishers is to assemble and implement a budget and schedule for the project that, according to the last section, can be chaotic. Typically, game work is organized around milestones or deliverables, finished elements of the production that must be given to publishers, as per the expectations of their contract with the affiliated development firm. A lead designer of a *CSI* game described the workflow process saying,

> we had deliverables so it wasn't like an open exchange it was more like we had to deliver something and they [Ubisoft] would have to get back to us within two weeks. [Ubisoft would determine] if we hit or not . . . I think that some of our income was actually tied to whether we hit the milestones, so it was extra incentive to make sure that we were hitting all the spirit of what they were looking for and over-delivering as much as we could.

Although licensed game makers engineer inter-firm deals that grant them exclusive interactive rights over IP from their studio partner, they, like all trandmedia makers, are still beholden to the ultimate approval/disapproval of agents of the original rights holders who must also sign off on all projects. This other layer of supervision is just one more step integrated into the process of making games. An executive at a major producer of licensed mobile games described licensor approval as a five-step process, focused on the hinge points of concept document, design document, graphics, alpha version, and beta version, before a project can officially be passed by the rights holders. However, exactly who communicates with the licensee, how often, and to what depth varies greatly from instance to instance. At one end of the spectrum is the simple selling of rights without subsequent support. Perennial tentpole TV writer Jesse Alexander dismissively characterized the *Alias* game as being produced with just such an arrangement stating, "the *Alias* console game came about because the media company who owned the license wanted to make a few dollars so it sold the license to a game company. It didn't really fulfill the promise of the medium" (Taylor 2007). The quality of engagement with the rights holder is often characterized as contingent on the dispositions of the creative core, that is, the writers and producers, of the on-air series. One executive at a development studio described the typical arrangement saying that the amount of contact between on-air show makers and video-game producers

> depends on how much they want to get involved. The interactive [licensing] people are always very, very cautious. They don't want to step on anybody's toes. I think, in general, they try to find out how involved the TV production wants to be and then depending on what they say, that's how involved they are.

The actual frequency of contact, too, is variable, ranging anywhere from 4 to 12 weeks between meetings in typical cases of licensed games.

While some licensed games do have an uncommon access to the creative core of the on-air series, most licensees only contact and meet with television writers and producers through a managed series of organizational firewalls. As in the case of tie-in novels and comic books, video-game developers most frequently deal with a system of middlemen, ranging from studio-licensing departments to talent agents representing IPs. Moreover, like these other transmedia creatives, video-game makers are often twice removed from the creative core. One creative lead on a *CSI*-themed program described this arrangement stating,

> at first our initial contact was our executive producer, Tony Van [from Ubisoft], and he was the guy who talked to CBS directly. The exchange was very distant on the CBS side, but its really collaborative on the producer side with Ubisoft.

This organizational and spatial separation is even more prominent in the production of *Buffy the Vampire Slayer* (Electronic Arts, 2002). One creative lead on this project claimed in an interview that,

> our leads worked closely with the agent [representative] from Fox Interactive, who was the main go-between from the producers of the show, actors/actresses, and the stunt team. We never met personally with the producers or the licensors, but we did work closely with the stunt team for the motion capture session.

Despite this emphatic separation of supervisory licensors/producers and freelance publishers/developers, makers of licensed games often do provisionally interact with the on-air creative core in a few accepted, ritualistic meetings. Video-game makers often describe going on "field trips," visiting the actual site of the series (Doukas 2002). Thus, producers of *LVD* sent a staff member to Hawai'i to take reference photographs of the locations and sets of the on-air series to facilitate the realism of the game (Peckman 2008). In this case and in accounts of other field trips (a term used by one maker of the *Buffy the Vampire Slayer* game), what is being exchanged is not simply images (surely these could be sent remotely), but also something more symbolic. In Nick Couldry's *The Place of Media Power* (2002), the sociologist describes the peculiar phenomenon of television fans visiting the sets of ITV's *Coronation Street*. Ultimately, Couldry argues that these visits can be best understood as rituals that reinforce the symbolic division of media and reality and the hierarchy between the two wherein media frames the social and the former is powerless to do the converse. I would similarly argue that video-game makers' pilgrimages to the site of television production reinforces another hierarchy, this one between media, where video-game makers are relegated to the end of decision making, impacting scheduling and contact between producing firms involved in licensing games.

However, licensed games of the last 15 years have enjoyed one clear connection with the creative core of on-air series; namely, nearly all were privy to either direct or indirect input from show writers on the construction of the game script. On the one hand, television writers are often employed to write game scripts directly. Describing this practice, one video-game executive claimed, "we almost always try to use writers that have actually written for the TV show. That's the first and best way to make sure that you have the right tone and you understand the characters." Indeed, this is the case with *24: The Game*, which was scripted by Duppy Demetrius, a junior writer from the on-air series. Although *LVD* was penned by video-game writer Kevin Shortt, multiple publicity pieces surrounding the games' release were insistent that, in an early story meeting, it was showrunner Damon Lindelof who conceived the game's cryptic ending (Totilo 2008). Even in cases where writers are not directly involved in story conceptualization, licensed game makers insist that all narrative elements (story, dialogue, etc.) are given close scrutiny by licensors and more often by the creative core of the series as well. For example, producer Patrik McCormack described his team's work on *Alias* stating,

> it was agreed that our lead designer would create the broad strokes for the story, based on the environments, characters and game ideas that were being conceptualized at the time . . . the show's script writers then carried out a second pass on the story, giving it the *Alias* treatment and slanting things more appropriately to the *Alias* style and pace. (Berardini 2004)

Similarly, one creative lead on the *CSI*-licensed games recounted to me the experience of being able to pitch his and his team's potential stories in the on-air series writers' room and then receive personal notes in a 20-minute meet-and-greet with series head honcho, Anthony Zuiker.

However, just how much these brief contact points impact the finished product creatively and how substantial the interaction between co-collaborators may be more of a technique of market positioning and endorsement is an open question. One video-game licensing executive discounted exactly these types of relationships stating that shared writers and their advice might help in ensuring non-repetition with the on-air series, but that ultimately, "they [television writers] don't bring much value to us in the game space." Here this executive is tapping into the larger debate in games studies as to whether video games are an expressive form better understood through a narrative frame or a so-called ludologist's one in which video games' essential features are not character, plot, and setting, but rules, player strategy, and gameplay (see Jenkins 2006 [1998]). With their focus on the textual/"script-ual" elements of game creation, licensors and the creative workers that they represent implicitly privilege a narrative understanding of gaming, eventually impacting the look and feel of licensed games themselves.

Implicitly referencing both the increasing technological sophistication of video-game consoles/formats as well as the digitalization of film and television production itself, Jenkins (2006) has recently discussed the sharing of digital assets across source and licensed texts, citing the particular case of Peter Jackson and Electronic Arts' *Lord of the Rings* series as exemplary in creating this visually seamless transmedia flow. Despite this utopian vision of shared transmedia production, the digital references shared in the case of TV-based licenses are typically limited to cast and set photography to check for realism; show scripts to check dialogue and prevent story contradiction and repetition; and some set blueprints to facilitate the construction of more accurate digital spaces. Moreover, any adaptation from on-air series to game is less frequently labor-saving than it is simply just a nuanced form of translation, particularly as game makers move from two-dimensional, constrained spaces and characters to "three-dimensional" playable spaces. Furthermore, intimate connection to the creative core in the manner of sharing assets can just as often cause as many problems as it allays. For example, one creative lead working on the console gaming adaptation of Peter Jackson's *King Kong* (Ubisoft 2005) describes the last-minute crunch to alter the character model of King Kong after some slight revisions on Jackson's creature in the parent film version (Poix 2006).

In 1982, Fox Video games developed an Atari 2600 adaptation of the hit CBS television program *M*A*S*H*. In this version, the gameplay is split between a pixilated helicopter picking up a series of human-shaped icons denoting injured soldiers in the field and a two-dimensional version of the popular board game *Operation* where players remove shrapnel from prone, lying patients. The elements of the series borrowed from the television series are confined to the show name (featured prominently on the game box art), the loose setting of a rescue hospital, and a monophonic rendition of the series title song, "Suicide Is Painless," which occasionally plays in the background. Beginning with the so-called sixth generation of gaming consoles, increasing visual sophistication and memory capacity have allowed for the integration of digital photography in the construction of character models, for increased fidelity of audio acting and for more complex scoring mimicking the on-air series. The sophistication of video games has made possible the sharing of digital assets while consequently adding yet another extra layer to the approval process. Agreements to license games are often modular contracts that guarantee some rights while others—particularly in the employment of acting and musical talent—must be negotiated separately. One development executive described these multiple layers saying,

> they [licensors] want to know in terms of talent and the music you want . . . For sure, you get to the logo and the name. In terms of Jerry Orbach, starring in *Law & Order*, we actually had to go and negotiate separately with Orbach for his likeness rights and we also had to negotiate separately for any sort of voice over work . . . In the old days, you used to just get the likeness rights, but I think that's probably changing. You have to negotiate with the actors.

Licensed game makers must scramble to secure the participation of actors who, when they decline to participate because of timing, lack of payment, and the like, are then replaced with so-called sound-alikes, actors paid to replicate the voice of on-air talent in licensed games. Indeed sound-alikes are used extensively in *LVD* and in the *CSI* games.

Many investigations into the business of video games have either focused on the industry's "upgrade culture" (Deuze 2007: 217) or its penchant for "perpetual innovation" (Kline et al. 2003: 66) to describe the way that rapid technological advancement is the principal method of competitive advantage. As a corollary to this drive, major game publishers and developers often have striven to create more and more photorealistic games. This aesthetic feature is the hallmark of this pursuit of technological supremacy.[3] When a game is licensed from a preexisting "photographic" medium, many elements potentially could be adapted in the process of translation from character, to story, to setting, to atmosphere. The practices of licensed game makers frequently overlap and collide with the industry's drive toward photorealism compelling developers to focus on the translation of actual actor likenesses into the digital realm through the mapping of digital photography on character models, the recording of actor dialogue, and in some instances, the recording of actual actor movement through motion capture technologies. This is comparable to comic-book producers' focus on motivation and tie-in writers' focus on voice; all transmedia workers seem to legitimate their work in the accurate translation of character. The integration of likenesses in video-game production adds one more layer of approval to the process and potentially puts actors in a veto position, based on precedents of publicity and privacy laws. Indeed, the use of digital likenesses has already led to a number of lawsuits as ex–National Football League player Jim Brown has sued Electronic Arts for his uncredited "appearance" in the *Madden* football franchise (Thomas 2009) and the rock group No Doubt has sued publisher/developer Activision for what the group sees as a misuse of the group's images as game avatars in *Band Hero* (Gwen Stefani would never sing "Honky Tonk Women") (Lewis 2009). In the case of TV-licensed games, one worker on the *Buffy the Vampire Slayer* game recounted that, "Sarah Gellar had a 'three strikes' rule where she could review the in-game model and could request major revisions three times [in the production process]." Similarly, Mark Green, a creative worker on *24: The Game* has described a recording session with series star Keifer Sutherland where the actor refused to read the lines of the script as written and demanded a series of on-the-spot rewrites before he would proceed (Bramwell 2006).

In summary, the approval process for video games echoes what we have seen in previous chapters in that contact is minimized by a series of middlemen and a system of inconsistent feedback. However, licensed games contain at least two significant clamps where activity by or on behalf of the creative core is uncommonly active, namely in the consideration of story/scripts as well as in the translation of character likenesses.

Armed with a deeper understanding of both the industrial and organizational questions at the heart of licensed game production, we can now turn to the games themselves. What is most noticeable at first glance at our sample of tentpole TV–based games is the sheer amount of visual fidelity between the television series and the games themselves. Won by the technological advances of sixth- and seventh-generation gaming consoles and compelled by the cultural virtue of photorealism, licensed game makers maximize connection with the on-air series through the strict digital translation of recognizable visual elements. For example, *Alias* incorporates interstitial titles in a font borrowed from the series and a vast amount of costume changes for the Sydney Bristow avatar;[4] *24: The Game* incorporates the use of multiscreen displays and the orange-hued, superimposed running clock to denote in-game save points; and *LVD* includes episode breaks between missions where players are treated, in the style of the on-air series, to a quick montage of what happened earlier and a deep baritone voice-over ("previously on *Lost*"). Furthermore, the producers of all these games went to great lengths to render characters photorealistic, mapping digital photography. As discussed above, this preference for photorealism is the overdetermined result of an organizational pull for brand integrity and the internal culture of video-game production where realism is the ultimate mark of craftsmanship.

Despite these visual flourishes, all three games, in terms of gameplay, visual display, and mechanics, ultimately operate in ways more typical to the larger field of games. In other words, licensed games typically translate their licenses into preexisting genres and formats. All three games (*Alias*, *24*, and *LVD*) present a player with a so-called third-person display (popularized by

Eidos's *Tomb Raider* series) where a virtual camera floats above and behind a character avatar and the player uses the character and limited control of the virtual camera to navigate three-dimensional represented space. The games play out spatially in the manner described by Greg Costikyan (2006 [1994]) where encounters with antagonists, NPCs, and successive environments are controlled by the rate through which a player "moves" an avatar through the virtual landscape. Furthermore, each game incorporates elements of both combat and object accumulation to move through these successive spaces. In *24: The Game*, a player must maintain an inventory of ammunition and health kits to survive a ceaseless succession of gun battles; in *Alias*, a player must find and use a series of gadgets and keys to move through a series of spatial boundaries; and in *LVD*, a player must collect several basketfuls of jungle fruits and scattered plane wreckage to act as currency to attain objects that allow for spatial passage. Each of these games is also organized in a series of discrete missions through which a player advances by way of the completion of clear goals. NPC colleagues inform players, through voice-overs and cinematic cut scenes, what they must do to advance and these objectives are saved for review in drop-down menus accessible in the games' pause mode. The convention seems appropriate to both *24: The Game* and *Alias* whose on-air plots are similarly constructed around professional, task-oriented missions; however, the game design is less suited for *Lost*, a program where the overarching plots are cryptic and difficult to boil down into objectives. These elements of display and gameplay may sound familiar to those with at least a fundamental understanding of contemporary video games, and that is precisely the point. Licensed games look and sound like the on-air series with an ever-increasing fidelity, but they are constructed and played in a manner common to video games. This result is greatly influenced by the recursive nature of game production and the limited/specialized contact with license owners/creators. In the first case, the rationalization of production by utilizing the concepts, mechanics, and the very code structures of previous games results in a final project that incorporates many elements from previous successful games. Moreover, since, as we have seen, licensor/ creative core contact is focused on the narrative elements of licensed games, game producers are left to their own devices with respect to the elements of gameplay and game mechanics, discussed above, again leading toward recursive production practices. All these point back to the deferential comic-book artists who produce "standard" layouts and tie-in novelists who hem to playing by the rules of the license. In each case, these transmedia creatives respond to minimized contact with a standardized output that avoids blatant experimentation or innovation specifically because of their unique organizational pressures.

All of these tentpole TV licensed games also heavily rely on the use of minigames. Minigames are play sequences that briefly diverge from the dominant visual design and game mechanics, often in the form of a narratively contextual puzzle. For example, in *Alias*, a player must crack a series of computer codes throughout the game on an interface in which a framed computer screen takes up the entire play screen. *24: The Game* also features a number of puzzle sequences where, for example, a player must use another framed computer within the screen to search a series of satellite photographs to detect possible sniper threats to the arriving Vice President. Minigames are most prominent, however, in *LVD*, where a player must fix a series of at least six electrical panels using a specific combination of coded fuses wherein the image of the circuit board encompasses the entire game screen. Such minigames certainly are not unique to these games, but I would argue that their frequent recurrence, especially in the case of *LVD*, indicates how they may be considered a textual solution to the difficulties born of licensed game production. With minigames, licensed game makers avoid the problem of narrative approval as game narratives literally freeze while they are played; minigames avoid the problems of likeness approval, as they are all played through a near first-person point of view where no likeness is visible in frame; and minigames avoid scripted elements more generally, as they are games in the most literal sense, more akin to *Tetris* or Tic-Tac-Toe than television serials. More simply, including minigames is a technique to flesh and fill out licensed games while avoiding all the organizational problems associated with them. The danger of using these sequences, however, lies in making sure that these minigames are not too far removed from the series narrative as, for example, when a player of *LVD* spends a significant amount of playing time doing virtual wiring, perhaps veering from the "spirit" of the property. Arguably, the construction of these pure gaming interludes also constitutes the leeway, the ability to craft segments outside the purview of license holders, which game producers have over their texts.

In terms of the actual game narratives, licensed game makers are under similar constraints that we have seen in other ancillary media texts. Licensed games of the past often replayed elements from the source material. In *Star Wars* (Atari 1983), players controlled Luke Skywalker's X-wing fighter as it took its final bombing raid on the Death Star and, more recently, in *Spider-Man* (Activision 2002), players replay the hunting down of Uncle Ben's killer. However, in the case of television licenses and more recent licensed games in general, developers are held under the constraint of non-repetition guaranteeing that they do not reproduce or reuse key plot elements.[5] For example, the writer of *LVD* justified his work stating, "we all know the story of Jack and Kate and all of them. We wanted to create the *Lost* experience and the best way to do that was to make you a new character who was one of the castaways on Flight 815" (Totilo 2008). This device allows the producers access to licensed characters and setting while avoiding actual narrative events from the series. On the other hand, licensed game makers are constrained from adding new elements that may contradict with continuity or future storytelling. Here we only need remember *LVD* producer Gadi Pollack's claim to "not to answer any questions related to the show, but really give everyone the experience of being on the show and on that island" (Peckman 2008). Similar to tie-in novelists placed between the constraints of non-repetition and noncontradiction, producers of *LVD* constructed a game that was based more on spatial exploration and a model of experiential gaming where narrative consequence to the series at large is constrained and freedom of action is limited. For example, a player is given only two consequential opportunities to fire a gun that the avatar carries throughout a majority of the game. Eschewing the action and adventure elements of the original on-air series, *LVD* instead operates as a *Zork*-like of spatial exploration. A player's perspective is ultimately not that different from the video-game developers invited to the field trip on set—you can look, but you cannot touch.

In the previous chapter, we discussed the use of dead-end continuity where narrative elements can be tied to the on-air series, but can never be tied from transmedia text back from the ancillary to the core. *24: The Game* uses this strategy by working backward, attempting to explain narrative events skipped over, but implied in the ellipsis between Seasons Two and Three: How did Kim Bauer come to work at CTU, how did Chase Edmunds become Jack Bauer's partner, how did Jack become a heroin junkie? Similar to the way that the prequel comic book *24: Nightfall* constructs a likely past from narrative hints in Season One, *24: The Game* fills narrative gaps in the series past that are not addressed on-air. With the exception of the example of Dr Caplan, a secondary character from *Alias: The game* who subsequently appeared on the on-air series, narrative elements from TV-licensed games rarely tie back into the on-air series, requiring a degree of coordination between game makers and video-game makers that simply does not exist.

TV-licensed games also navigate their imposed narrative constraints by clearly delineating the temporal relationship of game and on-air series events. *LVD* emphatically coincides with the beginning of the on-air series, depicting the series opening plane crash. *24: The Game* clearly sits in the gulf between Seasons Two and Three. According to *Alias* producer Patrik McCormack, that game takes place between Episodes 19 and 20 of Season Two (Berardini 2004). Like the writers of the APO novels, licensed video-game makers define time frames to avoid contradiction with serialized programs whose status quo rapidly changes on a schedule radically different from the much slower pace of game production. *LVD* takes a unique tact in dealing with these constraints by depicting an adjacent story with respect to the on-air series. Instead of taking on the role of a series regular, a player controls an avatar unique to the game whose backstory echoes the themes of the on-air series, most prominently by having a dark past that is addressed in a series of revelatory flashbacks. Similar to the *Lost* tie-in novel *Signs of Life*, *LVD* features this new character who only subsequently interacts with series regulars. In fact, the game, perhaps evidencing producers' overcompensation for the use of an original protagonist, overrelies on dialogue interaction with series regulars to advance the game story. Players must get direction for missions and motivations specifically through long dialogue interactions with NPCs representing series regulars (as performed by sound-alikes). Arguably, this also marks an overreliance on licensor interaction, squarely focused on scripted dialogue elements. This is particularly relevant when one remembers that a large majority of the remainder of the game is spent fixing fuse boxes.

All of the TV-licensed games of my sample were also constructed with limited variability, or in the parlance of video games, as non-branching. In other words, the path of progress in these games is more or less clearly prescribed with little consequence of player behavior attached to the larger game narrative. As a result, players must largely do what game makers want them to do, when they want you to do it. For example, early in *24: The Game* players must catch a possible suspect in a footrace and, if the player fails to do so, they fail, or colloquially, they die. There is no subsequent chance or alternate outcome. Similarly, in *LVD*, a player must, as in the on-air series, enter the proper sequence of numbers into the Swan hatch computer terminal, or they immediately and inexplicably die—an odd occurrence as the noncompliance of number crunching in the on-air series has decidedly variable and unpredictable outcomes. The lack of significant narrative branches is not altogether uncommon in action adventure games, like those of our sample, but contemporary games are increasingly including mechanics that allow multiple narrative paths, specifically in the movement through three-dimensional space. *LVD* again clearly butts up against this impulse when, for example, players are forced to replay missions if their avatar strays too far from a preordained path while navigating through the island's jungles. I would argue that this preference for limiting narrative consequence and even action is, in part, attributable to the layers of approval necessary for licensed texts. A truly branching game would be an organizational nightmare given the variable and inconsistent contact of licensors and the scrutiny given to narrative elements. Moreover, a true sandbox game, which gives players more freedom—albeit inscribed—as in the case of the *Grand Theft Auto* franchise, includes the possibility and likelihood of uncontrolled tampering with brand integrity and would unlikely be approved in the process of review indicative of licensed game production. However, the approval process is not the only mechanism studios use to evaluate and manage ancillary production. In the following chapter, we will examine the emergence of the mobile entertainment content and suggest how professional media research, subscribed to by Hollywood decision makers, too, plays a great role in the measured acceptance of streamability and transmedia in network television production.

4

Tentpole TV: The Mobisode

From its introduction, mobile TV—that is television either made for or played on mobile cellular devices—has been accompanied by the enthusiasm of professional media analysts. An early 2006 *The New York Times* article reported that, "analysts predict that the number of global mobile phone customers will double to four billion in five years" and that "the sale of mobile phone content by entertainment concerns and others directly to users could grow to 50 percent of all wireless content purchases by 2008" (Holson 2006). Reports in early 2007 continued to laud the emerging medium stating that its subscriber base had expanded from three to seven million users and the forecasts predicted a US$4.8 billion take for mobile advertising by 2011 (Kapko 2007, Whitney 2007). Most emphatically, Chris Khouri of the research firm Datamonitor opined that "the number of mobile broadcast TV subs is predicted to grow from a mere 4.4 million today to an estimated 156 million by the end of 2016" (Gibbs 2009).

However, it seems that by the end of 2008, the bubble had burst in trade press accounts as near-boundless optimism was replaced with apologetic recalculations. For example, one article rolled back expectations stating that, "spending on mobile TV services is expected to reach on $2.7 billion by 2013" ("Mobile TV uptake falling short" 2008), while a near-concurrent work published by the research firm Jupiter Research reported that, "adoption of wireless TV is languishing around 1%" ("Mobile TV suffers from lack of on-demand programming" 2009). These industrial trade accounts cast a picture of a medium that has been endowed with incredible promise, but after a sluggish adoption by consumers, has been reconfigured as a sort of cautionary tale.

The overenthusiasm for mobile TV during this early 2005–7 period may appear naïve from a contemporary perspective, but the attitude is more sensible when placed in the cultural context of the much-discussed death of network television, a discourse observed at length in the Introduction. *Wired* magazine, probably the most forceful herald of this presumed death, on the occasion of the US$1.65 billion purchase of YouTube, captured the revolutionary zeitgeist, stating,

> until about five minutes ago, remember, almost all video entertainment was produced by Hollywood. Period. That time is over. There was a time when advertisers could count on mass audience for what Hollywood thought we should be watching on TV. That time is all but over. (Garfield 2007)

This millennialism was picked up by academic media studies as well, significantly in the important volume *Television after TV* (2004), whose very title underscores the inevitability of a vast change in the business of television and whose every chapter is invested in chipping away preconceived notions of TV as an economic, a technological, and a cultural form. Specifically, each of the above-cited, over-effusive trade reports were based on market information supplied by professional media analysts and consultants, who also have a vested interest in the "death" of television. However, these significant consulting firms, important to cultural industries' transition to convergence and streamability, have been rarely considered.

In the following chapter, I would like to rectify this miasma while, at the same time, consider what has become, thus far, largely a dead end in the practice of transmedia, mobile TV. To begin, I will reflect on the tremendous amount of difficulties faced by the producers of mobile TV. This contextual review will conclude with the simple question: Why would network television bother in the face of such difficulty? To answer this question, we will examine the industry of media analysis and, armed with the sociological theory of Richard Peterson, trace how both the results and the methodologies of this industry leave their mark on cultural industries and their resultant texts. Ultimately, incorporating an understanding of these firms' work will suggest a revision of the traditional three-part model of production typical in media studies—that is, production–distribution–exhibition—by placing as a research phase a preliminary term. Additionally, we will investigate the role that professional media research has played in this over-eager adoption of mobile TV and how these research firms' methods of data collection and analysis may have predisposed them to advocate for such an adoption. Finally, we will review the two most prominent examples of tentpole TV mobisodes—that is, television programming designed specifically for the cellular phone—*24: Conspiracy* and *Lost: Missing Pieces*—to consider how each was influenced by the contextual regime of market information. As in previous chapters, we will attempt to demonstrate how texts both reflect and reflect upon these production circumstances. More specifically, I will argue that professional media analysis, as an element of production or preproduction, plays a significant role in determining how streamability and convergence have been adapted to network television as well as the character of what gets released. Arguably, many of these debates have lost a bit of their bite given the more recent uptake of mobile video devices, expanding broadband networks, and digital content services, which have left the mobisode as a sort of curious half-measure, a metaphoric part-talkie, and have rendered full episodes on-the-go an everyday reality. However, the conflicts and compromises that encompass this medium's fitful beginning remain instructive for the study of cultural industries and tentpole TV specifically.

In their important essay on the methodology of the production of culture, sociologists Richard Peterson and N. Anand (2004) introduced a six-facet model in the study of symbolic production. They argued that by tracing out the six contexts of technology, law and regulation, industry structure, organizational structure, occupational careers, and markets, a researcher could craft a holistic picture of how the unique circumstances of a given cultural industry shapes its eventual output. Like Wendy Griswold's (1981) important work on the American novels, the six-facet model complicates simple reflection models of the sociology of culture and opens up the consideration of any number of social forces that may have had a lesser or greater influence on a finished creative product. In the case of Griswold's equally important essay, the researcher demonstrates how the rise of the so-called American character in novels of the last century must be largely attributed to changes in the international copyright regime (the facet of law and regulation) that prevented American publishers from simply reprinting British works and compelled them instead to increase the production of a differentiated product (the facet of the market) that later became critically enshrined as a distinctly American literary style.

In the following section, we will similarly apply the Peterson–Anand model to the case of mobile TV and attempt to account for the medium's inconsistent results. Our overview will conclude with the simple notion that each of the facets surrounding the production of mobile TV has been fraught with so many profound difficulties and uncertainties that the very existence of mobile TV becomes more than a little enigmatic.

An early measured review of the mobile television market in *Forbes* magazine did an excellent job of enumerating the many technological problems preventing its smooth implementation (Brown 2005). The problems are presented as threefold: receiver battery life, reception, and interoperability. The first variable is easy enough to understand as the processing of audio-visual information is a large drain on power, so much so as to be at essential odds with what may be the most essential function of the cellular phone—to be in constant contact. Uncertainty of reception goes to the lack of a definitive standard of transmission. The competing mechanisms are considered in Oksman et al.'s article (2008) on mobile TV standards in Northern Europe. Simply, the alternatives for mobile broadcasting could be aggregated into four options. First, mobile TV could be "broadcast" over existing telecommunications networks and, indeed, the transition to so-called 3G, and eventually 4G systems, was prompted by the increased capacity for sizeable data transfer, as in the case of audio-visual broadcast. When in February 2005, Verizon broadcast *24: Conspiracy* through its V-Cast brand, it was via existing telephone connections and a transmission standard known as EV-DO (evolution-data optimized) (Robischon 2005). However, these mechanisms are plagued with the problems typical of earlier cellular connectivity: system overload, dropped signals, and the lack of coverage. Another option for mobile TV broadcast is the use of wireless access to the internet, colloquially WiFi. Yet, for as many problems of quality and consistency of service that plague preexisting cellular telecommunications, they are much more so when dealing with wireless internet. Alternatively, mobile TV could be broadcast according to a more traditional standard, namely through radio waves sent out from a central transmitter. This is the mechanism that has been implemented in both the European (through the Nokia-based DVH-B protocol) and the Korean (through the DMB protocol) media systems. Using this more traditional model frees broadcasters from worries of system capacity, but introduces its own pitfalls, including problems of poor reception and frequency allocation. This later problem was partially addressed by the 2009 transition to digital television broadcast that allowed the US government to auction off former television frequencies to movers in the mobile TV field. For example, the telecommunications firm Qualcomm paid US$554.6 million for the right to broadcast its MediaFLO mobile television service in several major American markets over what was formerly the television frequency UHF 56 ("AT&T launches cell video service" 2008). One last option available to mobile TV is asynchronous transmission via digital download for rebroadcast, or colloquially podcasting. Cheap digital memory in the hardware industry, based originally on the massive production capacity for consumer digital cameras, makes this alternative particularly practical. However, like the use of traditional broadcast signals, podcasting lacks the real-time adaptability and personalization, principal hallmarks and selling points of contemporary new media, of the first two broadcast models (phone lines and over internet). As of the writing of this chapter, no single delivery mechanism dominates the American market, owing partially to the technological drawbacks suffered by each, resulting in what appears like adoption indecision.

Issues of transmission standards and frequency allocation also suggest the pitfalls at play in the second facet, that of law and regulation. Historically, the US government has taken differing positions from a more laissez faire attitude in the case of emerging commercial radio (Barnouw 1982) to the more interventionist in the case of the support for emerging network television (Schiller 1969) when considering telecommunications policy. Thus far, its attitude toward mobile TV more closely resembles the former, a situation described by Greg Clayman, executive vice president of digital distribution at MTV, as a market "flooded with too many formats and too many models" (Kapko 2008). This hands-off approach contrasts starkly with the actions of the European Union Commission for the Information Society and Media who, in March 2008, declared DVB-H (Digital Video Broadcast—Handheld) to be the regional standard. Industry groups in the United States, such as OMVC (the Open Mobile Video Coalition), have attempted to fill the void of standardization, but with little consensus thus far. By letting the market sort itself out, policy makers have neglected to assist the mobile TV leaving it, again, in a state of perpetual indecision. The face of regulation, too, has impacted the exploitation of mobile TV in the case of network television through labor and guild agreements. Ultimately, the production of mobile TV was understood as being too similar to the traditional television production to circumvent pre-existing labor agreements, resulting in a multiyear delay in the filming of the *Lost* mobisodes as well as directly contributing to the inciting grievances of the 2007 WGA strike.

The industry structure of mobile TV has also contributed a series of inhibiting factors, primarily because of the industry's hybrid nature. Mobile TV ventures have awkwardly combined powerful telecommunications concerns, which have a wealth of experience in customer service, but very little experience in content production, with power entertainment conglomerates whose skill set is nearly inverted.[1] Although not directly connected to service operators, the telecommunication industry's prior experiments in entertainment, notably the rapid rise and calamitous fall of 900 numbers in the late 1980s and early 1990s, resulted in swift and harsh backlash. Prompted by public outcry over questionable advertising techniques that, for example, solicited children to call Santa Claus or the Easter Bunny, the FTC, in 1991, reigned in the third-party businesses using these new toll, long-distance lines (Andrews 1991). New York attorney general Robert Abrams lambasted the entire market saying that it had "attracted more scams in a shorter period of time than any other new industry" (Andrews 1993). Although telecoms have had little subsequent luck in transitioning to content production, this paradigm shift has been cast, in recent business research, as essential. One such brief has stated that, "UBS predicted that without an effective video strategy, the Bells likely will loose 30 percent of their telephone market to cable companies in the next thirty years" (Douglass et al. 2006: 13). The most important question may be how to arrive at an appropriate revenue-sharing model for both industries, telephone service and network television, which until relatively recently have both operated under the purview of a government-approved monopoly/ charter that gave each exclusivity over distribution in their respective fields. Indeed, one recent *The New York Times* article notes that,

> negotiations have long been testy as entertainment companies and their mobile partners, who invested billions of dollars to update their networks [namely in the purchasing of 3G and 4G service lines and the licensing of broadcast frequencies] for voice and video, argued over price and control. (Holson 2006)

In essence, the issue is similar to media companies' very public displeasure with the low price points and unfavorable revenue-sharing arrangements with Apple in regard to Web TV; reportedly, Apple is due 30 percent of each video download (Nail et al. 2005). In both cases, the problem is specifically media industries' reluctance to surrender their control over distribution, their traditional source of bargaining power.

Moreover, mobile TV has excited divisions between television networks and their parent studios, which are dense organizations with ofttimes conflicting divisions. Prominent among intrafirm debates is the question of media cannibalization, or whether innovations such as mobile TV and Web TV add new viewers to programming or whether they merely siphon off viewers from preexisting distribution mechanisms in an enormous shell game. While it is still an open and hotly debated question, the issue itself is potentially divisive between those divisions touting digital distribution methods and those whose business models rely on traditional advertising sales (e.g. O and O network stations as well as network affiliates) and subsequent market sales (such as syndicators and international distributors whose product loses value as their exclusive hold on programs' after-market evaporates).

Mobisode production also raises the organizational question as to who would be responsible for the segments creatively and where would their production be situated in the parent firm. This latter point became significant in the context of the aforementioned writers' strike where digitally distributed content was cast by allies of the producers' bargaining position against the collective writers as promotional and not creative, in the legal sense of the word. However, the drive for artistic integrity among tentpole showrunners countered this position and, at least in the case of *Lost*, disrupted smooth transition. This drive was described by showrunner Carlton Cuse saying, "conceptually, for us, the key was it had to be up to the quality standards of the series, and that required me and Damon [Lindelof, co-showrunner] to oversee it" (Manly 2006a). Late in this same article, Cuse obliquely cites the negative example of the *24* mobisodes which were devised and filmed by freelancers outside the on-air series proper, stating, "for us, putting two strange, non-SAG people on the island isn't *Lost* . . . we don't want people to feel cheated or ripped off."

Beyond the problematic questions of who will make mobile TV and how it will be made is the larger issue of Peterson and Anand's final facet, the market, or in the case of mobile TV, is there even demand enough to constitute a market? A significant amount of research has been directed at this and several related questions: When would people watch mobile TV, what would people like to watch on a mobile device, and the like. By monitoring a nascent global market, researchers have arrived at sometimes divergent conclusions with one project demonstrating how mobile is and will be a commuters' medium and will be used primarily for keeping in touch with live events (Carlsson et al. 2007), while another contemporary study argued that consumers use mobile TV just as frequently in the domestic space (Varlav et al. 2007). Such indecision seems inevitable while adoption rates and consumer interest remains low. On the supply side, there seems to be little agreement over the proper revenue model in the exploitation of mobile TV. Verizon's V-cast has used a subscription-based model mimicking a more traditional phone service. However, other potential models being considered and experimented with are "free," advertisement-supported systems as well as on-demand/single-purchase ones. Of course, the question of which business structure will eventually win out has to do with which technological standard is established (e.g. broadcast mobile TV makes advertisement support more practical) as well as consumer disposition (i.e. how willing are consumers to accept advertisements on their personal phones).

In summary, this prior section is meant simply to demonstrate that in the case of mobile TV in the United States, there is only confusion, indecision, and inconsistency with regard to how it will be made, what it will look like, or even who will buy it. This all begs the question: Why would anyone bother?

One possible solution to this riddle can be found in the early television studies work of Raymond Williams. Williams (1975) related the rapid advances of communication technology over the last century to the needs of expanded scope and scale of modern military and commercial enterprise (14). The sociologist demonstrated how a number of prior technologies converged by mid–last century in a tendency dubbed "mobile privatization"—essentially having to do with television broadcast—which provided a sense of private self-sufficiency based in the domestic sphere, while still being connected to a larger social center of power (20–1). Williams suggests that mobile privatization provided the economic and social underpinning for vast suburbanization. Arguably, one could adapt this term to the contemporary era, as mobile phone privatization. Williams's original notion attempted to demonstrate how individual mobility and private acquisition were bought by an intimate, televised connection to state and economic power. Sociologically, as a larger segment of the population becomes more and more mobile and even less connected to the traditional institution of the home, mobile TV could be cast as a way of bringing this mobile privatization even closer to its user on the go, to undergrid the ideological basis of the entire political–economic system. Theoretically, this plausible, if not speculative, hypothesis is, however, entirely divorced from the attitudes and dispositions of the actual decision makers behind mobile TV. Moreover, if advances in mobile TV are to be characterized as purely ideological, a hypothesis would also have to address the slow and fitful uptake of the form as it has occurred.

A more practical rationale can be found in the sheer volume of cellular phones in the world. Market research claims that approximately two billion mobile phones were sold in 2006 and 2007 alone, far exceeding the worldwide growth of personal computers and laptops (Reardon 2008), suggesting that the immensity of the potential market may be motivation enough. These market figures did not simply appear out of the ether. They were assembled by a vast system of industry research and analysis firms who wield a strong influence over the maneuvers of creative industries plagued with what economist Richard Caves (2000), following the screenwriter William Goldman, has called the "nobody knows" conundrum—that is, nobody knows the value of creative products prior to their release to consumers. Reliance on market data in the formation of firm strategy and project preproduction is a technique to avoid just this unsolvable dilemma of creative work.

The importance and potential impact of market research on creative industries was well demonstrated in another masterful essay by the sociologists Anand and Peterson (2000). Here the researchers argue that creative decision making is influenced by the "generation, distribution and interpretation of a web of information about activity in the 'market'," and, further, that "markets themselves are best understood as the mental constructs devised specifically from the conglomerations of this data" (271). In defense of the theory, the sociologists cite the example of the implementation of the Sound Scan metric of music consumption as it was adopted in the early 1990s. Sound Scan is a digital protocol that allows for the aggregation of the real number of point-of-sale purchases across all record retailers. The availability of these data challenged prior ranking systems in music consumption (i.e. *Billboard*'s

Hot List) that were based on reports by major market retailers and disc jockeys and pointed to a large, underrepresented market for country music in rural retailers. This change in reporting metric prompted a new understanding of the record market itself and directly impacted production, as the percentage of country music among the majors' catalogs grew and the public profile of country artists (such as Garth Brooks) greatly increased due to a proportional increase in label publicity efforts. Simply put, a change in market research techniques changed the conception of the market itself and the best practices pursued to succeed within it.

The marked importance of research and what amounts to the reflexivity, in the Giddens (1990) sense, of the television market is easy to reconcile with theoretical and historical work within television studies proper. Recently, John Caldwell has argued that the industry of media production is one that produces and consumes an enormous amount of self-knowledge and that this knowledge—coming in reflexive forms of rituals and repetitive self-narratives, as well as market research—constitute the industry itself (2006). While Caldwell's work here is mostly methodological, we can also point to several examples from the history of television and television studies that undergrid his and Anand–Peterson's hypothesis. Television producers have traditionally relied deeply on the third-party reporting of viewership, typically through the research firm Nielsen, to assemble a picture of the market, set advertiser rates, and make creative decisions. This relationship was emphatically underscored in Eileen Meehan's (1990) essay, "Why We Don't Count," which painstakingly demonstrated that programming decisions are based on these internal numbers gathered by researchers and only in the last instance are they based on anything resembling raw audience numbers or popular taste. Moreover, changes in these ratings in the early 1970s that supported more granular, demographic-sensitive data, famously encouraged CBS's movement from broad-appeal, so-called hayseed comedies to the slick, modern MTM and socially conscious Norman Lear product, in an effort to capture more upscale, urban ratings (Feuer et al. 1984). Like the example of the transition to Sound Scan, a change in the metrics used to calculate consumption greatly changed the picture of the television market—from one of a tremendously large, undifferentiated audience to one serving elite niches—and, thereby, creative decision making.

In the following, I would like to follow the lead of these previous studies and suggest a similar impact of market research on the adoption of mobile TV in US network television. The work of researchers is one of the only forces urging television producers in this direction in the face of its already enumerated difficulties. To capture a more precise picture of this influence, the following will review the predominant themes recurrent through a modest sample of publicly available professional media research on the subject and a small sample of personal interviews with research practioners. An effort will then be made to consider how these data and the implicit attitudes coded in their evaluations constitute, in the manner of Anand–Peterson, the market for mobile TV. Obviously, this can be seen in the manner in which any number of market forecasts (like those cited in this chapter's introduction) would encourage the exploitation of mobile TV. However, in the following, we will attempt to more precisely reconcile this research with their eventual results in our case studies of 24 and Lost's eventual mobisodes. The one methodological caveat that must be mentioned in the beginning: All media research, whatever other purpose it is meant to serve, is advertising for the researchers and, thus, the data and results are often peppered with what may seem like hyperbolic rhetoric and overstated claims. However, even these flourishes help shape attitudes and thoughts about the market and, thus, cannot be dismissed out of hand. Moreover, my reliance on what is publicly available may result in a slightly skewed image of the industry as so much of the work of business services involves direct transactions between analysts and client firms and the information shared in these interactions is where analysts create a bulk of their value. Moreover, since information is the key to their business model, analysts are sometimes reluctant to give details of their methodologies or their results away for free.[2]

Professional media research (not to be confused with academic media studies) constitutes a relatively unseen segment within the field of media production. However, these firms and their work are intimately connected to any number of vital decisions within the studios from assisting in tax preparation to conducting pilot testing. The business information industry is typically understood as being dominated by a Big Four comprised of KPMG, Ernst & Young, Pricewaterhouse Coopers, and Deloitte Touch Tohmatsu, of which the first three have very significant media divisions. These larger firms along with more specialized firms such as Nielsen, Yankee, and Gartner, do the bulk of the heavy lifting in the media research field. These firms typically employ a staff of economists to work on metrics, that is methods of quantitative data collection and reporting; forecasting, that is, the modeling of available data to make reasonable predictions about demand in the future; and white papers, that is reports summarizing findings of research projects related to data collection. These large firms, as well as smaller ones focused on studying specific industries also practice consulting in which they work closely with a single firm client to solve some particular strategic problem, develop executive strategy, or analyze business processes. Frequently, research serves consulting, acting as both publicity for the latter as well as providing the rudimentary tools to analyze and critique business performance.

In a recently published industry report, aptly named "The future of broadcasting" (Venturini 2008), the large business services firm Accenture constructed a simple economic model for the traditional television producers and networks that predicted and described a radical drop in these firms' enterprise and future values and a simultaneous rapid growth in current value. In other words, the value of what television makers have always done (enterprise value) and that business-as-usual projected into the immediate future are economic dead ends and that it is only through innovation, new revenue models, and the exploitation of emerging technologies that television producers can expect to thrive or even survive. In the words of the report: "the market place is increasingly favoring digital TV service providers over companies that continue to operate with a traditional, linear broadcast model." Here and in any number of similar reports, the television market is characterized as being at a vital moment of transition and change where those who fail to upgrade will not only lose competitive advantage, but will risk their very economic existence. Moreover, this threat applies not only to television makers, but to all companies that touch media. Telecommunications firms are similarly positioned in the jaws of this sink-or-swim moment. Another Accenture report declared "[telephone] carriers are finding themselves in a market where subscriber penetration is saturated, and they have to justify their investment in next-generation, high-bandwidth networks" (Douglass et al. 2006: 12). Both imperiled by the same transitional moment in which, as one Ernst & Young white paper put it, the "pace of change shows no sign of abating" ("Media and entertainment" 2008: 4), it seems plausible to assume that a hybrid solution should be sought between these two aging industries, that is television and telecommunications.

As mentioned above, these white papers and reports frequently act as advertisements for analyst firms and the vitality and necessity of the important moment imagined by these reports ultimately serve these information firms, positioned to guide media makers through the next market that their own reports served largely to create. Tempering their claims with competing evidence, however, suggests that the traditional, linear models of media business are still quite strong. For example, as recently as February 2005, cable network A&E paid US$2.5 million per episode to syndicate WB's *The Sopranos*, proving that traditional television sales still continue to exist and, in fact, dominate the balance sheet (Schneider 2007). Nevertheless, the picture given by business analysts is typically one of tremendous and immediate change.

The question then becomes: if the old way of doing business is positioned as "broken," what is the alternative? This is precisely the question posed by a recent Pricewaterhouse Coopers study entitled "Navigating the era of the empowered consumer" (2008). The results, or "key takeaways" in the parlance of media analysis, are based on the findings of a group of seminars comprised of industry executives who role-played nine alternative futures, all based on contemporary uncertainties. Outside the novelty of the research methodology, what is interesting about the conclusions is the openness and the multiplicity of the possible futures presented. Indeed, among the participants, there is no consensus about the best method or methods of adapting to this moment of so-called essential change. A like-minded report published by KPMG ("Consumers & convergence III" 2009) stated that, "all content providers, from providers to broadcasters, still struggle with finding the best, most efficient ways to monetize content online and now on mobile devices" (14). Again, this uncertainty partially reflects the nature of the data at the same time that it is subtly skewed to the advantage of the researchers by leaving the potential client in a state of indecision. In other words, the death of traditional media revenue models is a great cliff-hanger.

However, outside of just throwing up one's hands in regard to finding an alternative revenue solution for television producers, researchers seem to congregate around a similar set of solutions. First, although professional media research often discusses many of the same limitations cited earlier in the adaptation of TV to mobile, they cast these problems and their solutions as simply internal and strategic ones. This is unsurprising given that developing executive strategy and best practices is a large part of what business services firms do. Time and again, reports gloss over technological, cultural, and regulatory issues posed by mobile TV (the last omission is particularly glaring given the significance of the 2007 writers' strike), and stress that the important roadblocks to growth in mobile TV are ones that comprise the formation of the right business plan, the right partnership with other firms, and the right relationship with customers. Second, professional media research points not to a fixed path to lead firms to post-digital success, but suggests that solutions to the conundrum of streamability and convergence are multiple. Many studies agree with the sentiment shared with me by one researcher who stated that firms, "haven't figured out the whole revenue model—what's going to work and what people are going to pay for." Crisis coupled with uncertainty leads to a situation where the only poor move is the one that fails to innovate. Thus, market information represents, and arguably creates, a marketplace where alternative revenue streams are valued over and above their actual economic impact, which by most accounts is still relatively modest. However, these observations have to deal with the specific example of mobile TV specifically.

In 2006, *Time* magazine declared its person of the year to be "you" (Grossman 2006). The cover story refers to the increasing economic and cultural power of individual choice, selection, and modification available to the contemporary consumer, thanks largely to digital technologies. Indeed, the implicit promise of new media lies prominently in its malleability. Stressing this personalization, Shani Orgad (2009) recently demonstrated how the allure of a personalized "TV in your pocket" is being prominently cited in the advertising and publicity surrounding mobile TV (200–1). Professional media researchers spend a significant amount of resources tracking these more mobile, more empowered, and more digitally savvy consumers. Of course, market research has always been about tracking customers' desires, tastes, and habits. In interview, one researcher described his job to me saying, "that's what my works about, figuring out what consumers want and what consumers like and advocating on their behalf to my clients." However, there are two essential differences that distinguish the contemporary moment from consumer tracking of the past. One, consumer behavior is both easier to compile, but harder to track, thanks to the use of digital technologies that paradoxically both decentralize and monitor media usage. Second, researchers time and again advocate a new relationship between media firms and their buying public, moving it from a model of producer–consumer separated by any number of layers of internal exchange typical of mass production to one based on customer services where there is a direct interface between buyers and sellers. One emblematic study by KPMG states, "if convergence has given the power to hold the world in the palms of their [end-users'] hands, it has given them the power to dictate just what kind of world they chose to hold" ("Consumers & convergence III" 2009: 9). This representation of the market conveniently ignores the large capital investment that makes consumer empowerment possible and suggests a best course of chasing and courting customers as individually as possible—they were, after all, persons of the year. I would argue that, based on the picture of consumer power alone, the marketing of content over cellular phones, devices that are already abundant and typically personalized, seems like the most logical choice. Indeed, one researcher at a large business information firm expressed great optimism for television on the cellular phone to me saying, "it's the most personal device that's with you the most. People will leave their house without their keys, but not their cell phone." The market picture created by media research (in concert with, in the case of *Time*, popular culture) is ruled by powerful consumers with business tagging along behind. Mobile TV, though a complicated, underperforming sector, continues to be utilized partially because it fulfills this research mandate for, a potentially more "personal" relationship that is more customizable, individualized, and intimate (e.g. see Jenkins's [2006] discussion of emotional branding).

In the context of the empowered consumer, research firms also struggle to adopt new methodologies for data collection. In the past, media research firms gathered their data primarily from informant diaries in which participants recorded their consumption habits as well as from face-to-face and telephone interviews. However, as one Ernst & Young report ("Media and entertainment" 2009) put it, linear tracking itself, that is merely following a good through production to market to its eventual consumer, is inadequate in the era of media convergence, which allows for any number of engagements between media and consumer on any number of devices. As a result, many research firms have upgraded. For example, one researcher at a midsized firm described to me how, in the last 15 years, half of their work has migrated to the internet. Online work greatly reduces the need for worker-hours as they require no proctor and can be completed by any number of respondents concurrently. However, more importantly, these surveys give researchers potential access to consumers unreachable by landline telephones, a growing and attractive demographic. To deal with these new sources of data, firms have simultaneously developed new techniques of management and analysis. One novel white paper produced by Pricewaterhouse Coopers ("How consumer conversation will transform business" 2008) outlines the firm's new technique to monitor online conversations, called "voicescapes," across blogs and message boards to track hard to pin down cultural memes, called "whispers," like the phrase "go green" or the style of wearing a baseball hat backward as they traverse populations.[3] The study cites a sample of 75–100 million blogs and 10–20 million discussion boards, a wealth of information that comes with its own daunting problems of scale. Indeed, one researcher with one of the Big Four assured me in an interview that "data management is a huge area for us." In short, the moment of convergence seemingly provides as many challenges and opportunities to researchers as it does to their clients. Despite potential problems, professional media researchers often unproblematically embrace technological improvements. One such researcher in interview explained this preference stating, "if I ask you what you watched last night and put it down in a book, you may not put everything down. Whereas if we have a machine there that records it—everything is there." While such an attitude appeals to common sense, the slight technological bias in project construction (and truly there is no shortage of research on mobile TV and, especially web or IP TV) and increased access to digital media use/preference may have led researchers to overstate the importance of nontraditional television distribution. In other words, by quickly integrating digitally savvy methods of data collection and analysis and by giving voice to mobile TV use in an effort to appear ahead off the curve, researchers may have prematurely stoked the flame of interest in what is financially still a nascent industry.

Prior research into television production by Todd Gitlin (1983) as well as William and Denise Bielby (1994) has demonstrated the recursive nature of decision making, as discussed in the last chapter. To review, each sociologist found that, among the factors weighing on producers, the most predictive is the prior success of a particular story type or the exploitation of a particular star persona. The result is repetition and recombination of product and the cyclical reaffirmation and reestablishment of guiding mores and principles among producers. In essence, there is a strong ritualistic aspect to each network television pilot season. Like Geertz's (1973) cockfight that becomes a mirror of the Balinese, rearticulating the social structure and distance between those involved in either deep or shallow bets, television producers, according to previous studies, reestablish the basis for their own self-fulfilling logic, as Gitlin (1983) put it, "nothing succeeds like success."

I include this digression in order to point to a similar ritualistic component to data collection in media research itself. On the quantitative side, firms gather respondents in a number of ways, yet all the techniques betray a certain circularity. One researcher described to me the technique of soliciting informants from databases of participants in previous studies, notably through the online service E-rewards. Another researcher detailed a technique whereby clients share their own billing information with researchers who then attempt to draw findings from the internal numbers. In the first case, firms run the risk of overdrawing from a sample of willing participants and in the second case, researchers are, in essence, feeding their own information back, reprocessed, to clients. However, the ritualistic, recursive element to media research is much more present in frequent qualitative studies that often are based on in-depth interviews with industry leaders. For example, Accenture published a study in 2006 based on interviews with "130 of the most influential content executives in leading media and entertainment companies" and boiled these observations down into a small number of "key takeaways" (Edis and Mann 2006: 4). Similar to the scenario-building conducted by Pricewaterhouse Coopers discussed earlier, this study must, in part, be understood ritualistically; the methodology is simply getting media professionals together to reaffirm with each other, through the legitimate forum of media research, what exactly their business is and how it should operate. If we are to take Peterson and Anand seriously, these studies allow media professionals to literally shape and reshape the market much in the same way that recursive behavior works in the process of Anthony Giddens's (1979) structuration as well as Berger and Luckmann's (1966) institutionalization of everyday life. What this means more practically is that there is a conservative aspect to media research counteracting the field's eagerness to embrace new technologies, guaranteeing that ideas that predate and outlive their practical utility may survive by virtue of their status as talking points. This ritualistic aspect also begins to explain why so many studies of independent data, research agendas, and separate projects converge around the same conclusions.

All the producers and consumers of this research draw on the same symbolic universe reflexively fashioned by previous studies. And, despite the differences between the expectations in regard to the future of mobile TV, what may be more important is the fact that it is a topic of conversation engaged with no sign of abatement.

I argue then that the recurring attitude toward media research constitutes a significant influence on the preference for mobile TV among network decision makers. These reports collectively point to a fateful moment of potential calamity associated with media convergence, but fail to delineate the exact solution. I argue that mobile TV is put in this place because of researchers' preference for examining tech-savvy consumers and for personalization as a vital form of competitive advantage in the post-digital media sector. Moreover, the reflexivity present in many research methodologies tend to only restoke the preference for mobile TV in the absence of clear financial success.

Both trade reports and professional media research also have been preoccupied with the question of just how mobile TV should look, intuiting the ideal aesthetic utilization of the medium based on its unique technological, industrial, and organizational restraints. Despite little accord among the contributing voices, several commentators have coalesced around the idea of mobile TV as a so-called bursty medium. Mitch Lansky, an executive with the mobile entertainment firm Jamdat has described his own company's attempt to craft suitable content for the phone saying, "the idea is to find something viral and exciting that fits into a five minute burst" (Brown 2005). Similarly, Paul Palmieri, chief executive officer of another mobile entertainment firm, Millenial Media, recently discussed the adaptation of older media to mobile and opined that, "magazines translate very well because there are short, bursty little features that translate very well" (Gibbs 2009). In these comments and others like them, makers and commentators idealize the use of bursty (a term surely resonating throughout what PWC would call the industry's own "voicescapes") aesthetics, a term that could be translated to short hand for being brief in duration and instantly comprehensible, or more similar in style to a typical YouTube clip than a program from television proper. Media scholar Max Dawson (n.d.), in his consideration of digital shorts, too fixates on this hyped form pointing to the so-called aesthetics of efficiency at play in their construction.

Indeed the *24*-based mobile series, *24: Conspiracy*, certainly seems to be a bursty adaptation of the Fox series. The mobisode series depicts, over the course of 24-minute-long segments, an internal betrayal among a group of CTU agents and the violence resultant from its revelation. While the mobisodes do not depict any characters, primary or secondary, from the on-air series, the mobile series does share in the on-air series' fictional milieu as well as their same thematic concerns, all be they temporally contorted and condensed. Mimicking the plot mechanics of the on-air series, the mobisodes include instances of identity theft, secreted shadow government plots, and double agents—the latter two elements emerging in Episodes 11 and 19, respectively. Great pains were also taken to ensure a consistency with the visual style of the series (or as much as possible) complete with shaky hand-held camera work and a quick editing style replete with jump cuts and purposeful continuity errors. Moreover, perhaps most importantly, the episodes, like their parent series, again and again depict the protagonists in conversation with one another over cellular phones in an elaborate piece of marketing that cleverly fuses textual fidelity with product awareness. The bursty narrative is, in part, facilitated by one important aesthetic exception in the mobile series, namely the modification of the series' eponymous real-time format. While the mobisodes attempt to maintain the real-time, running clock device within individual episodes, timing between the mobile episodes is, instead, inconsistent. At least four of the episodes continue immediately following the previous installment, but the remaining 19 transitions cut to some indistinct time best characterized as "soon after." By adapting the real-time format in this way, *24: Conspiracy* is able to truncate the instantly recognizable elements of the series proper—from gunfights, to double crosses to heated cell-phone exchanges—into a bursty package, much in the manner of a feature film trailer.

Arguably, the more consequential industry buzzword used to characterize the *24* mobile series is "experiment." In a contemporary article, Daniel Tibbels, then head of the new media division of Fox Lab, states that, "*24: Conspiracy*, *Love & Hate* and *Sunset Hotel* (two other Fox mobisode series) were never dear to the consumers' minds . . . they were, however, great experiments" (Fitchard 2006). The term "experiment" was, as the acrimonious debate in the wake of the 2005 birth of the mobisode, anything but benign. A key creative working on the *24* series hinted at the subtext in a personal interview saying,

> we were working through the radar and its not like we were using union actors and saying they weren't union. But the way we had to go about the production was, because it was an experiment—if it was union it would have been a much more expensive experiment than it was.

During the protracted WGA strike of 2007–8, representatives fought strongly against contractual stipulations governing the creation of new media arguing that these products, derived from the on-air series, resemble more promotions than fictional products in themselves and that, because of their inability to create sizeable audiences, such ventures should be considered to be at an *experimental* stage, necessitating time for the market to sort itself out. These claims fly in the face of the more enthusiastic media research cited above at length, a discrepancy pointed out to me by one WGA administrator who stated that,

> it's almost as if they [studio executives and producers] have a California line about new media which is, "oh, it's poor, there's no money in it," and a Wall Street argument. And we love to quote their own Wall Street quotes back to them.

24: Conspiracy was staffed and produced in a way similar to the techniques observed in the creation of other transmedia works. The program itself was shot by a group of creatives who were related to the series proper, but were not from the show itself. In this case, the technical crew was tapped from those responsible for the production of the DVD extras features for its season long box-set compilations. These freelancers were brought into the series proper, but were, at the same time, kept at a distance. A freelancer on the series described his contact with the creative core of the series saying that scripts were simply signed off on in the preproduction phase. Just like the creation of novels and comic books, contact is limited to second-hand communication focused very early in the process. The textual result is seen in a program that is, on the one hand, distant from the on-air series' characters and personnel, but is, on the other, closely related to the series through repeated narrative and thematic elements that are practically much easier to translate and necessitate little coordination. Ultimately, because of the similarity of the on-air series and the finished mobisodes, the production of the mobile series enflamed the interest of the WGA in the lead up to the 2007 contract renegotiation and eventual strike. The same creative team responsible for *24: Conspiracy* was initially tasked to produce the *Lost Video Diaries*, a similar, proposed series of *Lost*-themed mobisodes, but was forced to bow out due to excessive union oversight and internal negotiations. According to one interviewed WGA official, the controversy over mobisodes and internet-based webisodes was based on members' concern over distinct pay for these additional assignments and showrunners' concern over creative integrity.

In the end, the *Lost* mobisodes, eventually titled *Lost Missing Pieces* (*LMP*), took a very different strategy toward staffing and production that vastly altered the textual possibilities of the series as a whole. Concurrent with the production of the mobile series, *Lost* showrunner Carlton Cuse commented upon the production of the mobisodes in the *The New York Times* saying, "conceptually for us the key was to be up to the quality standards of the [on-air] series" (Manly 2006). *LMP* was then written by show writers, featured on-air cast members in character, and was shot entirely by on-air series technical staff. The series comprises 13 short clips that have no temporal or causal relationships to one another; in other words, they do not constitute an independent story line. Moreover, the individual episode's temporal relationship to the on-air series is also variable. In the first case, five of the mobisodes appear to take place during what could be called the story present of the first season, three during Season Two, three during Season Three, and two before the beginning of the on-air series itself. Some of the clips, too, appear to be more narratively consequential than others. For example, Episode 11, entitled "Jun Has a Temper Tantrum on the Golf Course," depicts just that and nothing more. However, several other episodes depict events implied, but never explicitly shown in the on-air series. For example, Episode Five captures the dramatic moment in which Juliet reveals to series regular Jack that she is working as a triple agent against the series antagonist Ben Linus. In Episode Eight, series leads Michael and Sun share an adulterous kiss, depicting a romantic subtext that was frequently hinted at in the on-air series, but was never clearly established. Perhaps, most interesting is the final mobisode that depicts what appears to be the ghost of Christian Sheppard instructing a dog (Vincent) to wake up his son, Jack, prompting the famous opening shot of the entire series—an extreme close-up on Jack's opening eye. In essence, this clip retrospectively (over the course of several years of real-world time) establishes an enigmatic causal relationship to the initial shot of the series.

This unique production and texts of *LMP* suggest that the closer the transmedia producers are to the creative core of the series (here they are essentially one in the same), the lesser they are compelled to create stand-alone narratives and the more they can substantively interact with the diegetic world, here by literally filling in the more or less implied and unexpected story events throughout the course of the first three seasons. Or, unlike *24: Conspiracy*, which tells its own story in the style of the on-air series, *LMP* tells the exact story of the on-air series, becoming our sole example of a tie-in text that actually ties back.

Creating a mode of address that moves freely through the on-air series in terms of both spatiality and temporality, *LMP* is both echoing the narrative conceit of the series and another recurring meme in the business literature revolving around mobile TV. Shani Orgad (2009) describes this as the promise of TV anytime, anywhere—TV free from the spatiotemporal limits on consumption—recurring through the promotion of mobile TV devices and services. Indeed, capturing the potential nomadic consumption, made possible through swift advances in digital technologies and connectivity, is high on the agenda of media researchers and business information services. In fact, the telecommunications researchers at Yankee Consulting Group have gone as far as to trademark the term "The Anywhere Network" that encompasses the use of new products and services that allow content to be delivered to its consumer anywhere, the implementation of which is, in the firm's opinion, vital to future competitiveness. I argue that *LMP* is, in part, a textual adaptation of these exact same business principles. This inconsistency in the representation of time and space, uncommon in traditional television aesthetics, will be the topic of the following two chapters.

In his own sympathetic examination of short-form television adaptations, Dawson has projected a history moving from an era of hardware-based limitations to a stylistic regime of efficiency that is "characterized by a streamlined exposition, discontinuous montage and ellipsis, and decontextualized narrative visual spectacle" (206). What was a technological drawback is celebrated as an ideal form for attracting the attention deficient attention span of so-called digital natives. Above and beyond these informing contexts, as well as the drama of the related WGA strike that Dawson faithfully records, the strange history and aesthetics of the mobisode is equally inflected by the facets of industry strategy, firm organization, and specifically the traditionally ignored role of professional media researchers. By the end of his essay, Dawson nobly attempts to argue for a revised analysis of short-form TV as texts worthy of study, although he neglects to delineate exactly the methodological tools that can be used in such an effort. It is my hope that combining what constitutes the first and second halves of Dawson's essay—industrial analysis and textual analysis—into one seamless conversation wherein the latter is a reflection and a space for reflection upon the latter, I have offered at least one systematic strategy to attack media texts often ignored or dismissed. Indeed, this has been the overarching goal of the entire first section of this book. As we move onto Part Two, we will examine with a minute, analytic gaze the on-air texts of tentpole series themselves. Here, we will discover how textual innovation and business innovation converge in the unique formal strategies of the tentpole series and how these novel TV texts again reflexively comment back upon their disruptive, confused, and evolving art worlds.

PART TWO

5

Lost and Mastermind Narration

In a recent article, sociologist John Urry (2006) used a simple illustration from the field of technology to underscore what he calls the increasing complexity of contemporary social life. While the rifle of two centuries ago contained roughly 51 working parts, the contemporary space shuttle contains ten million components. In the following chapter, I would like to discuss a more modest example of increasing complexity in the field of television programming, a field that has similarly been vastly amended with any number of textual "components." Facing growing threats of obsolescence, US network television has collectively followed the example of other, adjacent entertainment industries in the attempts to expand the breadth of their programming, replacing hits of scale with hits of scope.[1] In the phenomena that we have called tentpole TV, programs are densely serialized and narratively connected to any number of off-broadcast iterations, many of which we reviewed in the previous chapters, from online, to traditional print, to video games. While none of these techniques are in themselves entirely new, it is the sheer number of significant, often scattered narrative parts and the manner in which they are interconnected that makes this trend worth studying. If *I Love Lucy* is the narrative equivalent of Urry's rifle (a viewer need only remember who Lucy is, who Ricky is, the recurring dynamic of their marriage, etc.), then a program like *Lost* more closely resembles Urry's space shuttle (a viewer needs to maintain a mastery over any number of intertwining, inconsistent character relationships through both on-air and online manifestations).

In the example of tentpole TV, programming, assembled for a multitude of texts and competing story lines that can be broken apart and exploited in separate streams, has become modular. Yet, this vastness and complexity, characteristic of tentpole TV has necessitated experimentation in the very techniques of storytelling, the organizational systems used to hold all these diffuse narrative components together, altering television's traditional representations of time, space, and character. In this chapter, we will track one set of recurring strategies deployed to organize nonlinear time we can call mastermind narration. Mastermind narration is marked by the retrospective shifting in valence of narrative information (objective sequences become subjective and unmotivated sequences become motivated ones), resulting in the positing of a ghostly agency guiding narrative from the margins of the diegesis. In the following, I will use *Lost* as both an illustrative and a limit case for this tendency, a program that both suggests the existence of a central mastermind and endlessly defers the assignation of such a character.

In response to the growing trend toward the serialization of network television dramas, *The New York Times* published a feature article that exposed the fact that, as of the writing of the piece (March 2005), four of these programs had not only *not* shot their May season finales, but that they had not even drafted scripts for said episodes (Martel 2005). The piece goes on to stress that even ABC president Steven McPherson did not have an inkling of how his network's *Lost* would conclude nor did he care whether the series creators themselves had a definitive idea of the conclusion. The journalistic lead of this article, and several others like it, was that tentpole TV writers were just making it up as they went along—an odd observation and not particularly newsworthy.[2] What the article is more indicative of is the perceived precariousness of writing television programs where, if we are to believe Jason Mittell's (2006) conception of the operational aesthetic, part of the appeal to the audience is to see whether or not the creators are to "pull if off," that is reconcile all the programs' many lingering plot threads and insinuations. This same precariousness has also contributed to an increased media scrutiny applied to series writers and, more specifically, to showrunners of tentpole TV programs. As if in response, *Lost* showrunners Damon Lindelof and Carlton Cuse have starred in a series of show-themed podcasts as well as network-aired clip shows, making the writers series regulars in their own right and serving to subtly reassure a viewer that the program (with proper instruction) will indeed make sense. On the opposite end of the spectrum, *Heroes'* showrunner, Tim Kring, has been frequently singled out and attacked for what fans of the program consider its falling quality, culminating in a October 2008 cover story for *Entertainment Weekly* that personally petitioned the showrunner to make a series of changes after the producer made a public apology for the so-called diminished quality of the program's second season (Jensen 2007). Similarly, in November 2008, *Variety* picked up the story of the firing of two *Heroes'* staff writers, Jeph Loeb and Jesse Alexander, an item reprinted subsequently by several online news outlets again underscoring the uncommon attention given to the business of writing tentpole TV (Littleton 2008).[3] In other words, much of this coverage in the popular media (and certainly much more so in online fan forums) addresses an anxiety over the writers' ability to manage a complex enterprise like a tentpole series. It will be the business of this chapter to briefly outline several aesthetic factors that contribute to this precariousness and to suggest how mastermind narration has been employed to contain just these difficulties.

The stated precariousness of the work of tentpole TV can be traced to several of the format's more unique aesthetic features. Specifically, the series' modularity is achieved through a combination of increased serialization, information multiplicity and real virtuality. Seriality and its use in programming have been much debated in academic television studies. On the one hand, critics like Glen Creeber (2004) describe seriality as a technique of narrative structure executed over a number of episodes that promises a conclusion. In clear contrast, Angela Ndalianis (2005), tracing the neo-baroque tendencies in contemporary television programming, follows Umberto Eco in casting seriality as the resistance of linearity and all ultimate closures. This latter author constructs a model of series storytelling that more resembles a network (in the sociological sense) in which episodes do not simply accrue one after the other in a linear fashion, but form a dense grid and relate to one another in any set of combinations, not guided by simple chronology. In other words, while the first author draws on the Dickensian tradition of seriality wherein installments eventually comprise a whole, the second draws more on the model of DC Comics' Batman where monthly adventures stretch into infinity and overlap in inconsistent ways. For our purposes, we can draw out what is indisputably common between these opposing characterizations; namely, that seriality involves the delay and extension of narratively pertinent details across a multitude of single episodes, regardless of whether such narrative concludes. The problem of conclusion is one we will examine more closely in this book's Conclusion. Serials, programs whose narratives are delayed and stretched across episodes, represent certain challenges in the maintenance of story information at the same time that they encourage viewer hypothesization and speculation. Tentpole TV programs, more than being simply serialized, frequently use unanswered enigmas, both short term (in the case of *Alias*'s cliff-hanging endings) and long term (in the case of *Lost*'s many, many unexplained riddles), to bridge episodes with another. Episodes must adhere to episodic format, but also to any number of minute details of continuity in order to achieve synthesis between installments. In fact this attention to details of continuity have reportedly had a significant impact on the division of labor within the series writing room. At a recent public forum for the writers' guild (March 26, 2009), *Lost* writers insisted that the lion's share of drafting and writing on the series is done collectively despite the individual writing credits on specific episodes due to the complexity of series mythology and minute continuity.

Additionally, these series feature an informational multiplicity with regard to both onscreen manifestations and their many ancillary manifestations. Information multiplicity is a term coined by the literary theorist John Johnston to describe a subset of contemporary novels that abandon the literary representation of individual consciousness, indicative of modernist texts, in favor of capturing the "culture of noise and entropic dissemination in which information constantly proliferates and representations insidiously replicate and in which human agency finds itself enmeshed in viral bureaucratic forms and transhuman networks" (1998: 3). Novels indicative of this tendency, like Thomas Pynchon's *Crying of Lot 49* (1966), focus on vast conspiracies that escape the comprehension of the protagonists and, like the same author's *Gravity's Rainbow* (1973), encompass a small army of characters (both human and nonhuman) whose connections to one another only slowly become clear over the work's massive page count. For Johnston, such narratives can be grasped not through the model of the single thinking subject, but through the example of contemporary media and information technology systems that model a decentered frame to manage information density. In other words, they present less a mode of address and more a mode of access.

Tentpole TV series share many aesthetic features in common with these novels and, arguably, take the larger notion of multiplicity even further by integrating any number of transmedia expansions on a variable scale of involvement. In the first case, many tentpole series, *Lost* in particular, are centered around conspiracies and plots over which onscreen characters often have very little control. Exemplifying what literary theorist Timothy Melley (2002) calls the "agency panic" typical of conspiratorial narratives, the programs' subject matter is often less concerned with individual characters than with the transhuman connections that combine these characters with the unseen and the often-times malevolent vertex of these connections. Even when tentpole TV series do shift focus to individual characters, programs like *Lost* and *Heroes* deploy what Robert Allen (1985), in his discussion of soap operas, calls paradigmatic complexity in which character relationships are continuously changing and evolving as, in the case of *Lost*, characters' pasts and futures that are increasingly depicted, making them more nodes in an intricate unfolding puzzle than independent actors themselves. And in the second case, the ideal perspective to see these programs is a decentered one that keeps one eye on the on-air series itself and the other on a computer screen viewing an episode guide or a wiki entry, simultaneously juggling a wealth of minute, visual details and character backstories, both explicitly shown and implicitly suggested. From very early in the series, it becomes clear that no single diegetic character would be able to reconcile all the plot information into a satisfying whole. Thus, by the series' end, the focus shifts to the ghostly Jacob, an immortal, ghostly figure who is both everywhere and nowhere and is thus able to model the ideal yet impossible mode of comprehending the series' vast, dense narratives.

In addition to maintaining consistency of these vast character networks and their shaping narratives, producers must attempt to oversee a similar consistency between the on-air series and their many ancillary manifestations. However, as we have seen in previous chapters, on-air creatives often minimize their contact with freelance, transmedia co-collaborators. Furthermore, in discussing their vast narrative worlds, series writers have often contradicted themselves publicly both acknowledging and disavowing these off-air works with regard to overall series continuity. For example, in an interview for *Entertainment Weekly* before *Lost*'s fourth season, showrunner Lindelof flatly stated, "the only true canon is the show itself" (Jensen n.d.). Yet, approximately a year prior, Lindelof claimed that,

> I would say in terms of the all the . . . background that we did [the *Lost Experience*—ARG], in terms of the Valenzetti equation and explaining the formation of the Hanso Foundation and doing the other films . . . we'd consider this stuff canon to the show. (*BuddyTV* 2007)

This issue of oversight becomes an important one in informationally complex texts where any pareidoiac detail can be construed as central to a larger mystery or in establishing a connection between members of the ensemble cast.

Tentpole TV creators further complicate their own tasks by deploying what can be termed real virtuality in their series (Castells 2000). This term was coined by sociologist Manuel Castells to describe the contemporary cultural moment wherein individuals and digitized content are increasingly connected to a seamless network. Castells uses the notion to critique the then-popular notion of virtual reality, that is seeing a Gibsonian hyperspace as replacing the lived world, by flipping the term and suggesting that real virtuality describes a "system in which reality itself (that is, people's material/symbolic existence) is entirely captured, fully immersed in a virtual image setting" such that, "electronically-based communication is communications" (Castells 2000: 373–4). Real virtuality, too, has consequences as to how tentpole TV is consumed. In real–virtual systems, there is no longer any hierarchy between so-called reality and virtuality, between analog and digital, or between on-air or off-air. Moreover, in real–virtual systems, all times and places are equally accessible, not linearly placed in a chronological mimicking lived time, but deposited in a database to be drawn to order. As a textual consequence, there is a certain omnipresence and omni-temporality in tentpole TV texts themselves. This can be seen in the repetition of events from multiple perspectives and frequent temporal jumps in *Lost* and *Heroes* as well as the quasi-real-time format of *Lost*[4] and *24*. The result is a textual field where every space and every time is hypothetically accessible, making the creators less responsible for a simple narrative and more for a narrative world, what critic Matt Hills has called hyperdiegesis (2002).

Given these unique pressures of seriality, informational multiplicity, and real virtuality, the task of drafting tentpole TV is indeed a precarious one. Media scholar Roberta Pearson (2011) has recently discussed the importance of the so-called producer brand, the acknowledged authorship, of early cult TV texts from *The Twilight Zone* to *Star Trek*, both important forbearers to tentpole TV. Pearson argues that an ideal reading of both programs necessitates the perception of Serling's or Roddenbery's voice, respectively, ironically using the conventions of science fiction to conduct social commentary. Similarly, I argue that the "authors" become present in the texts of tentpole TV series; however, I will endeavor to demonstrate through sustained textual analysis how this present absence is achieved. I argue that all of these programs privilege a set of recurring narrational strategies that address these endemic concerns. As a set of textual solutions to formal problems associated with narrative modularity, mastermind narration emerges as a technique to give order to seriality, multiplicity, and virtuality at the same time that it subtly suggests a supra-intelligence guiding narrative, thereby answering the same anxieties articulated in the above-cited *The New York Times* article. Mastermind narration works by retrospectively modifying the assignation of narration information and events as well as motivation, in the broadest sense referring to both character actions and shot selection. Furthermore, mastermind narration suggests a diegetically ambiguous entity (is it inside or outside of the storyworld?) that shares with the implied author the power to shape and guide plot and only eventually becomes present in the narrative proper. Lastly, the mastermind, certifies, like the cover of a puzzle box, that even the most obscure and smallest of details will eventually be reconciled with the larger narrative whole. The use of mastermind narration in tentpole TV ultimately can be read anthropologically, as a textual solution to an extratextual problem, namely, how to manage order in complex narratives and assert an assurance of authority throughout these dense and sometimes disconnected episodes.

The question then becomes where is one to find such a ghostly narrative abstraction and whether such a concept indeed clarifies the textual operations of the series. Theoretically, I am relying on the work of Edward Branigan (1984) who described narrative agencies as viewer-generated hypotheses assembled on the basis of textual evidence in the form of stylistic cues. For example, Branigan explained the "presence" of the author in a text calling it a subcode; "the 'author' is a hypothesis constructed by the viewer" (Branigan 1984: 41). Branigan makes similar claims about other hypotheses as complex as "subjectivity" and as a matter-of-fact as the "camera." In the following, we will chart how the series *Lost*, in what seems like an effort to maintain organization and purposefulness, suggests the presence of a certain narrational entity, a "mastermind," through story choices as well as minute use of stylistic devices.

I use the term mastermind as a reference to a number of characters in popular culture that serves as a model of the narrational technique. Traditionally, characters such as Fu Manchu, Mabuse, and possibly Lex Luthor are depicted in narratives where their influence to effect plot surreptitiously, often through the actions of others, is only gradually revealed and unmasked. They are the generators of conspiracy. One recent, salient example can be observed in David Fincher's *Seven* (1997), in which an acutely intelligent serial killer literally leads a duo of detectives through a series of crimes, reveals himself only partly through the film, and, in the end, compels the lead protagonist to complete his series of murders. The killer is the textual force that, retrospectively, motivates the entire film and its narrative events. The closest analogue in series television may be in Rod Serling's appearances in his *The Twilight Zone*. Serling, in his prologues and epilogues, exists in some hinterland between story and real world, between diegesis and non-diegesis and, through the rhetorical device of the parable and its moral, determines the purpose and, therefore, the motivation behind the episodic narratives themselves.

Many of the series that I would isolate as emblematic of tentpole TV utilize this technique of storytelling in some form or fashion. In *Heroes*, each of the first two seasons revolved around a central plot whose consequences are revealed as a possible future through the device of the flash-forward. Over the course of each season, the possible future is slowly revealed to be the motivating goal of a mastermind character, who is only introduced over the course of many episodes. In the first season, a plot involving domestic terrorism and electioneering is revealed to be the product of machinations of a devious, superpowered businessman, Linderman, who is only introduced into the series in its eighteenth episode. Similarly, in the second season, the protagonists are threatened by another possible future, the outbreak of a deadly virus, which is exposed as the masterplot of Adam Munro, a 400-year-old samurai with an axe to grind with series regular, Hiro Nakamura. Although less potent an example, *Alias* too uses mastermind narration through the entity of Rambaldi, an invented historical personage, equal parts Leonardo da Vinci and Nostradamus. The collection of Rambaldi's personal effects and experiments guides the series' overarching narrative at the same time that Rambaldi, himself, is cast as having "predicted" the actions of series regular Sydney Bristow and her colleagues. For example, in "Time Will Tell" (episode 1.8), protagonist Sydney encounters a man claiming to be Rambaldi's contemporary and is given a sketch by the long-dead inventor, a perfect likeness of Sydney herself. Again, the mastermind is invoked by presenting a character who shares properties with an implied author by foreseeing and guiding protagonist actions. Even the ABC series *Desperate Housewives*, which shares many features in common with our sample of tentpole programs, uses the device of an all-seeing, all-knowing deceased narrator presiding over all the program's plot developments, but existing in a place adjacent to the story world proper. However, perhaps, the most interesting example of mastermind narration occurs in the series *Lost*, precisely because the program has suggested a number of possible masterminds residing behind the curtain of the series, but, through five seasons, has resisted definitively marking one.

In the final episode of *Lost*'s third season, a sequence, in the style of the series' flashbacks, depicts series regular, Jack, visiting a rundown funeral home. Jack enters the building in long shot, allowing enough headspace to capture the overhanging sign of the establishment: "Hoffs-Drawlar Funeral Parlor." It is an odd name whose significance only becomes clear subsequently in the episode that concludes by revealing that Jack's actions occur in the story "future" and not in its past, making the sequences the series' first systematic flash-forwards.[5] This twist makes the conspicuous presence of the sign all the more significant, as "Hoffs-Drawlar" is an anagram for "flash-forward." The brief, but noticeable appearance by the sign is the clearest example of what one could call the emphatic presence of the implied author in the text of *Lost*. The sign with its decodable message is a comment by the creators on the textual construction of the episode itself. Such information would be absolutely meaningless to the characters in the diegetic world proper and can be then understood solely as an instance of the creators using the diegetic space as a palette to indirectly communicate with viewers over the head of fictional representation. Producers of *Lost* seem particularly partial to asserting their presence through these word games. In another similar example, a traitorous character named "Ethan Rom," an anagram for "Other man," discloses his allegiance to series antagonists, known then simply as the Others. Again, this anagram has no bearing on the diegetic characters (certainly Ethan would have altered his name if he thought that such a blatant tip-off was possible), and, arguably, serves as a surreptitious cue from the creators indirectly to viewers. Regardless of whether these cryptonyms reach their destination, they serve more largely as textual evidence of an implied author, that hypothetical narrational entity that Wayne Booth (1983) found lurking in all fiction, more or less detectable in acts of selection and moments of explicit and implicit commentary. These instances in *Lost* approach the level of explicit commentary, at least as close as one would expect to find in realist television narratives, and serve a similar function of underscoring narrative authority.

Moreover, these instances force us to rethink the work of 1970's enunciation theory in film studies that suggested that all classical realist narratives sought to suppress the act of narration or discourse, giving agency entirely, or as much as possible, to characters onscreen or established, explicit narrators (Gaudreault and Jost 2004). Theorists and critics of this loose discipline often sought out diectics, that is, traces of the presence of the "speaker" of discourse, in the guise of unconscious, ideologically loaded symptoms. Most notably, in the work of Raymond Bellour (2000), one can trace out the lingering psychoanalytic, often sadistic desire lurking underneath shot selection in the films of Alfred Hitchcock. However, our examples from *Lost* suggest an altogether different understanding of these seemingly purposeful "traces" of the creator in the text more akin to what has been called an easter egg in popular culture. This other concept was first used in the field of computer programming where nonessential sections of code were included in programs for nothing more than to mark the work of its author, but soon was applied to other media texts to refer to any element that is more or less secreted beneath the surface.

These easter eggs often contain a possible disruptive effect by virtue of pointing back to the text's very construction. However, disruption is not the rule. The first season of *Heroes* included an illustrative counterexample in the episode, "Godsend" (Episode 1.12). Near the conclusion of the episode, one character hands another a business card and the object is captured in extreme close-up. From the vantage, a URL address on the card—www.primatechpaper.com—is clearly visible. Furthermore, this website, if followed, ushers a visitor into the *Heroes* ARG. Here an easter egg is meant to filter viewers through a system of related, ancillary texts. Closer to the example from *Lost* is the use of what critic Neil Perryman calls (borrowing Richard Dawkins's terminology) memes in the current BBC incarnation of *Doctor Who* (2008). In this case, the term "BadWolf" was repeated in background details (e.g. in graffiti on a wall) or in incidental conversations only to be revealed as a central plot twist in that season's finale. By the end of the season, it is retrospectively explained that the meme was introduced by a colleague of the protagonist, traveling back in time to make sure that the series protagonists would not forget about the Bad Wolf, which is essentially a deus-ex-machina-like secret weapon. In other words, the repeated meme or easter egg is retrospectively coded as character-motivated. The use of wordplay, similar to the initial example from *Lost*, comments on the textual construction of the series and, as a result, also signals the hypothetical presence of an implied author.

More frequently, the seeming power of textual construction is ceded to surrogate characters that effect plot. However, this is precisely the larger technique suggested by enunciation theorists to be at work in so-called realist narration. *Lost* complicates categorization in this previous mode of thought by either delaying the revelation of the character ceded with this responsibility (as in the case of the use of confidence wo/men) or presaging it (as in the case of prophets). What I am arguing here is that series episodes frequently cast diegetic characters as masterminds who compel a viewer to reevaluate the narrational status of story events, often changing them from objective or neutral to subjective or character-motivated. *Lost* introduces its tendency to purposely mislead its viewers very early in the series. For example, "Walkabout" (Episode 1.4) depicts character John Locke, in flashback, being denied the opportunity to go on an Australian wilderness hike. The episode is crafted such that the compositions and blocking deny a viewer foreknowledge of Locke's handicap as a paraplegic. This bit of character information is only given away in the episode's final flashback radically and retrospectively altering both Locke's backstory and his ability to stride through the mysterious island in the story's present. Moreover, the revelation also begins to suggest an authorial entity withholding important narrative information from a shot selection composed in a more or less neutral or conventionally objective manner. However, more often, these tricks are perpetrated not by narration itself, but through author surrogates within show narratives, specifically in episodes centered on Sawyer, a series regular and professional confidence man, and John Locke, whose father, too, is a con man. Episode narratives frequently cast the former as a consummate manipulator of events and the latter as an easy "mark." In an episode entitled "The Long Con" (Episode 2.13), Sawyer is depicted as perpetrating a coup d'etat on island while intercutting a past instance where he bilked a rich woman out of her savings. The episode begins with a violent attack on another series regular, Sun. In the furor of response, Sawyer is able to clandestinely stockpile all of the island's firearms. Only in the episode's final shots is it revealed that Sun's attacker was not an interloper, but another series regular, Charlie, acting on Sawyer's instructions. Another exemplary episode, Season Three's "Every Man for Himself" (Episode 3.4), depicts, in flashback, an imprisoned Sawyer befriending a white-collar criminal in an effort to secure an early release. However, the episode's final flashback reveals that the ploy was really a con with a con, as Sawyer discloses his motivation. He was not driven to obtain a reduced sentence, but to secure a handsome reward for his estranged daughter, whom Sawyer disowned earlier in the same episode. In both cases, Sawyer is depicted as retrospectively having controlled events first coded as objective or at least unmotivated (Sun's attack or Sawyer's casual friendship with the white-collar criminal).

Lost also examines the opposite end of the spectrum with episodes focusing on the oft-persecuted John Locke. In an episode in Season One ("Deus Ex Machina," Episode 1.19), the orphaned Locke is reunited with his biological father. However, the blissful relationship is short-lived; after his father swindles Locke out of one of his kidneys, the old man cuts off contact. Sadly, poor John never seems to learn.[6] In Season Three's "Further Instructions" (Episode 3.3), a flashback depicts Locke living and working in an idyllic farming commune/marijuana manufacturer. This edenic existence, however, is ruptured when a hitchhiker Locke invited into the camp is outed as an undercover police officer. The agent explains that his initial meeting with Locke was not a chance occurrence, but that John had been singled out by his superiors as being "amenable for coercion"—a nice enough euphemism for gullibility.

This recurring theme of confidence tricks, their perpetrators, and their victims can also be traced in *Lost*'s larger, episode-spanning arcs. For example, late in Season Two, series regular, Michael, returns to gather help to search for his kidnapped son, Walt. It is only three episodes later ("Three Minutes," Episode 2.22) that Michael's lost time is depicted and that Michael's true motive—to release the captive Ben Linus and to hand over four of his fellow survivors to the antagonistic Others—is explained. In the same season, series protagonists are portrayed as interrogating a man claiming to be "Henry Gale" beginning in Episode 14 ("One of Them"). The characters investigate the holes in the captive's backstory, which increase until that season's finale, nine episodes later, which recasts the captive as Ben Linus, leader of the antagonists, who had himself "captured" for the expressed purpose of infiltrating the series protagonists' confidence. Perhaps, a better example can be found in the so-called hatch computer. In the first episode of the second season ("Man of Science, Man of Faith"), series protagonists discover a computer station buried deep in the jungle and the instructions to activate the system's terminal every 108 minutes to defray the effects of a vague geomagnetic disturbance. The characters, with varying degrees of dubiousness, comply; unsurprisingly, John Locke is the most enthusiastic button-pusher. However, 20 episodes later, the protagonists discover a second station, known as The Pearl, whose sole purpose is to monitor activities in this first hatch. The first hatch then is recast as nothing more than an elaborate Skinner box abandoned by a scientific collective that long ago disappeared from the island. In all these cases, the narrative proposes a reevaluation of events, actions, and motivations in the story near-past, once a mastermind entity is given agency after the fact over these same events, actions, and motivations. The final example further gives indication to a larger understanding of how the figure of the mastermind works in the series as a whole. While the surveillance monitors in The Pearl still function, no one is present at the panopticon's controls. In other words, the series simultaneously suggests the presence of a mastermind monitoring and manipulating characters at the same time that it refuses to name and defers the ultimate assignation of the mastermind. The control seat at The Pearl is significantly empty—a fitting metaphor for the narrational strategies of the series as a whole.

Although not as prominent a tactic in *Lost*, psychics, seer, and fortune-tellers are also used to organize and presort narrative information. I argue that these characters serve as an inverse of the confidence wo/man and, instead of giving order to actions and events retrospectively, they establish a sense of order prior to events' actual occurrence in story present and prior to their logic in the series as a whole. The use of such a technique begins early in the series when series regular, Claire, in flashback, visits a psychic who, after having a premonition, urges her into taking the ill-fated flight 815 ("Raised by Another," Episode 1.10). The depiction of prophets becomes more elaborate in later episodes which periodically represent characters Desmond Hume and John Locke as being able to access story-future through a series of flash-forwards. For example in "Further Instructions," Locke "sees" the image of an attacking polar bear, an image that is repeated as Locke later drags Mr Eko, another series regular, from the bear's cave. Desmond, too, can "see" the future and spends most of the third season predicting different deaths for series regular, Charlie, only to subtly elude their fruition.

More globally, the series suggests that predestation or an intended future may be the central mastermind giving shape to the entire narrative, a metaphor for narrative authority itself. Here one can most clearly intuit the connection between characters, urging the pursuance of a preordained path, and the series creators personified by this path. Throughout Season Three, John Locke frequently protests against his fellow crash survivors, saying that they are not "supposed" to leave the island. In the subsequent season, that objection is echoed in series regular Jack's similar cry that he and his companions were not "supposed to" have left the island (which they had done at this point in the story time). The series even goes as far as personifying this "supposed to" in the guise of an old woman by the name of Ms Hawking. In the episode entitled "Flashes before Your Eyes" (Episode 3.9), Desmond, in a flashback, attempts to buy a wedding ring for his long-time girlfriend,

Penny, from Ms Hawking, who is acting as a jeweler. When Desmond settles on a purchase, Ms Hawking protests, saying, "give it here . . . this is wrong, you don't buy the ring. You have second thoughts; you walk out that door. So, come on, let's have it." Here again a diegetically ambiguous entity (how can someone in the story world have access to the sequence of events?) is controlling events, yet the identity of the manipulator remains, like the control seat at The Pearl, conspicuously clouded.

Yet, there is an irony in constantly referring to *Lost* as a mastermind narrative considering the seeming subjectivity of narration in individual episodes. Here I am referring to the fact that from the series' first episode, narratives are punctuated by flashbacks, seemingly coded as character reminiscences. To resolve this contradiction, I, for this project, charted all of the first four season's 450 flash structures, that is radical temporal jumps either backward or forward in story time, and all 1,800 shots surrounding the jumps (in each instance: shot one, from the original story time; shot two, into the new story time; shot three, out of the new story time; shot four, back into the original story time) to discern the stylistic and narrational norms guiding this practice in the series and to take note of any significant deviances. Based on these data, I argue that to read these flashes as unproblematically subjective, that is, coming from the mind of the character whose past or future is depicted, is to ignore several other stylistic cues that suggest another narrational entity influencing these jumps. In other words, reading these flashes as subjective is only one narrational hypothesis, in a Braniganian sense, and one that, as the series progresses, is increasingly discredited. Of course, this is precisely the way that I have been trying to describe mastermind narration; the narrational valence of events shifts retrospectively. In the case of confidence tricks, unmotivated narrative events are exposed as being explicitly engineered. And in the case of flash structures, seemingly subjective recollections are recast as manipulations of a hypothetical mastermind.

The use of flash structures throughout is guided by several overarching norms that are infrequently broken. First, the flashes in any given episode depict narrative events concerning only one single character. The exceptions to this rule are episodes depicting flashes concerning couples (Sun and Jin, Bernard and Rose, Nikki and Paolo) and a small handful of deviant episodes, like the season finales of both the first and fourth seasons ("Exodus" and "There's No Place Like Home, pt 3"), which depict flashbacks and flash-forwards, respectively, concerning a number of series characters. Second, these flashes typically depict a single narrative with a set of elliptical fragments where the timing between the fragments is successive, but not continuous. There are, again, a small number of exceptions. It is arguable that several episodes fail to tell a complete narrative in the flashes and three episodes from the first seasons ("Raised by Another," Episode 1.10; "Whatever the Case May Be," Episode 1.12; and "Born to Run," Episode 1.22) as well as the pivotal episode of the fourth season, "The Constant" (Episode 4.5), which depict flashes that, if reconstructed, would represent continuous, or near-continuous time. Third, regarding the narrational access of characters to the flashes, the narrative information depicted in the flashes is not shared with the characters onscreen in story present and is only clearly "told" to the viewer. In all of the episodes of the first four seasons (approximately 60 hours of text), I only know of one exception. In the episode entitled "The Whole Truth" (Episode 2.16), the content of a flash is retold by one character to another in story present, in this case by Sun to Jin.

Even a cursory review of the flashes illustrates that there are multiple motivations proposed by the texts for the flashes themselves. In other words, the relationship of the flashes to story present is not consistent with any larger pattern over the course of the series. In some episodes, the flashes are emphatically character-motivated. For example, the episode "Greatest Hits" (Episode 3.21) depicts series regular, Charlie listing, in story present, the top five moments in his life and jotting them down on a scrap of paper as the program then depicts these moments in flashback. However, most flashes across the text of the series are coded as less subjective (i.e. narrated from a character) on a diminishing scale and can be more or less connected to the circumstances of story present. For example, Episode 12 of the first season ("Whatever the Case May Be") portrays, in the present, series regular Kate's attempts to regain possession of a toy airplane, while the emotional import of the object is elaborated upon in a series of flashbacks. In this case, the precise motivation of the flashes is a bit clouded. There are simply not enough narrative or stylistic cues to definitively attribute the depiction of the past to either Kate's memory or to a higher storytelling authority, although the former is arguably more likely. An even more complicated case can be observed in episodes in which the present and the flashes are connected only thematically. Theme, by its very definition, is an element created by the textual construction of an object; thus, characters, as elements of representation, would seem to be aware of theme only insofar as they "encounter" it in story events. As a result, attributing thematically linked flashbacks to character memory becomes even more tenuous. For example, in the John Locke–centric episode "Cabin Fever" (Episode 4.11), a series of flashbacks use fragments to depict Locke, at various ages, resisting a calling or denying some sort of innate nature. As a young boy, he fails to choose the correct item from a small gathering of artifacts because of his childish attraction to knives—an attraction that recurs throughout the series. Later, a teenage

Locke refuses to accept a science scholarship because he is still convinced that he can be the "star quarterback." These fragments all relate to one another and to story present, which depicts Locke accepting orders from a prophetic dream, through the overarching theme of inner callings. Making theme the connective tissue of events, I argue, makes character memory an even less tenable a narrative hypothesis. Moreover, this episode also includes two flashbacks to Locke's birth and infancy, capturing events that the character logically could not have first-hand knowledge of. Appropriately enough, the shots bookending these flashbacks avoid the thoughtful glance offscreen that traditionally signals character-motivated time shifts, and instead begins and ends with character entrances and exits from frame, making the cuts even more disembodied.

Lastly, there are a smaller number of episodes that more clearly signal another narrating agency organizing flashes outside and above the characters themselves. This countertendency begins in the seventh episode of the second season ("The Other 48") which depicts, in abbreviated fragments, events occurring on the other side of the island since the beginning of the series, that is, since the crash of 815. Here the flashes are preceded by sections of black leader and simple, white text numbering the days since the crash. This same, more omniscient technique is also used in episodes that similarly fill in lost time concerning Michael ("Three Minutes," Episode 2.22), Nikki and Paolo ("Exposé," Episode 3.14), and Locke ("The Brig," Episode 3.19). These cuts lack the more obvious cues (e.g. cutting from a shot of character A in the present to a shot of that same character A in the past) that would mark them as memory and the use of black leader and omniscient titles more likely signals another narrational agency altogether. In sum, the precise textual mechanism motivating flashes is quite variable and subject to interpretation.

In addition to these general norms guiding the use of flash structures, one can also detect several other interesting trends by way of a more systematic analysis. As the series continues, episodes evidence a slight reduction in the use of redundant cues signaling jumps in time. Specifically, the series reduces the use of soundbridges (sound overlap between timescapes, that is, between shots one and two or between shots three and four), crossmatches (graphic matches or inversions of spatial or compositional arrangements between timescapes), and origin matches (returning to the same or approximate time/space after the initial jump, that is spatiotemporal continuity between shots one and four) (see Table 5.1). I argue that these techniques are traditionally used to signal temporal jumps and that their reduction is likely explained with the assumed familiarity with the program and its typical structure. There is one cue, however, that remains consistent. Although the use of the soundbridge greatly diminishes, a whooshing, non-diegetic sound effect is

Table 5.1 Flash structures: Seasons One, Two, Three, and Four

Editing technique		Season	Instances	Total shots or transitions	Percentage
1	Soundbridge	1	53	260	20
		2	14	222	6
		3	18	284	6
		4	3	134	2
2	Crossmatch	1	23	260	9
		2	7	222	3
		3	5	284	2
		4	10	134	7 (8 in Ep. 5)
3	Origin match	1	27	130	21
		2	15	111	14
		3	12	142	8
		4	7	67	10
4	Opening black	1	21	130	16
		2	23	111	21
		3	52	142	37
		4	21	67	31
5	Closing black	1	12	130	9
		2	3	111	3
		3	4	142	3
		4	13	67	19

Table 5.1 Continued

Editing technique		Season	Instances	Total shots or transitions	Percentage
6	Gazes offscreen	1	165	520	32
		2	133	444	30
		3	163	568	29
		4	81	268	30
7	Blank/no gaze	1	210	520	40
		2	183	444	41
		3	302	568	53
		4	147	268	55
8	Disassociated matches	1	46	130	35
		2	52	111	47
		3	50	142	35
		4	19	67	28

applied to all temporal jumps and is only absent in a handful of special cases.[7] Furthermore, one can observe a slight statistical increase in crossmatches in the series' fourth season; however, this is due only to their extensive use in Episode Five, "The Constant." Interestingly, this single episode modifies the function of the device not simply to underscore the temporal gaps, but to visually depict the character Desmond Hume's ability to retain his consciousness across these temporal ellipses, in the manner of Kurt Vonnegut's Billy Pilgrim, an ability unique to this character.

The most common visual cue for temporal shifts in *Lost*'s flash structures is the character gaze offscreen. This image is traditionally invoked to signal the entrance into another layer of narration, whether used more literally in the case of the camera seemingly taking on the position of the gazer in point-of-view shots or, more figuratively, in the case of "looking" into the mental states of either recollection or fantasy. *Lost* frequently uses the latter; almost one-third of the shots cataloged in the flash structures contain a gaze off-screen wherein the object of the gaze may be more or less defined. Yet one cannot explain these images simply as memory cues, as it is just as likely that these shots are used to connect the story past back to the story present (the cut between shots three and four), a transition for which the term recollection would be illogical and subjectivity a mis-assignation.

The third flashback depicted in the exemplary episode "Walkabout" (Episode 1.4) illustrates what could be considered a conventional, closed, and more or less unambiguous flashback structure (see Figure 5.1). Here Shot A (from story present to story past) depicts John Locke in close-up staring glassily at some indistinct point out of frame, clearly mimicking reverie. We return to this same distant look in Shot D (coming back from story past to story present); Shots B and C that bookend the flashback depict Locke absorbed only in that past moment, focused on a simulated war game. This structure is the closest *Lost* comes to depicting radical time shifts in a conventional manner. The narrational cues positing the flashback as Locke's memory/mental state are also underscored by the narrative echoes resounding through past and present. In both timeframes, Locke is thwarted in his attempts at masculine authority: On the island in story present, his war party has just been scattered by a wild pig; in the past, his military board game and planned Australian walkabout are ridiculed by an unsympathetic fellow office drone. However, the use of these redundant cues is complicated in the series as early as this episode's very next flashback. In this case (see Figure 5.2), Shot A again depicts

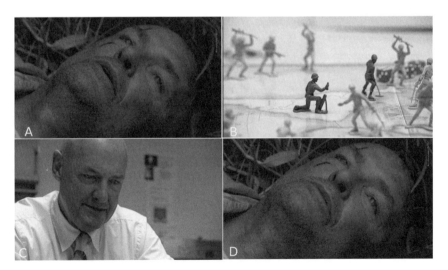

FIGURE 5.1 *From Season One, Episode Four, entitled "Walkabout."*

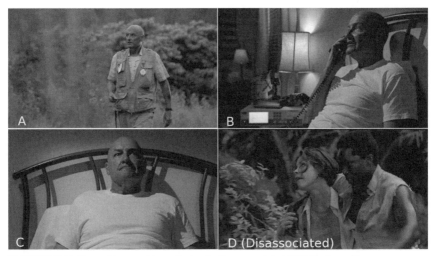

FIGURE 5.2 *From Season One, Episode Four, entitled "Walkabout."*

the character's distant gaze at some unclear point off frame, in this case as Locke exits frame left. However, Shot D neglects to bookend the structure and fails to depict our presumed recollector. The structure remains open in the sense that Branigan considers point-of-view structures that fail to return to the one gazing as somehow unresolved—a technique that we can call a disassociated match. Narrative redundancy still, however, weighs in the favor of the memory hypothesis. Once again past and present are bridged through implied character psychology; both timescapes depict Locke again desperate to assert his masculine mastery over charges of impotence. In the story present, he fearlessly continues to hunt the errant wild pig alone, as if responding to the shame handed to him in previous flashbacks by snide coworkers and uninterested phone sex operators. While this flashback's use of consistent character and theme papers over the connection of disparate story events, its use of a disassociated match early in the series suggests the fluidity of formal structure in *Lost*'s depiction of time.

Quite quickly, the pregnant offscreen gaze is compromised and loses its status as a clear narrational cue and its ability to signal character memory or subjectivity in any consistent way. For example, we can look to the fourth flashback depicted in Season Two's premiere, "Man of Science, Man of Faith" (see Figure 5.3). The first matched pair of shots (A and B) follow the traditional pattern; as Jack stares indistinctly into the dark abyss of the newly opened hatch (Shot A), the program cuts to a long shot of Jack entering a nearly empty stadium from far screen left in the story past (Shot B). This arrangement approaches what we have already considered typical character-

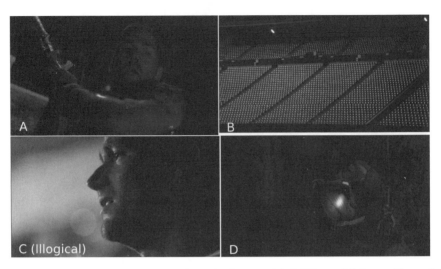

FIGURE 5.3 *From Season Two, Episode One, entitled "Man of Science, Man of Faith."*

motivated flashbacks: a distant gaze cues a memory. However, the structure unexpectedly inverts in the second matched pair (C and D) by placing the thoughtful offscreen gaze in the story past (Shot C) and a quasi-objective image, Jack falls into frame, in the final position (Shot D). In other words, the pregnant, meaningful gaze offscreen, which typically cues either visual or mental points of view and specifically reminiscences, illogically prompts the jump from story past to story present disrupting traditional narrational cues. The strange content of the flashback itself only underscores this inversion. In the past (from Shot B to C), Jack briefly encounters the character Desmond, who is only subsequently (in story present) revealed as being a lone inhabitant of the Swan Station at the bottom of the hatch. By placing the unmotivated memory of the past meeting with Desmond before Jack's present day run-in, the structure tips its hand, forcing a more direct intervention of an implied author by essentially (here again mimicking *Gravity's Rainbow* and its preoccupation with reversing of cause–effect, stimuli–response) placing the effect before the cause, complicating if not negating the possibility of the simple memory hypothesis for the flashback structures. This deceptively simple sequence then inverts the formal and narrative structures used to manage the shifting timescapes of flashbacks and subtly suggests another agency putting elements in (or out of) order.

These "illogical" uses of the device of the offscreen gaze also indicate *Lost*'s interest in what we can call the relativity of time. As mentioned above, the character Desmond is able to "predict" the story future because he is equally "present" in each of the series' timescapes, past, present, and future, evidenced through his continued consciousness through the program's temporally elliptical cuts. Similarly, in the aforementioned episode "Cabin Fever," young John Locke's childhood test is conducted by the mysterious character Richard Alpert, whom Locke will meet 40 story years hence, but will not have aged a day. In the test, Richard asks Locke to identify, out of a collection of knick-knacks, the object that was already his. In other words, Richard is asking Locke to become, like Desmond, equally present across time where it will become clear which object is, or will become, destined to become, or has already become his possession, depending on one's perspective. Here, again, the series is borrowing a textual feature from so-called postmodern novels, notably Philip K. Dick's *Valis* (1981) (a book that actually appears in the diegesis of the series) and Kurt Vonnegut's *Slaughter-House Five* (1971 [1968]), both of which feature protagonists who exist in multiple timescapes either by, in the former case, superimposition, or, in the latter case, by self-aware ellipses. However one interprets these disruptions of the traditional representation of temporality, they will remain just that: a matter of interpretation. What we can suggest is that when confronted with illogical uses of the offscreen gaze, we can attribute flashes only to an omni-temporal character (such as Desmond and, possibly, John Locke) or a higher level of narration outside and above characters arranging events.

One other surprising trend that can be traced across the first four seasons of *Lost* is an altogether consistency in the codes of representation in the depiction of both elliptical jumps backward and forward in time (see Table 5.2). Statistically, one sees a similar use of both offscreen and blank gazes (shots depicting characters, but no significant gaze, owing to either closed eyes or in-screen gazes) in terms of percentage. Moreover, one can see the inverse illogical use of the offscreen gaze in the first and fourth positions in the flash-forward structures, again illogically suggesting a

TABLE 5.2 Flash structures: Season Four

Flash-forwards	Instances	Total shots or transitions	Percentage
Gazes offscreen	48	168	28
Blank/no gazes	81	168	48
Black openings/closings	24	168	14
Disassociated matches	11	42	26

recollection of the future. This technique not only serves to further this aforementioned theme of the relativity of time at the core of the series, but also, I argue, retrospectively discredits the reading of previous flashbacks as character memory. By using the identical stylistic methods to depict temporal jumps backward (which use memory cues in terms of both style and narrative context) and forward (which use the same cues), the texts work to demystify the assumed tendency to attribute the former to character subjectivity. This stylistic echoing suggests that narrational cues can be manipulated and the flash-forwards in Season Four function to unmask the depiction of all the other flashes occurring previously. Indeed, this is exactly the central narrational gimmick of the third season's finale that depicts a series of fragments in flashes concerning series regular, Jack, that are only, in the episode's final moments, revealed as taking place in the story future.

The disruption of narrational cues of temporal organization reaches its apotheosis in *Lost*'s integration of flash-forwards beginning in Season Three. In these instances, the program frequently apes what we have called the traditional flashback structure, but inverts the timing to make the cues illogical and, I argue, retrospectively casts doubt on the motivation behind all of the flash structures. For example, the first flash-forward of Season Four's "The Economist" (Episode 4.3) (Figure 5.4) is constructed in a manner which echoes our first example from "Walkabout": jumps from and back to story present (Shots A and D) are cued with character gazes offscreen or near off frame. However, the content between Shots B and C is a depiction of story

FIGURE 5.4 *From Season Four, Episode Three, entitled "The Economist."*

future, rendering Shots A and D ambiguous. Clearly, character "memory" is an implausible motivation for the flash even though the formal structure suggests otherwise. Character agency over temporal organization is revealed as false and misleading, leaving a viewer with an inconsistent set of tools to distinguish timescapes and their relation to one another. This culminates in the masterful episode "Ji Yeon" (Episode 4.7), which alternates flashes of Sun giving birth and her husband Jin racing to get to the hospital. Only in the final sequences does the narration tip its hand and reveal that these two plot threads are not concurrent but are taking place in completely different timescapes: The birth of Sun's daughter occurs after the story future, while Jin's dash to the hospital took place long before the group ever crash landed on the island. Formal cues fail to distinguish the difference between jumps forward or backward in time as, once again, *Lost* mirrors its construction on the model of a confidence trick. Moreover, this episode's construction again strongly suggests the presence of a central trickster and implied author, much in the same way that *Twilight Zone* and *Star Trek* are "read" with the implied voice of their extratextual social commentators, purposefully rearranging time, not in accord with implied character psychology, but for the purpose of disorienting narrative gimmick that retrospectively changes the valence of prior story events—not untypical of art cinema, but quite uncommon in network television realist narrative.

Examining the results of my review of flash structures, we can also detect two smaller statistical deviances regarding the rendering of flashbacks and flash-forwards. First, one can observe the increased use of closing black in the fourth shot in the flash-forwards rather than opening black in the first shot for flashbacks. This first difference is easily enough explained as flash-forwards are, in a sense, inverting the structure of flashbacks and, thus, the position of the black screen is likewise inverted. Second, one can detect a slight decrease in what I call disassociated matches. By disassociated matches, I am referring to flash structures in which one of the four shots (or three shots if one shot of black leader is used) depicts a character different from the one that flash concerns. For example, the first flashback in Season One's "Tabula Rasa" (Episode 1.3) is structured around the following set of shots: one, a close-up of series regular, Kate, with no gaze; two, a medium shot of Kate asleep; three, another close-up of Kate with no gaze; and four, a close-up tracking with another character Hurley's feet. A disassociated match is similar to the above-mentioned deviant point-of-view structure that fails to conclude the sequence of gazer–object–gazer and, thus, leaves the narrational status of the object "open" and ambiguous.[8] Similarly, disassociated matches do not complete the structure (in this case of recollector–memory–recollector) and, thus, raise even more doubt and ambiguity concerning the relative subjectivity of the flashes. More simply, I argue that the more a text uses disassociated matches, the more unlikely is the memory hypothesis, that is, understanding flashbacks as memories. The twist in *Lost*'s depiction of flash-forwards is that the amount of disassociated matches actually decreases significantly. This is a strange irony given the fact that it becomes difficult or illogical to assign flash-forward information to character subjectivity at the same time that stylistic choices subtly suggest, through the decrease of disassociated matches, just such an understanding. This stylistic peculiarity can be addressed with exactly the same terms used to discuss the illogical use of the gaze offscreen. On the one hand, it again signals the theme of the relativity of time by suggesting that a character can "remember" the future. On the other hand, reducing disassociated matches in flash-forwards also unmasks and demystifies the use of what could be conversely called a closed flashback. The systematic use of associated, closed matches in the series' flash-forwards dismantles, retrospectively, willingness to attribute subjectivity based on this stylistic norm.

There are, then, several recurring stylistic devices at play in the flash structures that discredit the hypothesis of character subjectivity. Again, these include the illogical use of offscreen gazes, the stylistic continuity between flashbacks and flash-forwards and the peculiar use of closed (that is non-disassociated) matches in flash-forwards. However, what these tendencies do not manage is to give a viewer an alternative hypothesis; if these flashes are not the product of character of character subjectivity, to what narrational entity can we attribute them? These observed trends merely suggest that narrational agency may be subsequently replaced, but they do not necessarily name the replacement. Indeed, this is how conspiratorial narratives work. *Lost* begins with an airplane crash and the subsequent conglomeration of the surviving passengers, nearly all strangers to one another. However, by Season Four, it becomes clear that the crash was not an accident (in fact an entire substitute plane wreck was placed at the bottom of the Pacific Ocean as a decoy to mislead possible rescuers subsequent to the crash) and the people onboard the plane are, in fact, related in strange, unexpected ways (Claire is revealed to be Jack's stepsister, Locke's father is revealed to be responsible for the deaths of Sawyer's parents, etc.). What these story elements and the style of the flash structures collectively suggest is another narrating agency manipulating events on the fringes of the diegesis—a mastermind for the series as a whole.

Several episodes include stylistic deviances and plot devices that make the (non-)presence of the mastermind all the more noticeable. I have already discussed the narrational style of the episode "The Other 48" (Episode 2.7). It is the first episode to use flashbacks that entirely neglect visual cues to imply character subjectivity motivating the jumps. Interestingly, this episode also includes the first instance of the series' mysterious antagonists assembling a list of the protagonists, implying that they have intimate foreknowledge of the latter. In other words, in the same episode that first stylistically suggests a higher narrational authority, the story puts the antagonistic Others in a place of narrative knowledge that would make their mastery comprehensible. Later that season, the episode "Three Minutes" (Episode 2.22) mimics the same narrational style and, significantly, introduces a second list, reiterating the possibility of understanding the Others as a collective mastermind. Story developments in the subsequent Season Three only seem to reinforce such a hypothesis. For example, in that season's premiere, "A Tale of Two Cities," Ben Linus, leader of the so-called Others, reveals his possession of a set of personnel files on each of the crash survivors that contains personal, intimate details on each, exactly the sort of information that was frequently reenacted in the series flashbacks. Moreover, the comprehensiveness of the files exceeds even character knowledge as exemplified in the episode "The Man from Tallahassee" in which Locke reads his own file and learns that his father was responsible for the death of Sawyer's family, a fact not communicated in any of the series' flashes. Style and story converge to suggest an alternative narrational hypothesis, a conspiratorial mastermind.

What makes *Lost* uncommon, even among mastermind narratives, is its ultimate refusal to definitively characterize the mastermind. Instead, the series progresses, like a fractal, acknowledging and implying a possible center, but never giving it form. This can be seen through a cursory review of the series' ever-changing antagonists. The protagonists were first menaced by a group of savages somehow affiliated with a scientific collective named the Dharma Initiative. By Season Three, it is revealed that the Dharma Initiative was, in fact, killed off by the island's "original" inhabitants, led by Ben Linus. However, it is even later revealed in that same season that Ben takes orders from Jacob, a ghost who lives in a cabin that can never be found in the same place. Later, in the fourth season, the survivors are attacked by a group of late arrivals, prompted by an industrialist, Charles Widmore, who may be at the center of the conspiracy (but is more likely just one more false lead). The only thing that is certain is that the survivors are pawns in this larger plot being engineered outside and above their heads. And, although, the identity of the mastermind is unclear or undefined (like the absent occupant of The Pearl), it has been suggested, in the guise of Ms Hawking, that it is time itself or predestination that is guiding actions with an endless series of supposed-to's.

Furthermore, I would argue that this ceaselessly deferred mastermind, this way of hinting at a quasi-diegetic agency controlling onscreen events that is never entirely revealed, acts as a narrational technique answering the problems addressed in this chapter's introduction, that of deploying seriality, information multiplicity, and real virtuality, while maintaining a sense of central, controlled narrative authority. The mastermind, as an entity that moves in and out of diegesis with the shared powers of textual production becomes the perfect metaphor for *Lost* writers trying to control, or trying to give the illusion of control over the dense series. Indeed, nothing better answers this strange criticism of writers making it up as they go along as the emphatic cry of Ms Hawking to Desmond, "you're not supposed to."

In the final episode of ITVC's *The Prisoner* (ITV, 1967–8), the eponymous hero confronts the mysterious "Number One." Over the series' previous 16 episodes, "Number One," through the medium of his ever-changing henchman, "Number Two," has subjected the protagonist through a set of sinister mind games meant to break the latter's will. In this final confrontation, the protagonist tears a series of masks from the face of Number One only to find, at the bottom, his own face staring back at him. More specifically, the prisoner sees the face of Patrick McGoohan, the writer, director, producer, and star of the series. The revelation is a patently confounding turn in what is a difficult series whose ultimate significance is unclear. However, what can be pointed out is that Number One, the narrative's mastermind responsible for all the elaborate hoaxes perpetrated on the series protagonist yet never seen onscreen until these penultimate moments (in fact, each episode begins with the protagonist crying, "Who is Number One?"), shares his identity with the chief creative force of the series. While *Lost* has not gone so far as to unmask its creators in the context of the diegesis, I would argue that the series' use of the mastermind, a mastermind that is continually deferred and may be best characterized as the construction of time in the series itself, shares many similarities with the example of *The Prisoner*. In the end, the mastermind acts as both a surrogate for the implied author and his literal presence in the text influencing events and guiding character action from an ambiguous position between diegesis and the extra-text. The closest one can come to *The Prisoner*'s final revelation is, perhaps, the aforementioned presence of showrunners Lindelof and Cuse in several program clip shows constructed of previously aired material. In these episodes, the writers serve as quasi-masterminds certifying the cohesion of an often confusing narrative. In one such episode, *The Lost Survival Guide*, Lindelof comments that,

> the show is couched in mystery. It's probably the reason that a lot of audience members are intimidated coming in. The reality is, you're supposed to be a little confused. The show sort of reveals itself one layer at time.

Here, again, we return to the anxiety over the complexity of tentpole TV and here Lindelof responds reassuringly. There will be a unmasking, and although the face *Lost*'s Number One is unlikely to be represented as the face of the writers themselves, such a representation can already be discerned on a more figurative register. In the following chapter, we will further consider the unique storytelling problems and solutions associated with tentpole TV's particular textual form. However, we will shift our gaze from the problem of organizing nonlinear, vast time to that of expanding, inconsistent space.

6

24 and Tentpole Spatiality

To begin a discussion of the techniques of representing space in the tentpole TV, I would like to consider two examples of disruption. In his landmark essay "Narrative Space," Stephen Heath (1981) describes the peculiar moment late in Alfred Hitchcock's *Suspicion* (1941) in which two detectives call on the film's worried protagonist. Heath casts the scene as a model of classical construction, both visually—each shot rhyming the next as well as its inverse counterpart later in the sequence—and narratively—the whole event is clearly constructed on protypical lines of the classical hermeneutic that offers incremental information to push the plot forward. However, one moment, apparently useless in function, disrupts the economy of the sequence. One of the detectives is puzzled by an abstract painting in the protagonist's drawing room and spends a majority of the sequence giving it a series of sidelong glances. The film itself even cuts away to a set of closer angles on the painting and the perplexed officer. In considering this stylistic appendix, Heath suggests that the importance placed on the seemingly insignificant painting may be a displacement of the more narratively important painting, a portrait of the protagonist's overbearing father, or could be construed to underscore the overall ambiguity lurking throughout the film that never convincingly establishes whether or not the protagonist's husband is a murderer or not. However, more importantly, Heath concludes that the painting "has its effect as missing spectacle: problem of point of view, different framing, disturbance of the law and its inspectoring eye, interruption of the narrative economy, it is somewhere else again, another story, another space" (Heath 1981: 24). The example is instructive in Heath's larger attempt to chart how acts of narrativization contain, order, clarify, and restrain the possibilities of represented space; the very peculiarity of the scene from *Suspicion* depicts this system at its limits. Lingering on an apparently purposeless element of space threatens to disrupt managed order.

A comparably disruptive moment of spatial ordering occurs in Episode 12 ("Godsend") of the first season of NBC's *Heroes*. Near the conclusion of the episode, series protagonist Noah Bennet solicits the help of another regular, Mohinder Suresh. Mohinder refuses the gesture, but Bennet, undeterred, gives Mohinder a business card with his contact information just in case he decides to change his mind. As Bennet passes the card, the camera cuts in tight, lingering close enough and long enough to be in err of the narrative and compositional conventions of classical filmmaking and to render the website and phone number listed on the card clearly legible. In the context of the individual episode, the extreme close-up is superfluous, disruptive, and, like Hitchcock's painting, indicative of "another place." However, in this latter case, this other space is not just a hypothetical construct. The URL address given on the card leads to an actual website for Bennet's fictitious employer, Primatech Paper, and the phone number reaches a voice message from the same fictional business. Both contact points serve as entries into the *Heroes* ARG, which subsequently encompasses several other websites and private e-mail messages. Thus, while Heath argues that disruptions of classical space fray at the edges of narrativization and endanger its ability to order textual worlds (as well as ideological subtext), the *Heroes* example depicts the use of classical disruptive moment to vastly expand narrative space beyond the text and into unruly forms. Heath's other space has become clickable and navigable.[1]

In the previous chapter, I argued that the implementation of real virtuality in tentpole TV texts made any hypothetical story time accessible to on-air or ancillary texts, necessitating narrative innovations in the organization of potentially unruly time. In this section, I further argue that tentpole TV programs also have undertaken strategies to rein in vast and expanding space in programs that are made more textually mobile and are supplemented with any number of narratively significant, off-air manifestations, as exemplified in our introductory illustration. Specifically, we can look to the tentpole TV series *24*, which is truly a logistical narrative, one that foregrounds the problems of spacing, location, and scale to make sense of its own complicated narrative space. In this process, *24*, like our other tentpole series, crafts a hyperdiegesis that both reflects and reinforces concepts from contemporary theories of the social production of space. Specifically, all these programs break from the traditional representations of space in TV drama and recast it as amorphous, undergrid by constant recalculation and underscored by movement and contingency. It will be the exact business of the following chapter to consider these newer textual constructions of television space.

These innovations necessitate a quick review of traditional understandings of filmic space. Instructive in this regard is the work of Noel Burch (1973) whose deceptively simple observations on the conventional construction of narrative film are still unsurpassed. In his *Theory of Film Practice*, Burch proposes a taxonomy for understanding the spatial relationship of any hypothetical consecutive shots, ranging from continuous, that is, the shots share space either in part or entirely; to proximate, that is, shots that are coded as relatively near or related in space; to radical discontinuous, that is, the spatial relationship between shots is unclear or unimportant (9). Burch then proceeds to describe how makers of classical film innovated and perfected a set of visual cues to establish spatially continuous relations. And, to be fair, tentpole TV is clearly in this lineage to a large extent, as is a majority of popular film and television.

However, I further argue that tentpole TV makes systematic use of Burch's proximate and discontinuous cuts to expand narrative space. The clearest manifestation of this can be seen in tentpole TV's frequent use of split ensembles, that is the juxtaposition of character-centered sequences with ambiguous narrative and spatial relations that are only subsequently, after hours and hours of text, narratively and spatially reconciled. For example, the first five episodes of *24*'s second season intercut the work of the regular protagonists with the preparations for Kate Warner's sister's wedding. It is only in Episode Five (after approximately 4 hours of "real"/story time) that series protagonist Tony Almeida calls on the Warners and eventually exposes Kate's sister as an operative for a "sleeper cell" of terrorists. Similarly, the first five episodes of *Heroes*' first season leaves its protagonists in vastly different locations scattered globally in Tokyo in New York in Odessa, Texas, and others, and only eventually and intermittently allows its principal characters to co-occupy space.[2]

Increased reliance on proximate cuts between vastly shortened sequences alters the very scale of the narrative constructed. For example, in Season Two of *24*, series protagonists work to prevent a nuclear explosion in Los Angeles, an event whose impact, graphed on any number of diegetic computer screens, encompasses an entire geographical region. Similarly, *Heroes*' second season addressed the possibility of a global pandemic making any space at all narratively significant. Perhaps, the logical end limit of this impulse can be seen in ABC's *Flashforward* (ABC 2009–10), a series that begins with a global event in which all the world's population (or at least most of it) blacked out for 2 minutes and 17 seconds. With one deft move, every single human being and every location on earth were earmarked as involved in the series' premise, resulting in an immensely vast narrative space, one that was subsequently restrained by the more traditional procedural elements of police work and hospital drama in series episodes.

These changes, coupled with the decreasing use of traditional continuity editing in tentpole TV, underscores how the default of spatial relations of successive shots and sequences is moving from classical style's spatial continuity to an overgeneralized proximate space. Even within sequences, spatial continuity and spatial overlap are increasingly replaced with proximate spacing, indicative in *24*'s many scenes of telephone conversations (once a screenwriting taboo) and *Alias*'s frequent, similar use of walkie-talkie communications. On the inverse side, once every space and character is hypothetically propinquitous, there is very little possibility for what Burch calls a radical spatial discontinuity, outside of breaking with diegetic space entirely (such radical breaks may be found in *Lost*'s and *Heroes*' experimentation with multiple, non–mutually exclusive textual realities, that is, cutting between narrative "dimensions"). This point is emphatically indicated in *Lost*'s second-season finale, which concludes by leaving the narrative space of the island and its familiar characters to depict a telephone call from some unnamed frozen tundra to secondary character, Penny Widmore, or in the second episode of the program's fourth season ("Confirmed Dead") which cuts to secondary character, Charlotte, excavating an archeological site somewhere in Tunisia where she finds an artifact stamped with the Dharma logo. Both of these potentially disruptive shifts in vast space are reconciled as somewhat proximate either through a phone call or other trace physical evidence. No matter how vast the shifts, the spacing can be construed as proximate because *Lost* and other tentpole TV programs play out not in single texts, but across textual worlds where everything is eventually propinquitous.

The depiction of space in tentpole TV also begs a reconsideration of Burch's theorization of offscreen space. Burch famously stated that "offscreen space has only an intermittent, or rather fluctuating existence during any film" (21). For Burch, the space around the edges of the frame was either narratively activated or deactivated according to the use or nonuse of character glances, character exits/entrances, or incomplete framing that cuts figures off at the frame line. Such an observation is fair enough for individual shots separated from their context. However, the construction of tentpole TV narratives depends also on the replacement of a fluctuating textual off space with a hypothetical world surrounding individual texts, which critic Matt Hills (2002) has called hyperdiegesis. For example, the significance of the surrounding narrative worlds can already be observed in the expanded scale of the series narratives, ranging from the regional (*24*) to the global (*Lost*, *Heroes*, *Flashforward*). The widening of scale and the opening of the "world" results in confusion over what can strictly be considered off- and onscreen space. The increased tendency to intermingle the offscreen and onscreen can perhaps be best observed in the use of both literal and figurative multiscreen effects in *24* that juxtapose, in one frame, the image of several different spaces through either a non-diegetic or a diegetic device. Hypothetical world-space is further maintained, in part, by the existence of any number of transmedia texts that continue both to tell the series narratives and to dwell in narrative space off-air. In describing an early example of such an off-air extension, critic John Caldwell (2004) used the designation "after hours aesthetic"; however, as tentpole TV producers have sought to more aggressively enmesh their programs in transmedia, a tendency coupled with the increasingly nonlinear viewing habits of viewers, the style may be better termed a "24/7 aesthetic." In other words, the more tentpole TV series become vast fictional universes in their own right (much in the same way that, for example, the *Star Wars* Universe or the Marvel Comics Universe are discussed) and the more that they become multifaceted brands for their parent firms, the less sense it makes to distinguish simply between offscreen and onscreen.[3] Indeed, the "offscreen" may well become the "onscreen" of a subsequent novel, video game, comic book, and the like.

Beginning in the 1980s, intertextuality became an academic buzzword in television studies to describe both the way in which viewers read and understand texts by putting them into conversation with semantic webs of previously experienced cultural objects and the way in which producers of cultural objects increasingly included elements in their texts that rewarded or even demanded heightened cultural literacy (Ott and Walter 2000). Both theories conceive of the semantic ability of reference and imitation to create a metaphoric space between and around texts. Discussion of this latter aspect phenomenon was often posited as either an epochal stylistic advancement in television narratives (Williams 1988, Thompson 1996), or as the latest technique in luring upscale demographics (Caldwell 1995, Feuer 1995). These critical pieces reflected the sensibilities of contemporary series like *St. Elsewhere* (NBC, 1982–8), *Moonlighting* (ABC, 1985–9), *Northern Exposure* (CBS, 1990–5), and *Twin Peaks* (ABC, 1990–1), which were littered with glancing references to other media texts as well as self-reflexive humor, which is the critical hallmark of Brechtian aesthetics.

While these programs and their producers were working largely with what Jameson (1991) famously dubbed "blank parody," that is, parodic reference or imitation without critical intention (17), I would argue that tentpole TV narratives use intertextuality much more strategically in an effort to craft what Sara Gwellian-Jones (2004) has called virtual reality spaces. For example, Thompson (1996) discusses at length the final episode of *St. Elsewhere* and unpacks all the minute, passing references (mostly in dialogue in small elements of set direction) to other medical dramas that came before it as well as MTM's—the drama's producers—other series. Tentpole TV series, too, make use of these narrative hints, but they are more focused on the revelation of what is often called the program's mythology. A pointed example of this can be seen in *Heroes'* use of the repeated graphic motif of an open DNA helix—a riff on the Trystero symbol from *The Crying of Lot 49*. The symbol is continually introduced and reintroduced in diverging storylines, making sequences contain a conspiratorial, almost subconscious rhyming that is only resolved much later. Moments of off-hand intertextual reference in Thompson's so-called quality television are replaced with narratively significant details that work more intratextually, facilitating the construction of "fictional worlds to which the alchemy of textual data and imagination transports the reader, facilitating a pleasurable sense of 'being there'" (Gwellian-Jones 2004: 83).

In his own consideration of 1990s' intertextuality, Caldwell (1995) examines a single episode of *Northern Exposure*, demonstrating how its intertextual density can be understood as intellectual excess and "yuppie-bait," drawing in and gratifying potential upscale viewers. Certainly, *Lost* clearly follows in this tradition in the way in which, for example, it names many of its principal characters after Enlightenment philosophers (Locke, Bentham, and Rousseu). However, again, I argue that there is a qualitative difference between the tangential intertextuality of *Northern Exposure* that, for example, introduces Franz Kafka into the Alaskan landscape with the ponderous intratextuality and *Lost*'s use of philosophical namesakes in a series that foregrounds critiques of empiricism (the first episode of the program's second season was titled "Man of Science, Man of Faith").

Intertextuality is often explained with recourse to spatial metaphors that necessitate a slight modification when applied to tentpole TV. Discussing the concept in an early theoretical piece, Jonathan Culler (1976) states,

> the notion of intertextuality emphasizes that to read is to place a work in a discursive space, relating it to other texts and to the codes of that space, and writing itself is a similar activity: a taking up of a position in discursive space. (1382–3)

In other words, taking intertextuality seriously means understanding texts as being semantically located at the crossroads of any number of infinite texts, both actual and hypothetical, presupposed in the current text. The spatial model of reading here is entirely deterritorialized, allowing for an infinite sea of connections unchecked by the margins of the page. However, I would argue that tentpole TV has strategically used this intertextuality in an attempt to construct a new spatial model in which episode details lead not only back out into messy semiosphere, but also can be interweaved intratextually. One only need peruse the detailed sections on the *Lost*-fan-run *lostpedia* website on recurring symbols and themes to see such details at work. For example, the section devoted solely to eyes (http://lostpedia.wikia.com/wiki/Eyes) contains a detailed spreadsheet of all of the instances of graphic extreme close-up on eyes—the image that begins the entire series. This chart offers just one sort of map of the series that traces one intratextual detail. The series uses deferred, post-structural meaning not to explode texts into endless references, but to recycle details internally in a vicious cycle of reading and rereading.

In both its refiguring of the articulation of spatial connections, its reexamination of offscreen space and its spatial model of intratextuality, producers of tentpole TV are aesthetically testing and implementing the conclusions of recent innovations in the social theory of space. Many of these theorists have sought to rethink our traditional understanding of space, which has been cast as more fluid in the wake of modernity conceived broadly. Specifically, their collective work is concerned with the dismantling of the very notion of discrete space. For example, Anthony Giddens (1990) understands space as becoming increasingly "phantasmagoric: that is to say locales are thoroughly penetrated and shaped in terms of social influences quite distant from them" (18–19). More recently, sociologist Ulrich Beck (1992) has discussed a new indiscrimination of space with regard to risks, the increasing, and inescapable unintended consequences of modernity's "progress." The thinker describes the spatial vastness of the large-scale threats of radioactivity and global warming that have an indifference to class and wealth as well as an "inherent tendency towards globalization" (36). These threats demand an understanding of spatial connection as vast and interconnected, mirroring the expanding scaling and spacing of tentpole TV narratives. *Heroes* especially can be read as a fictional adaptation of Beck's (1992) theories. In Season Two, series protagonists struggle against a global pandemic glimpsed in a possible future. For Beck, risks similarly have a virtual existence given their similar existence as potential outcomes, which he calls the "not-yet-event" (33). Moreover, the series couches the responsibility of the characters' purpose within a discourse of fate. For Beck, risk positions are ultimately understood as a modern revision of fate, a destiny into which everyone is born and no one can fully escape. Also describing the unique spatial properties of the contemporary moment, sociologist Manuel Castells (1996) has argued that the more society is constructed around flows—flows of money, flows of information, flows of people—the more space, as an expression of this society, is constructed as a complimentary "space of flows." In this construction, communication itself becomes paramount in connecting hubs to nodes, that is, between social centers and margins. These connections are important as single places are no longer self-sufficient onto themselves (here Castells draws on conclusions based on the observation of the internationally intertwined nature of Big Business) and rely on any number of other spaces to derive meaning, importance, and utility. Castells exemplifies a larger trend of social thinkers who mark an elimination of distance, hereby replaced with a grid of quick accessibility (either corporeal or virtual), which arguably reflects and is reflected upon in tentpole TV series, which, as we have seen, eliminate the dichotomous logic of continuous/discontinuous space and replace it with the always and inescapable proximate.

In the above, I have attempted to demonstrate how the unique construction of space as vast, interconnected, and expanding in tentpole TV programs places the programs outside traditional understandings of filmic space, as understood by Burch, at the same time that these features put the programs into intimate conversation with contemporary theories of the social construction of space and situate their textual forms as nascent theorizations of a similar intention. As the model of the television program moves from a strictly textual one to one based more on the model of the world, or universe, with its fundamental depth and complexity of space and time, it may be increasingly necessary to deploy social theory to create frameworks to understand these phenomena. Moreover, it could be argued that these nascent theorizations could be understood as a reflection of the spatial arrangements of the work of tentpole producers as reviewed at length in Part One, which can be understood as an example of what Castells has called the "network enterprise" (187).

Before examining exactly the distinct ways in which *24*, as well as the other tentpole TV, produce textual space, it is necessary to consider the conventional constructions of space as they have developed in dramatic television. Although space itself is a deeply contested and complex term, in the following, we will refer simply to any number of techniques used by television producers in individual shots or across any set of shots, sequences, or episodes to cue a sense of realistic, lived space and the strategies of giving meaning to these hypothetical constructs.

The traditional depiction of fictional space in television has been greatly influenced by the organizational and technical limitations of the medium. In early television, shooting was done largely in metropolitan communication centers where large cameras were moved around cavernous studio spaces that had undergone a varying degree of dressing. Protypical here is the live TV drama and hybrid sitcoms (*The Jack Benny Show* [CBS, 1950–64], *Texaco Star Theater* [NBC, 1948–56]) of the commercial medium's first decade which traded on theatrical staging devices to capture all the relevant action in one performance space, complete with actor entrances and exits (Boddy 1990, Spigel 1992). The depiction of space in dramatic television altered with the introduction of what has been called the telefilm (Anderson 1994, Vianello 1994). These series, constructed with the resources and the techniques of the Hollywood studios, edited together a number of temporally diverse sequences drawn from any number of locations and professionally built sets. This organizational shift can also be cast as one of aggressive economic "routinization" (Hirsch 1991) wherein any number of elements, including plot, character, and genre, were grounded in formula in the service of staving off the inherent uncertainty of the creative process and the reception of mass culture. Arguably, this routinization also affected the depiction of space itself, liberated from the sound stage, but reined in by Hollywood convention. The concept or premises of telefilm series was typically ground down to three or four repeatable spaces, which would be contrasted with any number of occasional locations that, by definition, do not repeat through the life of the series. Therefore, Captain Kirk and the crew of *Star Trek* (CBS, 1966–9) can explore the most vast reaches of the universe while the majority of the narrative action takes place in the bridge, the teleporter room, the sick bay, and the unnamed hallway of the USS Enterprise punctuated by the occasional trip to "beam down" to an alien world or vessel.

This economic split between repeating and nonrepeating spaces in dramatic television also has an aesthetic function that gives meaning to narrative and helps to situate programs within a genre. In a rather resonate example, domestic sitcoms clearly articulate the differences between the private/home/repeated space and the occasionally disastrous foray into the outside world of chaotic/public/nonrepeated space, the protypical example being Lucy Ricardo getting herself into any number of priceless mishaps once she passes through the threshold of her apartment.[4] The same formula of inside space versus outside space plays out in any number of comedic series. For example, one memorable episode of *All in the Family* ("Archie and the Lock-Up," Episode 2.3) has Archie thrown in jail after he dares venture away from his sacred chair into the social world in a failed attempt to pull Michael and Lionel away from a student protest. Classically, the same observation holds whether the program is centered around a traditional family or a nontraditional work or leisure "family," as in the case of *Taxi* (NBC, 1978–82; ABC, 1982–3), *Cheers* (NBC, 1982–93), or *Friends* (NBC, 1994–2004).

Moreover, this description of the spacing of narratives holds relatively true for non-comedic, dramatic forms as well. Crime, legal, and medical dramas typically house their action in repeating, shared, quasi-familial spaces juxtaposed with contingent, encounter spaces. The deep structure of inside/outside even takes on a foregrounded narrative importance in *Hill Street Blues* (NBC, 1981–7), a program that is emphatically about creating order out of an urban chaos and how this same disorder infects and invades the sanctity of the police squad room, most prominently in the series pilot where a hostage crisis erupts from within the police station itself. Another interesting limit case can be observed in the series *The Rockford Files* (NBC, 1974–80) in which the protagonist's home, a decrepit mobile home on the beach in Malibu, is in constant financial peril and, as a running gag, is repeatedly broken into by a series of angry debtors and jilted lovers. Like *Hill Street*, *Rockford* foregrounds the distinction of inside/outside space as a repeating narrative problem. I would argue that this traditional distinction of inside/outside space and, more specifically, the redeeming of inside space at the expense of the outside is recurring ur-thematic that runs through much of filmed TV drama. Horace Newcomb (1974) famously discussed this dichotomy in terms of what he saw was the inherent "intimate" aesthetic of television form which favors narratives where "problems arise from 'outdoor' conflicts [and] are turned into problems that can be dealt within the confines of the living room or kitchen" (247). This thematic also echoes what is for Raymond Williams (1975) the ideological operation of the medium itself, the establishment and maintenance of private, domestic, and isolated spaces whose relation with the larger social world is hijacked by a direct communicative connection with the center of social power.[5] Traditionally, spatial organization in fictional TV similarly favors sets of isolated, domesticated spaces to house its action.

However, there is at least one other master spatial logic at work in dramatic series television, one that could be described as always-on-the-run. Simply put, these series of this variety refuse to rely on the use of repeating spaces for any number of production-centric or programming-centric reasons. Echoing the expanded, worldly consciousness of the New Frontier era, television programming of the 1960s, in particular, favored globe-trotting narratives and premises, as exemplified in programs such as *The Fugitive* (ABC, 1963–7), *Mission: Impossible* (CBS, 1966–73), and *I Spy* (NBC, 1965–8). The latter, specifically, was spatially diffuse, constructed with what amounted to travelogues as the two secret agent protagonists embarked on a never-ending series of road trips—as in their car ride through the Spanish countryside with absent-minded professor, Boris Karloff, in "Mainly on the Plain" (Episode 2.22)—or chases—as Cosby trails behind Culp through Western Mexico in "Bet Me a Dollar" (Episode 1.20). Later, this spatial logic was largely occupied by what could be called loner narratives (*The Incredible Hulk* [CBS, 1978–82], *Kung Fu* [ABC, 1972–5]), which also echoed similarly structured Westerns of the 1950s (as in *Rawhide*'s [CBS, 1959–66] endless cattle drives). From an economic standpoint, these programs can be understood as practicing, in contradistinction to routinization, a sort of heightened flexibility, in both the aesthetic and economic sense, wherein program narratives can take place in any number of competing studio spaces or live locations, whichever provides the best deal financially.

The spatial logic of tentpole TV can be understood as being at the vertex of these two traditions, using on-the-run spatiality to complicate the inside/outside binary logic typical of television programming. This is particularly evident in the narratives of tentpole TV that often revolve around the porous boundaries between the private and professional lives of the protagonists (discussed at greater length later in Chapter 7). The tendency can also be observed in the very textual construction of the programs that have used untraditional techniques to expand the texts' narrative space. Furthermore, just as the spatial representations of past television programs have reflected and reinforced the different economic and organizational decisions in their production, the spatiality of tentpole TV, too, implies similar decisions on the part of its producers. This rationale was suggested in a 2006 *Variety* article, which claimed that Fall television season, one filled "with intricate storylines, sweeping scope, large casts and $10 million marketing blitzkriegs," may be—at least up to that point—"the most expensive TV season in history" (Johnson 2006). The article proceeds to explain how network television programs are increasingly crafted as "events" calculated to maximize viewer investment and cut through increasing media clutter, with the side effect of greatly increasing production costs. In other words, these programs' producers seem less invested in maximizing routinization or capitalizing on competition between studio spaces (although this surely does happen to some degree) and more invested in creating a finished product that translates well to HD receivers and, like any good event, can be modularly expanded. Here it is important to remember that *Lost*'s US$13 million pilot included costs for shipping carved segments of a scrapped airliner from the west coast to their Oahu beach location, an extravagance altogether uncommon for an untested television series (Stewart 2006).

Using primarily a consideration of episodes from the first two seasons of *24*, we will examine at greater length the qualitatively new forms of spatiality indicative of tentpole TV. I argue that these programs, having left the traditional spatial logic of television drama aside, have pioneered new techniques for organizing fictional space that both reflect and reinforce the unique production circumstances of the programs themselves as well as contemporary theories of the social construction of space. Specifically, we will consider the textual world of *24* as containing examples of qualculative space, wherein location, distance, and proximity must continually be recalibrated; of in-between space, where characters, objects, and their surroundings are in constant motion; and as informationally rich space, wherein distance and difference are replaced with ubiquity and proximity through visual juxtaposition.

In a recent essay, Bruno Latour and two co-collaborators (Camacho-Hübner et al. n.d.) consider the implications of digital navigation on the concept of the map, an object that the authors call a "spurious referent" (8). The authors contend that the near infinite malleability and mutability of digital mapping—as in the experience of using, for example, Google Earth—reflects the fallacy that cartography should only be interested in resemblance. The sociologists contrast this single-minded operation of mapping with the messy acts of navigation that situate maps, instead, as assemblages of signs, what the authors call "dashboards of calculation," allowing for point-to-point movement (16). Implications of these notions loom large in the essay's conclusion where notions of Euclidean space itself are unmasked as nothing more than the false mimesis of combining all these spurious referents into one, merged notion of a continuous, cohesive world. To take Latour and company seriously would mean expelling all our static notions of defining space through concepts such as borders, territories, or maps, and recast it as something that is continuously reconstituted and reconfigured through use.

In this essay, the authors are echoing the work of sociologist Nigel Thrift (2004) who describes the contemporary era as one of "qualculation," one in which human activity is inevitably accompanied by unexamined acts of calculation and computation, giving social life a near infinite informational subtext. The consequences of such a development that makes this McLuhanite fantasy the stuff of everyday life are, for Thrift, vast and diffuse. Because data streams are unending, precision of analysis or spacing is less valuable than strategies to deal with vastness, complexity, and irresolvable ambiguity—such as in the example of getting directions on the fly from a smart phone. Like Castells, Thrift also suggests that how we organize our very lives, be it in physical spaces or in social formations, increasingly is constructed to accommodate flows—flows of bodies, information, and others. Courting Benjamin, Thrift even goes as far as to suggest the ubiquity of calculation and computation accompanies a different sense of space itself, which has become porous, more relativized and less grounded in location when given access to ambient information through any number of technological prostheses. All these social thinkers agree that contemporary uses of technology have led to a discrediting of notions of a stable, self-contained space. Furthermore, all suggest that space is less a mathematical concept than a social one and that spatial relations are increasingly understood as unstable, or made on-the-fly; or, in the parlance of Giddens, space is continually reconstructed through the act of structuration within navigation itself.

24 depicts just such a world, undergird by a vast, technological unconsciousness whose presence makes itself known intermittently in program narratives. For example, in Season One, an unending system of audio-visual surveillance devices allows gangster, Ira Gaines, to track, monitor, and control the actions of the series protagonist, Jack Bauer, from one public space to the next from a remote, indistinct location. Similarly, in the second season, this undetected technological undercurrent surreptitiously captures and records President David Palmer as he tortures the head of the National Security

Agency, an unintentional piece of data that becomes a primary piece of evidence in the President's subsequent impeachment.

More significantly, this technological subtext affects spatial representations. Above, I have referred to *24* as a logistical narrative, one that consistently foregrounds the ever-changing spatial relations between the large cast who are intermittently on the move. It is only through the use of the mobile prosthesis of the cellular phone, as both a textual and technological device, that the complex logistics of the narrative world coalesce. It is then unsurprising that the cellular phone is singled out for narrative importance in series episodes. Early in Season One, abductees Teri and Kim Bauer spend several episodes fighting for control of a mobile phone from their captors, culminating in that season's tenth episode, which is entirely predicated on the narrative conflict of trying to stay on the phone line. Later, in the same season, terrorist Victor Drazen uses a cell phone as a vehicle to send an explosive to the offices of the then Senator David Palmer. More importantly, the cellular phone and its omnipresence within *24* allows for the constant recalculation of the spatial relations of characters of these dispersed, widely cast narratives in a program that, for all its variation, is primarily an endless series of coordinated pursuits. This dispersion is evidenced in the fact that *24*, in its first two seasons, coordinates action between two principal protagonists (Bauer and Palmer) who are only copresent in a handful of episodes and, instead, synchronize their efforts over a series of brief phone-calls. These phone-calls, as well as Jack's calls to any number of colleagues, frequently begin with the program's familiar refrain, "Jack, where are you?"[6]

Traditional representations of space as discrete and stable are further complicated by what has become the stylistic hallmark of *24*, the use of multiscreen effects. A formal examination of these images that juxtapose multiple images coded with three dimensions on a single two-dimensional frame is noticeably absent from Burch's consideration of space in film. While the technique is utterly passé in the context of nonfictional TV and new media, it is a rare occurrence in fictional, filmed programming outside the specialized cinematic work of Brian De Palma or Able Gance. *24* uses the device frequently for one of several recurring functions. Multiscreen effects are used to signal act breaks. They are used to cut to a new scene that is spatially distant and temporally continuous (all edits in *24* occur in continuous, progressing time). They are used to juxtapose adjacent spaces with shared character knowledge, as in pursuits, or without shared character knowledge, as in suspense effects. They are used to render several, simultaneous perspectives on single events that are motivated not by character perspective, but, arguably, by a generalized sense of the surveilled society. Furthermore, in relatively infrequent cases, the multiscreen is used to give what Edward

Branigan (1984) would call a "total point of view" (75), depicting both a subject looking and the object of that gaze simultaneously.

However, by far, the most common use of the multiscreen effect—by my rough count at least one-third of the multiscreen effects in the program's first two seasons conform to this logic—is in depicting telephone conversations, juxtaposing the party on either end of the line and aligning these spatially dispersed characters in the shared context of a single frame. Examining the use of telephones in an early narrative film, Tom Gunning (1991) suggested that the technological device was used to justify the newly conceived textual device of crosscutting at the same time that it reflected the anxieties accompanying a modern understanding of time–space, altered by the action of connecting discrete points on a telephone, telegraph, or rail line. I argue that 24's use of the mobile and the textual convention of the multiscreen follows a similar theoretical logic, reflecting and reinforcing what has been called qualculative space, which has replaced a mode of discrete spaces accessible along a grid with a model of porous, inconsistent spaces where, thanks to instant access, here in the form of mobile networks, even the frame lines of the film image may reconfigure themselves around the actions of the characters onscreen.

In an attempt to remedy a significant oversight in social theory, John Urry (2007) has recently attempted to integrate the notion of mobility itself. Urry's general argument is simply that movement and circulation cannot be understood as incidental or interstitial to social life, but are absolutely essential in its operation. Movement and access to movement weigh heavily on the construction of social differentiation and identity formation, concepts that have traditionally occupied a majority of social research. In his effort to move sociology from a study of what he calls simple propinquity, Urry takes special note of what the author calls "inter-spaces," zones that, as a result of the sophistication of transportation and communication systems, are amorphous places that are not entirely work, not entirely leisure, and are often considered to be without specific locations in themselves. The prototypical example is found in the airline commuter waiting in a terminal who, when coupled with a wifi-enabled laptop or a smart phone can peruse any number of work tasks, acts of social bonding, or idle play. Thanks to our technological subtext, what was generally thought of as dead or down time and uneventful takes on an enhanced importance.

Reflective of an earlier era of commuting, the opening credits of The Bob Newhart Show (CBS, 1972–8) depicts the eponymous protagonist leaving work at his downtown psychiatric office, moving through urban Chicago, taking the elevated train, and arriving at his posh high-rise apartment. These credits reveal what is repressed in every episode, specifically the character's movement through interspace that, overdubbed with a jazzy 1970s' score and superimposed with graphic titles, is marked as narratively insignificant, underscoring what I have suggested is the traditional, binary spatial logic of television programming. The same scheme is echoed by any number of television dramas. For example, *The Rockford Files* depicts its protagonist moving in and around Los Angeles freeways, images largely removed from the subsequent program narratives. *24* could not be any further removed from this technique. Instead, this program stages a large share of its action in cars or in planes en route. Protagonist Jack Bauer acts in a similar way to Urry's contemporary commuter; his movement through interspace does not beget narrative pause to be excised, but is filled with narratively significant moments where all his ad hoc goals and affiliations are established and reaffirmed.

A counterargument could be raised suggesting that the movements of Bauer contrasted with the stability of the CTU office in Los Angeles, or David Palmer's hotel room in Season One and his western bunker in Season Two, may be understood as yet another example of the binary spatial logic of inside/outside. However, I would argue that while representation of the regular, repeated spaces certainly borrow on this traditional structuring of action, the scheme of rendering space is better understood as a model of informational hubs where the spaces are not as much discrete places as they are the vertex of flows of information, communication, and bodies. The very narrative importance of these spaces lies not in their distinct spatial identity (in fact, CTU's offices are decorated with bleak, modernist cubicles, largely unmarked by personality of individual use), but in their ability to access any number of other spaces, mimicking what Castells has called "hubs" that act as "exchanges . . . playing a role of coordination for the smooth interaction of all the elements integrated in the network" (413). Nothing exemplifies this more than the program's coordinated use of diegetic cellular phones and multiscreen effects that visualize the space of the network and the CTU home office's role as its intermediary hub. For example, in Episode Eight of Season Two, Bauer returns to Los Angeles via airplane with series regular, Nina Myers, and a terrorist suspect in custody. While in transit, Bauer receives a call from his collaborators, George Mason and Michelle Dessler at CTU in Los Angeles. In their conversation, depicted in both intercutting and with multiscreen effects, Mason and Michelle monitor the conversation of Nina and her accomplice, translate it from Arabic, and feed the information back to Bauer. Concurrently, Kim Bauer, on the run from the police, calls into CTU where her call is then transferred over to Jack en route; this conversation is also depicted with both intercutting and multiscreen effects. In this one, very complicated sequence CTU acts as an intermediary for Bauer and his near space as well as for vast space, allowing work and family life to coincide in the inter-space of a moving airplane cabin. Here the action takes place through and in a literal network of interconnected spaces. A similar effect is achieved in the inventive conclusion of the second season in which the president's ex-wife tricks an oilman into implicating himself in a domestic terrorist attack during a clandestine meeting at the LA Coliseum. A secreted microphone captures the off-the-cuff confession and workers at CTU Los Angeles rebroadcast the information to Jack laying in wait near the site; to David Palmer in his western bunker; and to a direct line to Washington, DC, where the acting president halts a military invasion on the basis of the confession. All five sites are juxtaposed in one overcrowded multiscreen effect, again literalizing networked narrative space and CTU's role as hub in this network.

As a testament to the relative complexity of *Lost*, network programmers were worried enough about its appeal in rerun to supplement the episodes' image track with a series of superimposed narrative hints. Mimicking VH1's well-remembered *Pop-up Video* (1996–2002), the rerun segments were overlaid with similar written tags indicating the deeper narrative significance of characters, events, and objects in the frame. However, while the pop-up videos' captions provided information that ranged from the tangential to the non-sequitor, *Lost*'s messages are, arguably, vital to a preferred decoding of the series and model the ideal hyperaware viewer of the series. These consequently layered, informationally rich images are also one more convention meant to deal with what we referred to in the previous chapter as informational complexity.

A similar argument can be made with regard to the representation of space in tentpole TV. Above, we have highlighted how tentpole programs deal with vastness of both scope and scale and how they, in this process, have eschewed traditional navigational tools of mapping narrative space. One more aesthetic tool in this capacity could be traced in *24*'s similar use of informationally rich images. Above, we have discussed the uses of multi-screen effects and how the device underscores an image of space that is both porous and vastly interconnected. However, the series almost as often uses what could be termed quasi-multiscreen effects by filling the *mis en scene* with any number of smaller frames, chiefly computer and television monitors that depict other spaces that, like our introductory example from *Heroes*, are only a click away. These diegetic pop-ups function similar to the more emphatic multiscreen effects in that they frequently are used to reorient space and spatial relations in the context of a single frame.

One particularly complicated sequence in Episode 17 of Season One uses this technique to great effect. In this episode, Jack and Nina set up a sting to trap war criminal, Alexis Drazen, by using one of David Palmer's senatorial aides as bait. The entire operation encompasses two adjacent hotel rooms connected with a small fortune of audio-visual equipment. The film uses every convention available to underscore the nearness of the two spaces: the film intercuts between the two, it depicts each space simultaneously with multiscreen effects, and, more interestingly, the *mis en scene* of Jack's hotel room is littered with television monitors focused on the room next door that are intermittently just one more element of the décor at the same time that they are individual frames within larger non-diegetic frames (which, vertiginously, are sometimes integrated into a multiscreen composition). Table 6.1 attempts to translate the density of the 10-minute sequence. In this transcription, letter denotes the character captured in frame with a single setup (A is Jack Bauer, B is Nina Myers, C is Alexi Drazen, and D is Elizabeth the senatorial page), the use of the "+" symbol denotes a two or three shot, the use of the soft brackets "{ }" denotes that the image of the characters is recorded from a diegetic frame, namely Jack's security monitors, and the hard brackets "[]" denote that the image of the characters is recorded in a non-diegetic frame, namely the use of multiscreen effects. The segment plays out in the successive setups as one reads from left to right down the page. Over the course of the sequence, nearly all the combinations of the listed variables are exploited on level or rising complexity over the course of time, graphed moving right and downward on the chart. The first third of the sequence incorporates the different combinations of screens within screens, but as Elizabeth begins her mission to clandestinely find Alexi's wallet, the form also begins to integrate its multiscreen effects both in conjunction and independent of the screen-within-a-screen effects. The most notable feature of the sequence, evident only after its transcription, is its use of rhymed transitions where the valance of the image is switched between setups. For example, the beginning of the sequence relies on a rhymed couplet of moving from a shot, or set of shots of Alexi and Elizabeth to a shot or set of shots of Alexi and Elizabeth on a diegetic monitor (or C+D is followed by {C+D}). Even after the introduction of the mutliscreen effect, this tendency continues. Thus, setups 49, 50, and 51 on the chart move Alexi and Elizabeth from being a live element of a multiscreen composition [C+D], to a recorded element of a multiscreen composition [{C+D}], to a live element encompassing the entire frame, C+D (see Figure 6.1). Accompanied with a running soundtrack that combines the live sound of both Jack's room and Alexi's, this overlapping of characters in different valences across subsequent setups serves to give a textual equivalence to the shots and underscores the technologically enabled spatial overlap between the two spaces which are never distinct from one another. In essence, the sequence is also a contemporary revision of the traditional crosscut rescue, described by Gunning, where distance need not be traversed by the advancing protagonists because the spaces overlap and are never entirely distinct.[7] Moreover, the sequence begins by depicting Bauer in control of the narrative, engineering the sting operation, and figuratively

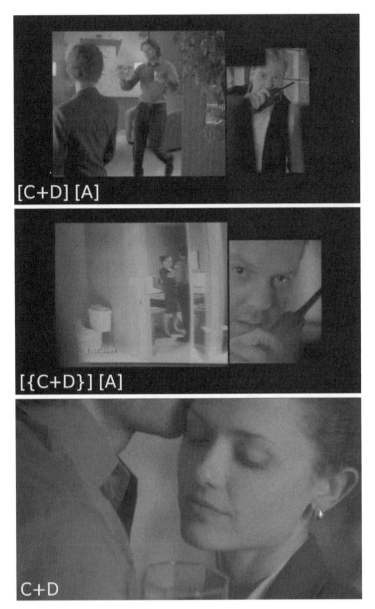

FIGURE 6.1 *From Season One, Episode 17, entitled "4:00PM–5:00PM".*

the shot selection from his immense monitor bank, which looks suspiciously like a television control room. However, as the scene plays out, Bauer loses control of his undercover agent (Elizabeth unexpectedly stabs Alexi Drazen) at the same time that the form discredits Bauer as a focal center of textual construction. With regard to the latter, simple point-of-view structures are

TABLE 6.1 Season One, Episode 17 (25:30–35:30)

[A+B] [C] [D]	A+B	{C}	C
{C}	B	A+B {C}	A
C	B {C}	B	D
C	B	A+B {C}	D
C+D	B	{C+D}	C+D
A+B {C} {D}	A+B	{C+D}	C+D
{C+D}	A+B	{C+D}	C+D
A	{C+D}	B	C+D
{D}	[{D}] [A+B]	B	B {D}
D	C+D	A+B	{D}
D	C+D	A	{C+D}
D	C+D	[B] [D]	[B] [C+D]
[C+D] [A]	[{C+D}] [A]	C+D	A
B	A	{C+D}	C+D
A	B {C+D}	C+D	[B] [D]
[B] [C]	C	D	C
D	{C+D}	[A+B] [C+D]	C+D
[A] [{C+D}]	[B] [{D}]	[B] [D]	D
{C+D}	[A] [{C+D}]	C+D	C
D	C	D	B {C+D}
A	C	D	A
A {C+D}	C	D	C
[{C}] [D]	[{C}] [C]	[D] [A]	C+D
A	{C+D}	A+B	B

C+D	A	{C+D}	C+D
[A] [C+D]	[B] [C+D]	[B] [C+D] [C]	A {C+D}
C+D	A+B	A {C+D}	[C] [D]
[{D}] [C]	[{D}]	A	[{D}]
C+D	A+B	C+D	A+C+D
B {A+C}	A+C		

replaced with "impossible" points of view as single images juxtapose live and recorded perspectives on Elizabeth and Alexi's exchange, a combination of images that simply cannot be reconciled in the singular figure of Bauer. Instead another narrative agency seems to take over one that could be better understood as the network itself, above and beyond individual characters who move from being manipulators of the technological unconscious of surveillance to just another observed element of some other distant, yet absent surveilling mastermind.

However, this example is perhaps complicated by the fact that the two overlapped spaces are not that distant in implied story space. The same technique, however, holds in cases where the implied story distance is vaster. Episode 21 of the second season contains several more restrained examples of the same device. In this episode, David Palmer is impeached and put on trial by the members of his cabinet who appear from distant locations, teleconferenced and converged on the many screens of the presidential meeting room in Los Angeles. Once again, Los Angeles serves as the hub for any number of flows of communication, here rendered in diegetic screens. The net result of each example, however, is the same: an informationally rich image filled with smaller frames renders space porous, shifting, uncontrolled, and nonisomorphic with anything resembling physical boundaries.

In these examples of multiscreen and quasi-multiscreen effects, several spaces literally interpenetrate and coexist on another in the context of a single image. These images model Latour's (2005) emphatic desire to keep the social "flat," or specifically, to avoid the theoretical error of moving swiftly in social studies from the micrological to the macrological with the result of overrelying on the mechanisms of reduction and determination in describing the local instance. For Latour, both the global and the local are constantly constructed anew in each social encounter through a series of actor networks.

What this means for our purposes is that encounters are understood as activating a number of local or distant (temporally or spatially) agencies that are used to localize the local or articulate a relation to the global—both of which are understood to exist on the same flat continuous plane. In Latour's words: "face-to-face should be taken as the terminus point of a great number of agencies swimming toward them" (2005: 196). It is precisely this complexity that is modeled in *24*'s and tentpole TV's unique construction of flattened, always proximate space. In the final chapter, we will examine a similar complexity at play in the work of characterization adapted to streamable and modular tentpole TV series.

7

Alias and Reflexive Uncertainty

In the conclusion of the second season of ABC's *Alias*, series protagonists, secret agent Sydney Bristow blacks out only to wake up two story years later. After this radical narrative ellipsis, Sydney finds that her entire life has been disrupted and torn asunder. Her arch-nemesis, criminal genius Arvin Sloane has reformed and has become a celebrated philanthropist and humanitarian. Her former partner and romantic interest, Michael Vaughn, has moved on and married another woman working for the National Security Council. Her father and fellow spy, Jack Bristow, has been incarcerated in a maximum-security prison. And her former supervisors at the CIA are more interested in lobotomizing Sydney to surgically extract memories from her intervening two years than helping the protagonist readjust and regain her previous role as the agency's top operative. Surprisingly, this was not the first time that *Alias* had changed its entire premise, nor would it be the series' last such effort. The series included premise-shattering reboots in both its second season, as Sydney and her collaborators successfully dismantle the terrorist organization, SD6, and in its fourth season, as Sydney and company all quit the CIA and join a "black ops" within the government dubbed APO. This willingness to rip it up and start again indicates the two central themes of the series: one, the fragility and permeability of institutions and organizations, here in the guise of the structure of the series itself; two, the consequences of this disintegration upon concepts such as individuality and motivation, which become more fluid and less consistent. These two thematic concerns situate the series squarely in its historical moment, a moment wherein social theorists have openly questioned the legitimacy and effectiveness of a number of broad social institutions from work, to family, to class to aggregate experience and understand everyday life, a diagnosis that we can call, following Anthony Giddens, the crisis of post-traditional order.

In the following chapter, I would like to consider not simply how *Alias* offers a potent social mirror, but to suggest how the series can be conceptualized a site where creative workers, who have particularly felt the uncertainly and impermanence associated with post-traditional order, have interrogated the condition of their own working lives. In this project, we will deploy a Geertzian (2000 [1973]) analysis that casts *Alias*, as well as the other tentpole TV series of our sample, as both portraits of and models for their "native" cultures (400). In other words, I argue that the makers of *Alias* actively deployed the themes of post-traditional order, pervasive broadly in culture at large, but particularly developed in the television industry as we seen from our Introduction, to reflect their own work conditions, but also to model ways of being in the industry and new modes of representation more amenable to the challenges of current network television. In this chapter, we will be pursuing both a weak and a strong thesis. The weak thesis, that is the speculative thesis, is that the program's key thematics reflect upon the lived experiences of the television creatives. As a brief example, consider the characterization of Arvin Sloane, who is depicted as having a radical change of heart in the elliptical gap between the second and third seasons. His inconsistency is typical of the series that casts characters as adapting and improvising in the present and reconfiguring their past. Also, like other series characters, Sloane's narrative power is cast in his ability to be two personae at once, specifically to be a double agent for the CIA. I argue that this mode of characterization reflects the conditions of the tentpole TV professionals who must adapt to the changing nature of their medium to the extent of becoming double agents, for example, working for the program proper as well as being increasingly responsible for any number of the series' transmedia manifestations. The stronger, or more conclusive thesis argues that this program and the other tentpole programs use these thematics, recurring through their personal and aesthetic lives, to reconfigure the use of character in serial, dramatic television to ultimately make them more modular and streamable. More specifically, I argue that the use of character inconsistency is a representational technique that facilitates this expansion. Unlike hermetically sealed series with classically "whole" and clearly motivated characters, tentpole series more frequently use inconsistent characters whose open nature and unclear psychology allow for the near constant rearticulation of motivation and reexamination of backstory. This reconceptualization of character and motivation constitutes one more formal innovation on the part of tentpole TV makers—in addition to the greatly expanded uses of temporality and spatiality discussed in the previous chapters—that positions programs as more amenable to the vicissitudes of brand expansion at the same time that it reflects the production realities of the on-going presumed crisis taking place in US network television.

In its presentation of disintegrating and fluid identities, *Alias* is echoing a recent trend within social theory that has sought to come to terms with the exact same phenomena. Despite great differences in final valuation and political agenda, several social theorists examining these problems have often come to similar observational and methodological conclusions. In the first case, these authors find the world to be composed of conceptually looser social bonds. In *Modernity and Self Identity*, Anthony Giddens (1991) isolates what he calls an existential dimension of social life where individuals are continually asked to reflexively monitor their own biographies and intentions with respect to what the author calls abstract systems, shared institutions freed from the specificity of time and place. This investigation leads Giddens to examine the uniquely contemporary practices of divorce and therapy as indicative of both the evaporation of tradition and the demands of constant individual self-reflexivity in modernity. Considering a much more constrained historical period, Manuel Castells (1996), in his multi-volume discussion of the rise of informational capitalism, makes similar observations. Castells also sees the contemporary era as one marked by the dissolution of the powerful intermediaries of socialization. And like Giddens, Castells latches onto identity as the central question of sociological thought. In the author's words:

in a world of global flows of wealth, power and images the search for identity, collective or individual, ascribed or constructed, becomes the fundamental source of social meaning . . . [identity is the] source of meaning in a historical period characterized by widespread destructuring of organizations, delegitimation of institutions, fading away of social institutions. (3)

Zygmunt Bauman (2005), too, has written extensively on social disintegration and delegitimation and its effect on individuality. The theorist uses the term *liquid modernity* to describe the contemporary era wherein social change comes so rapid and with such unrelenting consistency that it precludes actions and processes from every solidifying (thus, the fluid metaphor) into habit, routine or tradition. Bauman singles out the post-globalization nation-state as a symbol of the cracking façade of what he calls solid modernity; "no longer in full charge of the economy, security, or culture, the state cannot promise its subjects the whole-life protection from cradle to grave that it not so long ago strove" (45). Turning the Frankfurt School analysis of the dehumanizing effect of mass production on its head, Bauman claims that social subjects are now caught in a trap of constantly policed individuality wherein one is forced either to adapt, change and re-skill or be resigned to irrelevancy. Without the clear guiding institutions of solid modernity, this process, in Bauman's analysis, is a trying one. Despite the varying tones and intentions shaping the work of these and several other like-minded thinkers (e.g. Bauman is clearly a critic of contemporary culture of the Marcuse/Adorno mold, while Castells, in the Weberian tradition, approximates value neutrality), they all agree that the contemporary social world is best characterized by the nadir and dissolution of traditional institutions of socialization and order—from the state, to work, to the family—and the consequent and often frantic efforts of individuals to fill this gap.

Concomitantly, many of these same thinkers have assembled new research methodologies to better capture the operations of this altered picture of social reality. Often these methods are posited as moving beyond the traditional binaries of micro/macrological studies and conceptions of structure/agency in sociological research. Without definitive or consistent social intermediaries the macro and the micro always coexist and are reconstructed in the lived instance.[1] A more nuanced understanding of the individual has led to the interrogation of the models of complete determination (structure) or freedom (agency) and the establishment of theories of action that incorporate the coexistence of both. Drawing on Berger and Luckmann's (1966) theory of social construction, Giddens assembled his own system of structuration, which eliminated the virtuality of structures and functions and replaced them with the instantiation of action in definitive time-places. The result is a cycle wherein social order is continually achieved through recursive action; or, in the author's words: "rules and resources are drawn upon by actors in the production of interaction, but are thereby also reconstituted through such interaction" (1979: 71). This theoretical model gives the existence of a continuous social world a certain fragility, prompting Giddens to claim that, "the orderliness of day-to-day life is a miraculous occurrence" (1979: 52). These conclusions also bear several similarities with the theorization of habitus assembled by Pierre Borudieu (1977), who also stressed the centrality of concrete practice in the creation of seemingly objective structures and the room available for individual improvisation and adaptation within the rules and regulations of a given society. These theories of action further the central thematic preoccupations already introduced: the diminished capacity of traditional institutions to definitively guide actions and the increased attention paid to the individual addressing this motivational gap.

These changes are particularly felt in the institutions of work and family. Giddens (1991), in fact, refers to the latter as a "shell institution," an institution that fails to serve in its previous capacity of socialization and of providing a relative safe haven from the larger social world. Similarly, many sociologists have examined the expansion of work life into all neighboring spheres of life. What this means is that neither work nor family is the powerful lens to provide order to experience and that, moreover, they are more than likely to bleed seamlessly into one another. Following the initial insights of Lash and Urry

(1994), Mark Deuze (2007) isolates media work in general and employment in the film and television industries in particular as the vanguard of the post-traditional workplace that is marked by a combination of contingency and boundarylessness. According to Deuze, media work is exemplary in its fusion of the formerly distinct spheres of life, play and work. Given the liquidity of the media industry at large, particularly in its use of temporary workers and project-based employment, individuals without consistent work in terms of either time or space reflexively manage their own portfolio-based careers much as all individuals living in post-traditional order reflexively and recursively manage their own biographies without the clear frames of powerful, determining social institutions. In Deuze's words: "the individual, not the firm, has become the organization—a company that needs to be ran efficiently and smoothly, where order and control can only be individually established and disciplined to lead one into a supposedly productive and secure future" (84).

Even a cursory glance at the series *Alias* will see these same themes at play in the central conceits of the series. *Alias* is largely concerned with the fractured, dysfunctional relationship between two spies, father and daughter, Jack and Sydney Bristow. The source of their conflict comes as a result of the progressive invasion of the Bristows' home life by their work life, so much so that the former disappears. By the end of the first season, it is established that Sydney's mother, previously assumed dead, is actually alive and was acting as Jack's spouse and Sydney's mother only in her capacity as a KGB double agent. Essentially, *Alias* can be understood as a genre hybrid combining professional and personal lives in the context of an hour-long drama, along the lines of a *thritysomething* (ABC, 1987–91) or a *NYPD Blue* (ABC, 1993–2005). What distinguishes *Alias*, as well as the other tentpole TV series, from these earlier series is that while the personal often redeems the professional in these previous examples, in *Alias* the mixture is tragic as the latter devours the former. The eclipse of family life by work could not be more literal—Sydney's mother was always just "on the job." This destruction of family life is furthered in the series' first two seasons that progressively eliminate Sydney's "civilian" relationships: Danny, her fiancée is murdered when he learns of her clandestine work; her best friend, Will, after uncovering a related conspiracy is forcibly drafted into the CIA before being put into protective hiding; her roommate, Francie, is assassinated and replaced with an enemy agent doppelganger who underwent a procedure to become Francie's identical clone. A similar problematic is developed on other tentpole TV series, notably through the imperiled relationship of Noah Bennet and his daughter on *Heroes* and death of Jack Bauer's wife, Teri, in the first season of *24*. Plausibility aside, these plot developments all point back to the disintegration of the family and the increasing boundarylessness of work.

But *Alias* is not simply a narrative about the totalitarian control of the workplace. The institution of work, in final estimation, is also disintegrating. This distinguishes *Alias* from espionage series of the past, such as *Mission: Impossible* (*M:I*), where the covert organization was never imperiled and the protagonists' roles or tasks within the organization were ever questioned. This antecedent series, *M:I*, was broadcast in the same historical moment in which Erving Goffman (1961) introduced his concept of the total institution (TI) and the series, through its representation of an ultra-secretive government hit squad, arguably offers an illustrative example of this classical sociological formation. *Alias* too invokes the image of the TI through its many depicted covert agencies, however, the concept is at the very same time systematically undercut. Goffman described the many ideal typical features of TIs, such as boarding schools, hospitals, monasteries, and prisons in his masterpiece *Asylums*. Here the author isolated TIs as a particular set of institutions that erect high barriers separating themselves from the rest of the social world; that operate through a strict bureaucratic control over large groups of individuals through a monopoly on information and the practice of surveillance; and that effect a breakdown between the preconceived, independent spheres of life (work, sleep, rest) all monitored by the central institution. We have already noted the manner in which Sydney's occupation slowly devours her civilian life. Strict controls on information are evinced in the series' exacerbating incident in which Sydney reveals her secret life to her fiancée Danny, resulting in the latter's death at the hands of Sydney's employers. Goffman also describes the practices of exposure in TIs wherein the body of the inmate/prisoner/etc. is stripped of any sense of privacy and is invaded, both figuratively and literally. And, indeed, even Sydney's mind is fair game for her employers as she, through the course of the series, goes through any number of interrogations, polygraph exams, and, in a memorable episode of the third season (Episode 3.9, "Conscious"), a chemically induced form of experimental hypnotherapy (conducted, appropriately, by David Cronenberg). Moreover, Sydney is under constant surveillance by forces both active and passive, acting with both benign and malevolent intentions. In fact, this constant monitoring is essential to the stylistic construction of the series and its unique use of editing. No scene is too intimate not to be captured by some unseen observer. For example, when Sydney and Michael Vaughn first make love, the act is recorded by a clandestine video camera installed in Sydney's own television set. Goffman was interested in TIs principally because of their profound effect on individuality; "in our society, they [total institutions] are the forcing houses for changing persons; each is a natural experiment on what can be done to the self" (12). Sydney's incorporation into the life of espionage takes on a similar aspect.

Yet at the same time that Sydney's employer is given the veneer of a TI, its representation equally debunks and dismantles the powerful image of these social formations. In TIs, inmates experience a loss of independence even in the conducting of the simplest of actions (when to bathe, when to sleep, etc.). *Alias*, in its initial conception, was a narrative of double agency; Sydney posed as a member of a terrorist organization, SD6, while secretly reporting back to the CIA. Both organizations ape some features of the TI; however, Sydney's efficacy in the plot has not to do with the activation of orders, as in the case of *M:I*'s technocrats, but in her ability to move from one organization to the other. Also, Goffman's TIs are marked by concretized spaces, regularized practices, and definitive hierarchies. However, SD6 and the CIA, in their architecture and their actions are based on spatially diffuse networked alliences between single individuals. In the series' second episode, protagonist Michael Vaughn explains the operations of SD6 to Sydney. To do this, he uses a diagram made up of a vast series of lines which all represent personal, individual relationships between coconspirators—it is the chart from the courtroom scene in *Godfather II* blown up one-hundred fold. A more simple example resides in the fact that *Alias*'s vast, powerful criminal organizations are cast as fragile, crumbling, or even as collapsing over the course of the series. In the series' first season, K Directive, SD6's Russian counterpart is entirely dismantled with the quick execution of a handful of key leaders.[2] More significantly, SD6 itself is eliminated halfway through the series' second season, fundamentally changing the central conceit of the narrative. The other tentpole programs of my sample also tend to depict what we can call failed TIs, or just disintegrating institutions. For example, *Lost* frequently refers to the Dharma Initiative, a scientific commune living on the crash survivors' island years before the chronological beginning of the series and prior to begin slaughtered by the island's "original" inhabitants, the so-called Others. The Dharma Initiative is depicted as a self-sustaining commune that sought to control and measure all aspects of life for its members before being undermined by later plot developments. More comparable to *Alias*'s failed TI is *Heroes*' Primatech Paper, a clandestine, covert agency that seeks to control and monitor the activities of individuals with superpowers, for some unrevealed purpose. Yet from the very beginning of the series, the organization is also depicted as fallible and porous. For example, series protagonist and Primatech Paper employee, Noah Bennet is able to keep his super-powered daughter, Claire, out of the hands of his employers throughout the course of the first season, going as far as having his own memory erased to facilitate her dramatic escape.

I have drawn on these two extended examples, of the melding of work and family life and the dissolving of total institutions, to underscore *Alias* as well as the other tentpole series as particularly apt mirrors of their production context. Although these readings do by no means exhaust the symbolic value of the series, they do point to the productive ways that *Alias* can be understood as reflexively examining its own context. The disintegration of stable institutions can be read through the lens of a troubled television industry where producers, often within the same conglomerate as their broadcasters, increasingly change or reboot the model of their business from the ad-supported transmission of signals to the creation and exploitation of branded entertainment (or whatever will come next). However, an even more precise integration can be made between the series and the work of its staff. We have already seen how the series' disintegrating institutions represent and reflect a life where family is devoured by work, a social reality keenly felt in the case of media workers. I would also connect series themes of character inconsistency and double agency to the social world of creatives on tentpole programs who are similarly asked to re-skill, retrain, and work across agencies. Whether creatives do accept this aegis of expanding the program or not—and it seems that workers on *Alias* did if we are to believe series writer-producer Jesse Alexander who has been quoted as saying, "We [the staff] tried to get the network and studio pregnant with as much *Alias* stuff as we could"—is irrelevant (Dahlen 2007). I argue that anxiety over nothing less than the "death of television," or at least business as usual lurks behind the crises and conflicts of *Alias'* narratives with its failing institutions.

However, without access to the creative decisions and rationalizations to say nothing of the personal and professional lives of those behind drafting and producing *Alias*, it is difficult to take such an examination further. Instead, I would like to go deeper into the texts of the series themselves and to analyze them, anthropologically, as the ritual, artistic life of the community of its creators, offering insight into what Geertz (1976) called the "native's point of view." Similarly, in the field of television studies, John Caldwell (2006) has pointed out that in media production, an industry built on pitches, meetings, notes, and fateful conversations, informants are less able to give traditional empirical data than ritualistic meditations on the industry and its very reconstitution. This insight smartly echoes Geertz who, debunking the myth of anthropological empathy, claimed that the more reliable method of understanding the native's point of view was to interpret their symbolic forms. In this theory, cultural artifacts are cast as circular, embodying the collective thought of the community at the same time that they reinforce these same ideas. In a certain regard, Geertz's work harkens back to Emile Durkheim's (1995 [1915]) theory of religion which cast theological cosmologies themselves as outward representations of the collective itself at the same time that these representations provide moral guidance to members of the community, literal instructions in ways of being. In what follows, I will look more closely at the specific textual form of *Alias* and consider how it embodies and reinforces the beliefs of its "native" community, the television industry.

The most compelling model that Geertz (1973) provides for such an endeavor can be found in his analysis of the notion of Balinese personhood, in his essay "Person, Time, and Conduct in Bali." What makes this study so compelling is the way in which the author is able to deeply examine the specificity of a number of cultural forms, namely the practice name-calling, the cultural experience of time, and the monitoring of interpersonal conduct, and to tie this diversity back, without reduction, to a central insight about the fundamental understanding of the Balinese conception of identity itself. Drawing on Geertz's model, I will argue that *Alias*, through the textual practices of character inconsistency, double agency, and ever-present temporality, as well as the recurring thematics of brainwashing, cloning, and lost time, similarly suggests a notion of personhood within television work that both reflects and reinforces the particular stakes of working within the industry in general and within the paradigm of tentpole TV in particular. These unique textual features can be understood as reflections of these altered conditions of production as well as innovations and aesthetic solutions that make these exact same changes possible.

First, we can examine the distinct use of character inconsistency and problematic motivation at work in *Alias*. In his examination of the narrative construction of serial television, Michael Newman (2006) isolates the beat as the smallest unit of story meaning. Newman finds these beats to be frequently repetitive, saying, "television's redundancy has its causes in making narratives intelligible, but it turns out that it can also allow even regular viewers to be gratified by being reminded constantly of who the characters are, what they do, why they do it, and what is at stake in the story" (19–20). Certainly, this repetition occurs in *Alias*, but just as often the mnemonic function of beats is ignored and characters are, instead, represented with contradictory motivations and inconsistent desires. On a micro level this occurs in every episode as Sydney temporarily takes on the disguise of any number of other roles and monikers. This should be relatively unsurprising given the title of the series. What is more significant is the program's willingness to leave character motivation undefined, or endlessly shifting throughout the course of several seasons, or even the entire series itself. For example, we can scan the shifting characterization of Sydney's mother, Irina Derevko. Over the course of the first season, it is slowly revealed that Sydney's mother is not deceased and that she was Jack Bristow's wife only in her capacity as a KGB double agent. In the conclusion of that season, Irina emerges, in league with international terrorist Kasinow, only to shoot her captive daughter. However, in the following episode, the second season's premiere, Irina reappears, assassinates her accomplice, Kasinow, assaults several CIA agents and then calmly surrenders herself to the American government. In subsequent episodes three and four of the season, Irina insists that she has turned herself over to the authorities solely to help Sydney and the CIA and she does just that by surrendering information on her former coconspirators and facilitating Sydney's escape from a covert mission gone wrong in Moscow. Yet the goodwill garnered by these actions does not last and, by episode four, she is being blamed for blowing Sydney's cover within SD6. In episode nine, Irina claims that she only shot her daughter to maintain her own cover and to ensure that no great harm would befall Sydney. But by episode seventeen her loyalties are again put in flux when she engineers an escape from custody. After charming Jack into removing a tracking device, Irina slips away with series archfiend Sloane. Irina continues to elude recapture in the following episode and sends a cryptic, coded message to Sydney that reads, "truth takes time"—a mysterious promise to reveal motivation 20 episodes after her introduction. However, Irina does not fulfill her promise by the season's conclusion. In the penultimate episode, Irina blackmails Sydney into helping her. And in the season's finale, Irina feeds Sydney bad information that leads Jack and the CIA on a fool's errand, allowing Sloane to steal a set of priceless medieval artifacts. In the conclusion of the episode, Irina again avoids capture by Sydney and insists that her daughter needs to stop Sloane, the man who was presumably her accomplice. As Irina exits the episode and the series, it is still absolutely unclear where loyalties lie: were her affections toward Sydney legitimate or feigned, was she facilitating or sabotaging the CIA, was she in league with Sloane or was she attempting to thwart the series antagonist? Who knows?

There was probably a historical moment when this style of characterization may have been dismissed as "bad" writing, however, I would argue that the character inconsistency in *Alias* became an important aesthetic prototype for the tentpole TV series. Bordwell et al. (1985) have famously described how classical narration is guided with goal-oriented protagonists with discernable, regular traits where "traits are only latent causes" arranging plot development (14). And in his examination of the art cinema mode of production, Bordwell (2004) suggests that "serious" filmmakers conversely use amotivated characters to simultaneously increase the expressivity and the realism of their films. I would not propose a similar reading as *Alias* veers from the model of classical narration, but instead suggest that character inconsistency is deployed to reflect and reinforce a way of being in the television industry. We can mark Irina as an expression of liquidity—she is unprompted by traditional categories of wife and mother in her actions—and nondetermination—she ultimately refuses to be attached to any single agenda. Just as television creatives are unlikely to be attached to one project, or to a single medium, Irina is an avatar of adaptability, reflecting the imperative to and reinforcing the need to keep one's options open to avenues of re-skilling and reeducation. In other words, Irina models the most fruitful way of operating in a liquid world: remain inconsistent.

Different from episodic television, which relies on its characters' more or less known qualities and predictable motivations that are shaped into plot, most serials rely on the ability of characters to progressively change. What makes character inconsistency appreciably divergent is the ultimate refusal for character to ever settle; characters rather promise that "truth takes time," that all will be revealed, retrospectively, from some moment in the future, echoing mastermind narration's implicit promise that everything will make sense eventually. One can find these chameleon-characters in all tentpole TV series. In *Heroes*, one can look to Noah Bennet's shifting loyalties between his employer and his daughter. And in *Lost*, one can look to Benjamin Linus, whose only consistent trait seems to be his amorality.

Moreover, the use of character inconsistency constitutes a divergent form of storytelling that textually facilitates multiplatforming, thus becoming, again, a model for exactly the same social world that it creates. The less consistent a character, the more the text begs speculation on the part of a hypothetical viewer, the more it begs character rearticulation in any number of forms, and the more license it gives to vast plot twists. This style of storytelling deliberately leaves holes in classical narration's goal-oriented characters, replacing them with inconsistent ones who need to be filled in later, in other texts both off-air and on-air. More simply put, character inconsistency reflects and further promotes the very streamability and modularity of tentpole TV programming.

Character inconsistency is also foregrounded as a plot device in *Alias* through its many scenes of brainwashing, memory alteration, and hypnosis, which disclose the malleability of character intention, will, motive, and even personality. The best example of this can be observed, again, in the two-year ellipsis between the second and third seasons. In Episode 11 of the third season, "Full Disclosure," a CIA supervisor explains that Sydney was working deep undercover during her lost time and even plays for the agent an video recording of Sydney herself explaining the intervening two years, becoming another example of Philip-Dickian paranoia—even our body is not our own. At the end of the two years, Sydney had her memory erased, in an attempt to hide the location of a dangerous device; however, Sydney's efforts to uncover her own lost time compromise the location and sabotage her own past self's plan. This adds a strange wrinkle to the goal-oriented character, essentially making the protagonist work against herself. Similarly, brainwashing recurs again and again throughout the series as a technique for abolishing character consistency. Bit by bit it is successively revealed that Sydney herself was preprogrammed to be a spy from a very early age through a clandestine social-conditioning experiment dubbed "Project Christmas" (an ironic title which inverts a parental secret hidden from children, to a childhood secret hidden from adult sleeper agents).[3] In Episode 2.5, "The Indicator," Sydney uncovers the remnants of the project and confronts her father exclaiming, "you took away my choices in life." Here, as in other instances of brainwashing, inconsistency is invoked by revealing a portion of the mind unaware of or at odds with the more conscious and well-defined representation of the character. An illustrative example of the latter can be seen in Episode 1.7, "Color Blind," in which Sydney allies with another agent, tortured by the memory of a murder that he was mentally programmed to commit. As fate would have it, the victim was Sydney's fiancée, Danny. It is not enough to say that these characters are cast as ambivalent or conflicted, as characters often are in serial narratives. In character inconsistency, characters' psychologies are fire-walled and divided into portions essentially at odds, which, like Irina, cannot logically be reconciled into a cohesive whole. Motivation and character traits become impoverished conventions to guide the action of the plot and are replaced with echoed events, mirrored characters, vast plot twists and, to some degree, transmedia rearticulation.

Closely related to this thematic interest in brainwashing is the series' recurrent use of out-of-control action and clones. The most salient example of this occurs in the first half of the third season in which Sydney attempts to decode her own purpose for assassinating a Russian diplomat, an action caught on a surveillance camera during her experience of lost time. This narrative conflict of own's body out of one's control was taken even further in *Heroes* through its inclusion of a character, Nikki Sanders, who suffers from a condition which results in black-outs during which her body is literally taken over by an alternative personality. Similarly, Sydney's sister, Nadia, in Episode 3.22, "Resurrection," is drugged to the effect of being inhabited by the spirit of a fifteenth-century prophet, Milo Rambaldi. The series also replaced several principal characters (first Francie and later Sloane) with clones that metaphorically underscored this same sense of inconsistency in traits and motives.

Another reflexive feature of the series that leads to a set of uncommon narrative and textual strategies is its use of double agency. In this series, character agency is won through individuals' ability to move between organizations and institutions. This should be fairly obvious given that the program is clearly one about the problems of clandestine, undercover work. Nearly all the characters act, either for a brief or a prolonged duration of story-time, in this capacity; in the initial series both Jack and Sydney are agents of the CIA working within SD6; in the third season Sloane is an agent of the CIA working within a terrorist organization known simply as the Covenant; and Lauren, Michael Vaughn's wife during the third season, works for the National Security Council, but is eventually revealed to be Covenant double agent. This leads to an implicit theory of action that situates agency, in the sociological sense, as preconditioned on mobility, or liquidity of allegiance/motive. This technique of action is clearly played out in the typical narratives of *Alias* mark I, which is the series of the first season and a half. In this incarnation, Sydney conducted missions on the behest of SD6, but, with the coordination of the CIA, both sabotaged these stated missions and facilitated the case of the CIA against the terrorist organization in the process. A typical double cross can be observed in the series' second episode, "So It Begins," in which Sydney returns from Moscow after having stolen a set of intelligence documents on the orders of SD6. While at the airport, Sydney secretly hands off the data package to her CIA colleagues who copy the original information and then encrypt Sydney's source, before clandestinely returning it to her, all before the protagonist leaves the terminal.

I would argue that, like character inconsistency, double agency reflects and reinforces a way of being within its "native" producing culture. Again, television creatives of this era work in a world marred with particular uncertainty, an uncertainty that is even more palpable during the era of tentpole TV, as what exactly constitutes a television series is up for open debate. The only definitive response to this open question is that a television series is more than that thing which airs on broadcast signals at a certain time each week and can constitute any number of branded or licensed texts. And although the movement of television creatives into other media has been slow and measured, I would argue that the use of double agency in tentpole TV reflects the perceived need to embrace the multiform aspect of television and reinforces a model of being that exploits movement between these forms as a way of increasing power over a series (remember Alexander's quote of flooding the authoring studio with ancillary texts). More simply, *Alias* valorizes the ability to effortlessly shift from one guiding organization to another, a useful skill in the liquid world of media production and even more imperative in a world where TV series are increasingly exploited as all-encompassing brands.

Double agency is achieved textually through constant rearticulation of allegiances and feigned allegiances by way of what is arguably the series' most pronounced formal feature, rapid editing. More specifically, double cross sequences, as outlined above, are built around meticulously intercut sequences where there is a temporal simultaneity between the efforts of SD6 and the CIA. This formal cross-cutting structure is nearly as old as narrative film itself, but I argue that one can isolate an interesting difference in *Alias*'s use of the device. This difference is most evident through comparing the series with the conceptually similar, historically antecedent *Mission: Impossible* (*M:I*).[4] This earlier series also featured scenes of espionage rendered through measured intercutting. In these sequences, *M:I*'s series protagonists would separate and coordinate their efforts to some larger goal. Thus, Barney, the electronics expert, for example, would disable the phone lines, while Cinnamon, the only woman of the group would charm some foreign official, etc. Each protagonist had a clearly delineated task to perform. The temporal simultaneity between the multiple perspectives was won through the use of a handful of formal techniques, but was more a product of narrative context and generic convention. The shared present tense was rendered through series narratives that stress synchronization and deadlines. The overall effect is one of order, control, and mastery. All the work of timing and synchronization is achieved through the expertise of one-dimensional, espionage technocrats.

For example, the series' second episode, "Memory," depicts the efforts of the protagonists to prompt the overthrow of an Eastern European dictator through the use of disinformation. The team enlists the help of Joseph, an impoverished circus performer with a photographic memory, to play the part of a captured clandestine agent to supply the antagonistic government with the faulty intelligence after being purposely captured. To ensure that Joseph's story is believed by his captors, the protagonists engineer a prison escape, preconceived to fail, to lend credence to his false confession. The escape attempt begins sometime after Joseph's initial capture and after his initial interrogation, once the rest of the protagonists are sure that he is indeed in custody. It plays out over several intersecting perspectives of Joseph and his interrogator (A); Barney filling the prison with smoke (B); of Cinamon, Bridges, and Willy distracting the nearby firemen (C); and of the prison guards (both D and E). Charted and read from right to left down the page out it appears as in Table 7.1.

The first half of the sequence plays out like a series of "meanwhile's" where the only definitive temporal relation is narratively coded, we all know that this at least going in the same night and is part of the same "mission." The actions of the protagonists play out in a series of dependent, synchronized steps that must follow one another. Joseph must be captured and deliver the misinformation, then Barney must create the false fire, then Bridges et al. must blend in with the fireman to gain access to the prison. The actions, here a planned failure, are so neat and orderly that when Joseph tries to alter the mission objectives midstream (in the course of his capture, he secures some reliable intelligence and must be extracted), the team, instead of adjusting, retreats and reassembles to concoct an entirely new escape plan. The actions

TABLE 7.1 From Season One, Episode One, entitled "Memory"

A	B	A	C
B	C	C' (Wily leaves)	B
C	**B**	**D**	C
B	E	**C**	D
C	**A**		

of the first half of the sequence display no outward coordination of efforts, nor any outward explicit signs of temporal instantaneousness. This changes slightly in the middle of the sequence (denoted by bolded text) when Barney releases a smoke screen. From this point, the presence of smoke, the reaction of the firemen, and the sound effect of the fire alarm, recurring through all the perspectives ensure that all perspectives are simultaneous. But still there is no overlap in the depiction, protagonists stick to their own preassigned tasks, and perspectives, and, only in the last recurrence of perspective A, in which the interrogator reacts to the fire panic, is the contiguity of the sequence as a whole ensured.

Alias diverges from this other system of representation in at least two significant ways. First, in terms of narrative context, Sydney is frequently described as a master improviser. Unlike the members of the Impossible Missions Force who treat their job as a 9–5 affair, demanding only a Fordist expertise in one specialist's field, Sydney lives her job and is forced to do anything from speaking fluent Mandarin, to defusing a nuclear warhead, to brawling with a broomstick. The larger point being: Sydney is another representation of and avatar for the professional liquidity and adaptability of flexible specialization. However, one can also detect an even more significant difference in the editing of the intercut sequences that, in the case of *Alias*, could be described as emphatically simultaneous. In its intercut sequences, *Alias* deploys any and all formal cues to establish and reestablish simultaneity between perspectives, including spatial overlap in shots, destination matches (the convergence of any number of perspectives into a one), origin matches (wherein multiple perspectives derive from a single one), and spatial repetition (wherein successive perspectives depict the same space as in a pursuit). But most prominently, temporal simultaneity is won by a constant contact of perspectives through characters by way of communications and surveillance technology. In other words, a viewer knows that successive

TABLE 7.2 From Season Two, Episode 18 entitled "Truth Takes Time"

A	B	A	B
C	D	C	D
C	B	C [B]	D [B]
A+B	C	D	A+B
D	C	D	C
A+B	B	C' (Sydney alone)	A
C'	C" (Vaughn alone)	B	C"+B+C'
F	C'+C"+A	D	A
C	D	F	C
F	C	F	C

perspectives are precisely simultaneous because of the definitive overlap of sound and image. An illustrative example can be seen in the episode "Truth Takes Time" (Episode 2.18). Here Vaughn and Sydney track and pursue Irina and her accomplice, Julian Sark, in Stuttgart, Germany. The sequence begins with an A-B alternation of Irina and Sark, spatially distant, but connected via walkie-talkies and surveillance monitors. The sequence then cuts to Sydney and Vaughn, together (C) who are tracking Irina (A) through a homing bug and are similarly later connected by communication technology to their superiors watching their activities from Los Angeles (D). The action read from right to left down the page plays out as shown in Table 7.2.

Every cut between A and B or between C and D is motivated by instantaneous communication. At the same time, the cuts between A/B pairs and C/D pairs are motivated by the surveillance of A and B by C and D, until the surveillance is sabotaged. And the hard brackets imply the use of diegetic surveillance monitors in frame; C [B] then translates to Vaughn and Sydney (C) watching a monitor of Sark (B). But the simultaneity cues do not end there. In the second half of the sequence, the text augments its assumed instantaneousness by deploying nearly every other convention to underscore the intercutting. The use of the + symbol denotes the use of a destination matches and the use of apostrophes denotes the use origin matches. Moreover, there is continual spatial representation in the second half as C pursues A. And, borrowing from an earlier mode of representation, the sequence uses the context of the deadline, here depicted with the disembodied perspective (F) depicting a bomb's ticking timer. This is a considerably elaborate, but in many ways typical intercut sequence of the series that well demonstrates emphatic simultaneity, achieved through both a preponderance of cues, but also and more uniquely through the use of the present-tense connections of diegetic communication and surveillance. We have already observed a similar obsessive use of communication technology and its effect on form in the case of cellular phone use in *24*.

I argue that this difference in editing style returns us to the social theory addressed in the Introduction. Again, *M:I* depicts intercut sequences with minimal cues of simultaneity between perspectives while *Alias* deploys redundant cues to maintain instantaneousness. *M:I*, through its editing illustrates an unproblematic division of labor with prearranged tasks accomplished by experts. The organization of work in *Alias* is radically different. Tasks are not coordinated by specialty, but through the constant contact between coworkers. In *M:I* roles, tasks, allegiances, and the firm itself are unshruggingly consistent, as are the protagonists' plans. Constant intercutting is narratively unnecessary, as Barney can be absolutely sure that Cinnamon is accomplishing her tasks and is not changing sides midstream and vice versa. Conversely, where roles, tasks, and allegiances are permanently inconsistent, coworkers must remain in constant contact to coordinate efforts and, perhaps more importantly, to make narrative comprehensible. This attitude toward the coordination of action reflects the conclusions of Giddens who, in his theory of structuration, discounted the existence of consistent, virtual structures guiding human behavior, claiming instead that, "structures do not exist in time-space, except in the moments of the constitution of social systems" (64–5). Emphatically intercut sequences are representations of just this, relationships, roles and organizations are constantly updated and resolidified, most commonly through individual, face-to-face interaction, here mediated by communications technology.

The representation of work can also be understood as a reflection and reinforcement of the network (in the sociological sense) form of organization. The notion of the network is a sociological concept of binding marked by nonlinearity, indeterminability, and the central importance of individual relationships. Again, this is well demonstrated in intercut sequences in *Alias* where social relations are maintained only by constant interaction. This picture also illustrates Deuze's (2007) characterization of media work in general which is marked by its individualization—each participant is solely responsible for his/her own success or failure, as opposed to the embedded bureaucrat—and by its semipermanence—all work is managed by what Deuze calls semipermanent work groups. My argument then is that the very formal structure of *Alias* can be understood as a valorization of the native network of its production. Arguably, the network-form is more keenly felt in tentpole TV where the mandate is clearly to expand the series beyond broadcast.[5]

It is unsurprising, then, that all of the tentpole TV series analyzed include their own valorization of the network form, mostly through the depiction of vast systems of character interrelations. For example, both *Lost* and *Heroes* begin with a set of geographically distant characters and then, in the following episodes and seasons, reveal how the protagonists are, in fact very much related to one another. The "long lost" motif is frequently deployed, as *Heroes*' Nathan Petrelli is revealed as Claire Bennetts' biological father and *Lost*'s Claire is revealed to be Jack Sheppard's half-sister. One can again read reflexivity at play in these programs where vast, sometimes occluded individual connections are recurrently depicted as the most fateful and meaningful means of social organization.

The particular use of intercutting in *Alias* also begins to suggest the series' and its producing culture's distinct construction of temporality. Geertz, in his examination of Balinese personhood, marks the cultural expression of time as particularly indicative of the Balinese way of being and the organization of social behavior; here I argue that we can learn something similar through the construction of time in *Alias*. I have glancingly mentioned the relative rapidity of the series; however, there are also several other unique temporal features at play. *Alias*, like its historically antecedent James Bond films, includes the use of more or less plausible gadgets to make Sydney's impossible-seeming missions possible. In the 007 films, Bond is commonly introduced to these miracle machines somewhere early in the film and eventually, later in story-time, he will find an opportunity to use these items. *Alias* shares in the convention high-tech gadgetry, but treats these objects different textually. Most commonly, Sydney is depicted in the throes of her mission and, only when she needs to use a device or a particular technique to surmount a certain narrative challenge, will the episode quickly flashback to the exposition of the mission briefing or the description of the vital gadget. For example, in Episode 2.10, "The Abduction," Sydney plays the part of a road surveyor in Paris before the text flashes back to Marshall (007's Q) explaining the operation of a magnetic tear gas mine, mere moments, in plot time, before the mine detonates back in the "present." In other words, the past, treated like one of Giddens' reflexive biographies, only exists as much as it serves the immediate present. Sydney's mental life is assembled in a similar manner, as she is often given immediate expertise to any number of obscure spying skills only in the instant that there are vital to the present, mirroring the use of plug-ins in new media. This conception of character and temporality is made more literal and more simplistic in the later tentpole series, *Dollhouse*, which featured protagonists whose entirely personalities were literally rewritten and reprogrammed between each episode to suit the needs of the current narrative.

This manipulation of the conventional depiction of temporality has important consequences for the implicit social theory at play in *Alias* and tentpole TV more generally. One can again read this formal feature with respect to structuration, as consistent time is not so much structurally determined, but temporal relations are only articulated in the concrete instance in which they are recalled, lived, or predicted. We have already seen how emphatic intercutting can underscore the fragility or impermanence of institutions or organizations. In the case of the ever present of these quick flashbacks, I detect a similar quality in the depiction of the individual. Again, what we returned to is yet another avatar of impermanence and adaptability that literally takes and leaves what it will of its own past for the benefit of the present. The depiction of an all-encompassing ever-present—echoing Chapter 5's real virtuality—that includes accessibility to all times and places is a textual impulse that recurs throughout all tentpole programs: in *Lost*'s flashbacks, in *24*'s real time format, and *Heroes*' narrative use of plots of time travel.

In sum, I have sought to demonstrate how *Alias*, in general, reflects the larger social circumstances of disintegrating institutions and, in specific, the instable work conditions of tentpole TV production, and its effects on individuality. Following Geertz, I subsequently attempted to illustrate how these programs can be seen as, not only reflecting these conditions, but conceptually reinforce them through repeated representations and, arguably, exacerbate them through formal innovation. *Alias* was cast as a model of and model for tentpole TV through its use of character inconsistency, its representation of double agency, its valorization of the network form and its temporality of a continuous present tense. In addition to suggesting ways of being in the industry, these formal techniques also provide the aporias and opportunities for expanding the texts of the series, leaving motivation blank and in need of articulation, leaving open the availability of vast plot twists, allowing the existences of holes in narration to be plugged, implying a real virtuality of spatial and temporal vastness to be subsequently exploited. More simply, I have sought to argue that *Alias* can fruitfully be understood as an alias for the creatives behind the series itself.

Conclusion

The fourth installment of *Jericho*'s third season radically changes the series' plot through a sustained flashback depicting the backstory of the mysterious John Smith. The previous season revealed Smith as the author of the secret shadow government plan to annihilate several US population centers in order to rebalance the nation's power structure. In other words, Smith acts as the series' mastermind, eventually discovered as having composed the inciting incident and premise of the entire program. During the flashback, Smith is depicted as a disgruntled employee of the vague nongovernmental organization/think-tank Jennings & Rail, who not only drafted the attack plot for his employer, but while later reeling from disillusionment with his immediate bosses and grief over his wife's murder, also used his expertise to put his plan into motion. The nuclear attacks that begin the series then were not engineered by an evil cabal of government ghouls and soulless technocrats, as suggested by the previous season, but by an alienated, anomic loner. Significantly altering the series' implicit political stance, this twist moves the newly emerging federal government, dubbed the Allied States of America (ASA), from Malthusian supervillains to mere opportunists trying to erase their relationship with Smith and his master plan. This substantial plot twist is typical for our sample of tentpole series that, like *Alias*, featured any number of conceptual reboots and, like *Lost*, refused to definitively name clear antagonists. What makes this plot development even more significant, however, is the fact that it takes place in an on-air episode, but in a comic book. *Jericho*, the television series, was cancelled after an abbreviated second season, but *Jericho*, the story, was continued in a comic-book series, subtitled Season Three, produced by publishers Dynamite Comics and IDW. This attempt to conclude or at least continue a tentpole series terminated prematurely serves as a final example of both the organizational and aesthetic constraints at play in deploying transmedia in the context of network television.

While there have certainly been unsuccessful or unsatisfactory conclusions to television series as long as there has been a medium, I argue that the very streamability and modularity of tentpole series make this particular format of programming specifically plagued by possible irresolution, encouraging the producers' and consumers' desire to wrap it up or to tie up loose ends. Above, we have referred to tentpole series as being both streamable, that is, available for exploitation in other media, and modular, that is, composed of disintegrative narrative parts disconnected with regards to traditional representations of time, space, and character. This leaves the series a disparate set of interlocking texts that often lack eventual synthesis (see, for example, the far-reaching criticism of *Lost*'s finale). When tentpole series are terminated without an attempt to at least provide closure, both fans and creators have appealed for opportunities to "wrap up" the program narratives. Thus, when *Heroes* was cancelled after a fourth season, showrunner Tim Kring immediately announced that he was in negotiation to "finish" the program as a miniseries (Logan 2010). Similarly, the narratively premature cancellation of NBC's *The Event* led to speculation that the series would be subsequently picked up by the parent conglomerate's own cable network, SyFy (Harnick 2011). It seems as if the hypothetical wrap-up has replaced that other televisual undead text, the reunion show. Several creators have favored the medium of comic books as offering an opportunity to tie up loose ends. After the premature end of the well-liked ABC series *Pushing Daisies*, showrunner Brian Fuller quickly announced plans for a 12-issue DC Comics series extending the on-air program, which never materialized (Melrose 2011). Several writers from FOX's *Dollhouse* have recently filled in the multiyear ellipsis between the series' penultimate episode and its flash-forward, coda-like finale in comic-book form.

Ironically, *Jericho: Season Three* (*JST*) fails to conclude the series narrative; in fact, it only more deeply complicates any such resolution. The on-air series culminated with protagonists Jake Green and Robert Hawkins fleeing to the restored independent republic of Texas with evidence to incite the reemerging state into conflict with the corrupt ASA. However, before this seemingly inevitable war begins, the comic-book series depicts the ASA preemptively bombing Texas, eliminating them as a credible threat. Changing course, *JST* then follows Jake and Hawkins as they rescue the imprisoned John Smith in an effort to rally the still existing eastern states against the ASA, a mission that is only beginning as the comic-book series concludes. All this underscores the difficulty of resolving tentpole narrative despite the overwhelming desire to do so and the critical preoccupation with "the end" (as seen in the strange criticisms levied against *Lost* showrunners in Chapter 5).

Whether or not such a conclusion could ever be applied to vast and expanded narratives, the production of both these proposed and actual texts returns us to the simple observation offered in the introduction—simply that a television series is not just a thing that you watch each week on television. The very idea that one could conclude a television series in a completely different medium echoes the popular industrial and academic chatter that has cast the boundaries of discrete programs as porous and indeterminate. However, we should also note that the case of *JST* does not represent the vaunted transmedia synergy of on-air and off-air texts posited by Jenkins that sees a diversity of media complicating and complimenting one another. *JST* was plotted by series writers Robert Levine and Dan Shotz only after the on-air series was definitively cancelled, casting the comic-book series as a authorial court of last appeal. In other words, *JST*, like our many examples throughout Part One, did not signal a new cooperation between media creatives, but simply reiterated an implicit hierarchy as a terminated narrative, in a sense, was imposed on another adjacent medium. While many of our examples in Part One reinforced this hierarchy through minimized contact, *JST* gives an inverse example of hierarchy maintained through excessive closeness, one could even say colonization, reinforcing what we have previously termed the dead end of continuity, the fact that the narratively significant events only emanate from the creative core outward. In sum, the more streamable and modular a television series, the more one is compelled to tie up loose ends and, conversely, the less one is willing to truly collaborate across media—a paradox at play again and again throughout Part One.

If Part One suggests that the industrial and organizational structures of media production impede the integration of transmedia, then I would like to suggest one final provocative hypothesis; namely that the very form of tentpole TV, as outlined throughout Part Two, equally complicates narrative transmedia by its incorporation of a conspiratorial rhetorical mode. *Jericho* is perhaps the most outwardly conspiratorial of all our tentpole seires. The program follows a survivalist's worst-case scenario of elites in the shadow government and Big Business actively plotting to take over the country, leaving middle-American citizens to rely on their immediate community and their old-fashioned do-it-yourself ingenuity to survive and, eventually, revolt. Season-long story-arcs concern themselves with the very problem attaining reliable information from official sources. The first season featured the inhabitants of the town of Jericho desperately trying to piece together the sequence of events that resulted in the nuclear attacks: Who was responsible for them, which US cities survived the blasts, and the like. This void of information is symbolized in the program's title card that depicts the title's letters in a field of televisual static/snow. *Jericho*'s second season then concerns itself with the debunking of the official story of the attacks given by the provisional ASA, emblemized in the town's resistance to freshly minted history books that tacked on the corrupt government's version of the nuclear assault. Even *JST*, in its own way, apes this fevered interrogation and suspicion of information by displacing it onto series protagonists, Jake and Hawkins, who suppress John Smith's responsibility in the attacks in a larger effort to discredit the ASA. By engaging in all the uncommon formal practices enumerated at length in Part Two, from nonlinear time, to expanded space, to inconsistent characterization, tentpole TV series manifest what could be termed a conspiratorial rhetoric and mimic the very form of conspiracy theory. I argue that vast texts necessarily invoke implicit rhetorical modes to give textual worlds cohesion. For example, Tanya Kryzwinska (2006) has argued that the diffuse experience of the massively-multiplayer online role-playing game *World of Warcraft* is solidified through reference to visual and discursive elements of legend and myth. Or we can think of soap operas in the on-air and the off-air digest forms as being held together by the generic speech genre of gossip or rumor. In the case of tentpole TV, conspiratorial rhetoric's constant misdirection, expansive plotting, and conniving masterminds help to hold the narrative enterprise together. Several recent critics (Mason 2002, Melley 2002, Kahn and Lewis 2005) have demonstrated that the contemporary use of conspiracy theory has increased as a method for both understanding an individual's imperilled position in and possibility for meaningful action within a world economic and cultural system that complicates both. Conspiracy theories then assemble and narrativize complex and contradictory information into far-reaching and interlocking hypothetical systems of control and resistance, echoing the same critique of structure and agency and of the micrological–macrological logic at play in tentpole TV series. As Mason elegantly put it, conspiracy theories work when, "paranoia provides coherence for subjectivity by providing coherence to society" (47). Similarly, secrets, lies, and speculative hypotheses often act as the communicative glue that holds together the disparate narrative elements of tentpole TV and their hyperdiegetic worlds.

Specifically, tentpole TV programs incorporate elements of conspiracy theory in their narratives, their preferred reading practices, and most importantly, their very construction. Tentpole TV narratives often function like conspiracy theories, problematizing the very possibility of individual, meaningful action. Most radically, *Lost*'s second season depicts its main protagonists pushing a button on a mysterious computer terminal every 108 minutes, an action that may or may not do anything. Conspiracy theories also hinge on the revelation of mind control and the powerful institutions that inflict it. It is the very disruption of mind control that is the necessary precondition for all such theories and the stickiness of this presumed control that constitutes the conspiracy. As we have seen, *Alias* narratives feature many instances of mind control and brainwashing, while *Lost* is constructed almost exclusively through a series of evolving confidence tricks. Furthermore, in all of our sample programs, individual characters are menaced by shadowy, malevolent, yet fragile institutions that seek to dominate protagonists' lives.

Stereotypically, conspiracy theories operate by attempting to reconcile and rationalize minute detail and instance, finding motivation where most (those still under "mind control") find none. I would argue that tentpole TV series encourage a similar mode of address by including a wealth of pareidolic detail in visual design and characterization. "For example in *Lost's* second season finale, the Swan Hatch explodes, but not before a ticker-counter briefly replaces numerals with words rendered in ancient Egyptian hieroglyphics. Barely legible on first viewing, the provocative message suggests an overactive reading practice that must rewatch and freeze the fleeting image to literally decipher its content.

However, conspiracy theory and conspiratorial thinking are more than just a set of stereotypical story elements and depth details; they are, I argue, a technique for organizing a flood of seemingly irreducible information. As Mason puts it,

> conspiracy theory provides archeology in narrative form, locating causes and origins of the conspiracy, piecing together events connecting random occurrences to organize a chronology or sequence of sorts, providing revelations and denouements by detailing the conspiracy's plans for the future. (2002: 43–4)

Tentpole TV programs similarly break up their fictional worlds into vast seas of modular texts at the same time that individual texts break apart the traditional representation of time, space, and character, resulting in a dense, contradictory textual system. By invoking conspiracy theory, tentpole TV makers suggest methods for reconciling this vastness by papering over seeming confusion and inconsistency with a central plot (as a definitive plan) or plotter—"Its all being engineered by the Dharma Initiative/Primatech Paper/war profiteers/the CIA/Jennings & Rail/etc." However, as I have argued, the density of form more often points outside of the text to the implied, hypothetical author as the central locus of the conspiracy implicitly promising a synthesis and begging the viewer that truth takes time.

On-air tentpole TV programs present a deep narrative and thematic suspicion toward attempts to control and contain information. Those in control, in the broadest sense of the term, are consistently debunked and rendered false in *Lost*'s endless series of con games, through *24*'s compromised moles, through *Heroes*' philanthropist supervillains, and through *Alias*' duplicitous covert organizations. This atmosphere of suspicion, I argue, can be displaced onto texts themselves resulting in fannish preoccupation with the canonicity of texts (this seems to be a particularly strong issue with online enthusiasts of the work of Joss Whedon). In other words, viewers conditioned by an interplay of conspiracy and revelation are hypothetically predisposed to view transmedia with a jaundiced eye, trained, in a sense, to question texts for their supposed "truth-value."

On the other hand, on-air tentpole TV series in their construction rely on author surrogates and authorial interventions to posit a possible truth behind the seemingly endless layers of lies and conspiracy. *Lost* had its Jacob, *Alias* had its Rambaldi, *Jericho* had its John Smith—mysterious, plotting characters surreptitiously shaping show narratives. As I argued, these figures compliment an increased virtual presence of the programs' writers both implicitly in textual construction and explicitly in show intertext that similarly act to authenticate the "true" story that remains hidden behind the plots and machinations of individual texts—they're not "just making it up." I would suggest the possibility that viewers in this case may, in effect, be predisposed to accept the existence of central masterminds who are solely responsible for the hidden core of the series; preoccupation with these creators was indicated in the extensive media coverage of the *Lost* writers remarked upon in Chapter 5. The result is, again, a hypothetical spectatorial suspicion of anything not clearly attached either diegetically or extratextually to this mastermind figure. I speculate then that the all-pervasive suspicion and central masterminds used to construct vast texts may have equally complicated the smooth integration of an idealized, cooperative world of transmedia workers and texts.

This final example was constructed to reiterate what have been the overarching theoretical and methodological goals of this book, namely the search for nuanced ways to use production data to complicate textual analysis and to deploy textual examination to similarly complicate understandings of the production of popular culture. I anticipate that this book may be cast as somewhat heretical from opposing academic camps for mirrored reasons. On the one hand, it may strike textualist as too preoccupied with social context and on the other it may strike more cultural studies–minded scholars as being too caught up with minute textual analysis. However, I, echoing a number of prior scholars (Kellner 1995, Spigel and Curtain 1997), insist that the future of the discipline hinges and the integration of these two valuable traditions. Simply we are increasingly caught in a world of media abundance where, one, texts themselves can no longer be pinned down to single objects, streaming from one to the next and, two, texts themselves as well as production information is increasingly available at the click of a button, resulting in a veritable glut of data. It is my hope that my quasi-anthropological models will be seen as a way of dealing with this abundance by both following texts through their multiple manifestations, by situating them in the context of their production, and incorporating social theory in a manner that allows these aspects to illuminate one another.

Notes

Introduction

1 An informal, expanded list of these programs would include *24* (FOX, 2001–10), *Alias* (ABC, 2001–6), *Day Break* (ABC, 2006), *Dollhouse* (FOX, 2009–10), *Drive* (FOX, 2007), *Flashforward* (ABC, 2009–10), *Harper's Island* (CBS, 2009), *Heroes* (NBC, 2006–10), *Invasion* (ABC, 2005–6), *Jericho* (CBS, 2006–8), *John Doe* (FOX, 2002–3), *Journeyman* (NBC, 2007), *Kidnapped* (NBC, 2006), *Kings* (NBC, 2009), *Life on Mars* (ABC, 2008–9), *Lost* (ABC, 2004–10), *The Nine* (ABC, 2006), *Push, Nevada* (ABC, 2002), *Prison Break* (FOX, 2005–9), *Reunion* (FOX, 2005), *Surface* (NBC, 2005–6), *Traveler* (ABC, 2007), and *Vanished* (FOX, 2006).

2 Charles Hatfield (2012) has recently argued that Mark Gruenwald occupied a similar position at Marvel Comics in the 1980s helping to usher in a period of tighter continuity, that is more intertextual connections between the firm's many comic-book titles. All of these examples beg for an extended study of the practice of the cultural archivist within media industries.

Chapter 1

1 One major exception to this rule was comic books based on animation properties that frequently tapped moonlighting program artists to draft comic pages (Arnold 2011).

2 Informants have been left anonymous as per their request.

3 This observation and its theoretical consequences are perhaps most examined in works of art history that often minutely consider the exact influences and bodies of knowledge informing individual artists and their works. For example, Claude Cernushi's (1992) authoritative book on the work of Jackson Pollack includes a chapter on the artist's so-called primitivism based on close readings of the anthropological texts literally found on the artist's bookshelf after the artist's death.

4 A term mostly used in software production, time crunch, or the adjective crunchy, refers to a rush to meet deadlines at the end of a production schedule that results in long nights, overtime, and potential abuses of labor law. For a discussion, see Dyer-Witheford and de Peuter (2006).

5 Here I make the distinction of primary and secondary based on credit roll of the on-air series.

6 The character Gitelman initially introduced in the *Heroes* ARG and later briefly appeared in the on-air series as well as several of the webomics.

Chapter 2

1 Film theorist David Bordwell, in his book *On the History of Film Style* (1997), recommends a similar problems/solutions model to understand changes in film aesthetics. However, Bordwell's system is problematic in the way that he conflates his own interpretations of film elements with the hypothetical "solutions" of historical film workers. I will attempt to minimize this problem by working only with the variables of the conditions of the production (so much as they can be reconstituted) and the manifest content of the books themselves and avoiding (as much as possible) contributions based on my own analysis.

2 Exceptions exist as on-air programs are cancelled and writers "descend" into the printed medium in order to complete their stories, as in the case of *V: The Second Generation* (2008) written by the original show-writer Kenneth Johnson.

Chapter 3

1 This was the reported price tag for Take Two Interactive's *Grand Theft Auto IV*.

2 The old media analogue for this practice is unclear. It could be described as a way of borrowing technique (in the same way, for example, that Jackson Pollack borrowed drawing and sketching techniques and brought them to the medium of paint) casting previous code as a tool, or as a way of borrowing content in the manner of pastiche or collage. Or, perhaps it is best understood as a resource, a sort of copy–paste, unique to digital production.

3 With the notable exception of the Lego franchise of games (*Lego Star Wars* [Eidos, 2005], *Lego Batman* [TT Games, 2008]), most licensed games of the last 15 years are rendered with a high degree of photorealism.

4 In interview, producer Patrik McCormack has boasted that the costume designer for the on-air series worked on the game to ensure the fidelity of these costume changes (Berardini 2004).

5 This contrast is also attributable to the difference in adapting feature-film source material that has a central, definitive narrative and television texts, which contain a multiplicity of story material and, thus, no clear narrative for adaptation.

Chapter 4

1 There are some small exceptions such as Fox's satellite television services and WB's broadband services.

2 In fact, one of my interviews was cut short when the interviewee suspected that I might be conducting industrial espionage—a miscommunication that was resolved through a subsequent background check.

3 Oddly enough, the example of the backward baseball hat is also used in William Gibson's *Pattern Recognition* (2003), a novel set in the world of contemporary market research and advertising. In the novel, the protagonist discusses tracking down the very first person to wear his hat in this inverse fashion—a teenager living in rural Mexico.

Chapter 5

1 This technique shares much in common with blockbuster films in motion pictures, blockbuster writers in print publishing, and the sometime endless sequalization in video-game publishing.

2 A similar observation was made in another *The New York Times* piece (April 25, 2004) concerning the ABC program *Alias*, which quoted a series writer, Rober Orci, stating, "we've mastered the art of having the characters say things that are vague and open-ended because we don't know what's happening next."

3 Both of these writers are notable for their work in furthering the use of transmedia; Loeb, for his work bridging the fields of comic books and television; Alexander, for his pioneering work on expanding the series *Alias*.

4 The story present of the series through the first four seasons spanned approximately the first 100 days after the airliner crash.

5 However, the series includes brief flashbacks in the third season in Episodes 3.3 ("Further Instructions") and 3.17 ("Catch 22").

6 Significantly, Locke and Sawyer swap roles in Season Three's "Man from Tallahassee" (Episode 3.13), wherein Locke tricks Sawyer into killing his own father who had mysteriously appeared on the island.

7 These special cases can be found in Episodes 22 and 23 of Season Two; Episodes 14 and 19 of Season Three; and Episode Five of Season Four.

8 Interestingly, *Lost* also contains several unconventional uses of ambiguous point-of-view structures. For example, the first season concludes with a backward track down the so-called hatch. Four real-world months later, in the second season's premiere, this shot is recast as an expressionistic point-of-view shot from the character Desmond's vantage in the hatch.

Chapter 6

1 Of course, nonfictional television genres have too experimented with this technique, in the case of local television news, by soliciting viewers to follow stories of interest further on station websites.

2 Such narrative constructions most likely owe some of their novelty to the hip nonlinearity of such prominent film auteurs as Quinten Taratino (*Pulp Fiction*, *Inglourious Basterds*) and Wong Kar Wai (*Ashes of Time*, *Days of Being Wilds*) whose films only eventually reveal the spatial and narrative links of their dispersed characters.

3 In this way, the challenges of constructing a tentpole TV series shares many of the problems facing contemporary makers of massively-multiplayer online games whose primary objectives are to produce a cohesive, vast, and populable world.

4 More recently, boundary pushing, so-called single-camera sitcoms (*Malcolm in the Middle*, *Arrested Development*, *Scrubs*, *Modern Family*) have complicated this dichotomous logic and, in the process, share features in common with tentpole TV, particularly spatial and temporal experimentation.

5 Such a spatial dynamic is even at play in the conventions of network television news, which contrasts the recurring newsroom with the variable, messy social world outside covered by intrepid electronic news gatherers.

6 *Lost*'s fifth season replaced this use of spatial recalculation with temporal recalculation, depicting a set of characters repeatedly forced to determine what year they are in while their island home jumped through timescapes in the manner of a long-play record skipping.

7 Significantly, the sequence also retrospectively foregrounds the relationship between Nina and Jack by mirroring it with that of Elizabeth and Alexi. By the end of the first season, it is revealed that Nina was acting as an antagonistic informant during her own previous romantic relationship with Jack.

Chapter 7

1 This, too, echoes the flattened social space of *24*'s multiscreen effects examined in the previous chapter.

2 Such a fate would be inconceivable for KAOS, or UNCLE, or any other fictional spy organization of the past.

3 Interest in social conditioning in general is another thematic debt present in tentpole TV (particularly in *Lost*'s Skinner boxes) that relate the programs back to the fiction of Thomas Pynchon.

4 Unsurprisingly, *Alias* showrunner J. J. Abrams has gone on to direct the feature-film version of *Mission: Impossible*.

5 The survivors of 815 in *Lost* can, too, be conceived of as a thrown-together, semipermanent work group and, indeed, the impermanence of the "team" is well demonstrated as the survivors subsequently separate into rival camps.

Bibliography

Activision. 2000, 2001, 2002, 2003, 2004, 2005, 2006, 2007, 2008, 2009. Form 10-K, commission file number 0–12699. Retrieved February 13, 2010 from Activision website: <http://investor.activision.com/secfiling. cfm?filingID=1104659–07–47752>.

Adlain, Josef and Michael Schneider. 2007, May 17. Fanciful fare, not crime, highlights lineups. *Variety*.

Adler, Moshe. 1985. "Stardom and talent." *The American Economic Review* 75(1): 208–12.

Alberto Giolitti biography. [n.d]. Retrieved February 29, 2012, from Alberto Giolitti's website: <www.albertogiolitti.com/bio.php>.

Alexander, Jesse (w), Aron Coleite (w), and Jordan Kotzebue (a). 2007, January 29. How do you stop an exploding man? part 2. [*Heroes*] #18.

Alexander, Peter J. 1996. "Entropy and popular culture: Product diversity in the popular music recording industry." *American Sociological Review* 61(1): 171–4.

Alexander, Victoria D. 2003. *Sociology of the Arts: Exploring Fine and Popular Forms*. Oxford: Blackwell Publishing.

Allen, Robert C. 1985. *Speaking of Soap Operas*. Chapel Hill: University of North Carolina.

Alvey, Mark. 1997. "The independents: Rethinking the television studio system," in *The Revolution wasn't Televised: Sixties Television and Social Conflict*. Ed. Lynn Spigel and Michael Curtin. London: Routledge, pp. 138–58.

Anand, N. and Richard A. Peterson. 2000. "When market information constitutes fields: Sensemaking of markets in the commercial music industry." *Organization Science* 11(3): 270–84.

Anderson, Chris. 2006. *The Long Tail: Why the Future of Business is Selling Less of More*. New York: Hyperion.

Anderson, Chrisphter. 1994. *Hollywood TV: The Studio System in the Fifties*. Austin: University of Texas Press.

Andrews, Edmund L. 1991. FTC obtains concessions on children's "900" TV ads. Retrieved August 26, 2009, from *The New York Times* website: <www. nytimes.com/1991/05/09/business/ftc-obtains-concessions-on-children-s-900-tv-ads.html>.

— 1993. "900" telephone business withers as problems rise. Retrieved August 26, 2009, from *The New York Times* website: <www. nytimes.com/1993/04/21/business/900-telephone-business-wither s-as-problems-rise.html>.

Arnold, Mark. 2011, October. Evanier, Spiegle and a dog named Scooby-Doo. *Back Issue* 71–7.

"AT&T launches cell video service." 2008. Retrieved August 26, 2009, from Variety website: <www.variety.com/article/VR1117984938. html?categoryid=1009&cs=1>.

Atkinson, Claire. 2007, May 10. Is prime time past its prime? *Television Week.*

Ayers, Jeff. 2006. *Voyages of the Imagination: The* Star Trek *Fiction Companion.* New York: Simon and Schuster.

Baetens, Jan. 2007. "From screen to text: Novelization, the hidden continent," in *The Cambridge Companion to Literature on Screen.* Ed. Deborah Cartmell and Imelda Whelehan. Cambridge: Cambridge University Press, pp. 226–38.

Baker, Chris. 2008. Meet Leland Che, the *Star Wars* franchise continuity cop. *Wired* September 16.

Barnouw, Erik. 1982. *Tube of Plenty: The Evolution of American Television.* Oxford. Oxford University Press.

Bauman, Zygmunt. 2005. *Liquid Life.* Cambridge: Polity.

Baxandall, Michael. 1972. *Painting & Experience in Fifteenth Century Italy.* Oxford: Oxford University Press.

Beck, Ulrich. 1992. *Risk Society: Towards a New Modernity.* London: Sage Publications.

Becker, Howard S. 1984 [1982]. *Art Worlds.* Berkeley: University of California Press.

Behind-the-scenes: Disney interactive talk pirates. 2007, May 11. *Game Biz Daily.*

Bellour, Raymond. 2000. *The Analysis of Film.* Ed. Constance Penley. Bloomington: University of Indiana Press.

Berardini, César. 2004, March 17. *Alias*: Patrik McCormack interview. Retrieved February 13, 2010 from IGN website: <http://interviews.teamxbox.com/ xbox/754/Alias-Patrik-McCormack-Interview/p1/>.

Berger, Peter L. and Thomas Luckmann. 1966. *The Social Construction of Reality: A Treatise in the Sociology of Knowledge.* Garden City: Doubleday.

Bielby, William and Denise D. Bielby. 1994. "'All hits are flukes': Institutionalized decision making and the rhetoric of network prime-time programming." *The American Journal of Sociology* 99(5): 1287–313.

Birdwell, Ken. 2006 [1999]. "The cabal: Valve's design process for creating *Half-Life*," in *The Game Design Reader: A Rules of Play Anthology.* Ed. Katie Salen and Eric Zimmerman. Cambridge: MIT Press, pp. 212–25.

Boddy, William. 1990. *Fifties Television: The Industry And Its Critics.* Champagn-Urbana: University of Illinois Press.

Booth, Wayne. 1983. *The Rhetoric of Fiction.* Chicago: University of Chicago Press.

Bordwell, David. 1985. *Narration in the Fiction Film.* Madison: University of Wisconsin Press.

— 1997. *On the History of Film Style.* Cambridge: Harvard University Press.

— 2004. "The art cinema as mode of film practice," in *Film Theory and Criticism: Introductory Readings, 6th ed.* Ed. Leo Baudry and Marshall Cohen. New York: Oxford University Press, pp. 774–82.

Bordwell, David, Janet Staiger, and Kristin Thompson. 1985. *The Classical Hollywood Cinema: Film Style & Mode of Production to 1960*. New York: Columbia University Press.

Bourdieu, Pierre. 1977. *Outline of a Theory of Practice*. Trans. Richard Nice. Cambridge: Cambridge University Press.

Boyes, Emma. 2008, January 22. Q&A Gadi Pollack on *Lost: Via Domus*. Retrieved February 13, 2010 from Gamespot website: <www.gamespot.com/news/6184937.html>.

Brady, Matt. 2007, January 17. Taking the novel approach with Greg Cox. Retrieved October 24, 2008 from Newsarama website: <http://forum.newsarama.com/showthread.php?t=97865>.

Bramwell, Tom. 2006, January 25. 24: The Game interview. Retrieved February 13, 2010 from Eurogamer website: <www.eurogamer.net/articles/I_24_markgreen>.

Branigan, Edward. 1984. *Point of View in Cinema: A Theory of Narration and Subjectivity in Classical Film*. New York: Mouton.

Brown, Erika. 2005, May 23. Coming to a tiny screen near you. *Forbes*. Retrieved March 21, 2012, from Forbes website: <www.forbes.com/forbes/2005/0523/064 ml>.

BuddyTV Interviews LOST's Damon Lindelof and Carlton Cuse—and Gets Answers! 2007, March 7. Retrieved January 22, 2009 from BuddyTV website: <www.buddytv.com/articles/lost/buddytv-interviews-losts-damon-4766.aspx>.

Burch, Noel. 1973. *The Theory of Film Practice*. Trans. Helen R. Rane. New York: Praeger.

The Business of Novelizations & Tie-Ins, Part One: The Deal [n.d.]. Retrieved October 24, 2008 from The International Association of Media Tie-in Writers website: <www.iamtw.org/art_business_deal.html>.

The Business of Novelizations & Tie-Ins, Part Three: The Characters [n.d.]. Retrieved October 24, 2008 from The International Association of Media Tie-in Writers website: <www.iamtw.org/art_business_characters.html>.

The Business of Novelizations & Tie-ins, Part Two: Deadlines [n.d.]. Retrieved October 24, 2008 from The International Association of Media Tie-in Writers website: <www.iamtw.org/art_business_deadlines.html>.

Caldwell, John. 1995. *Televisuality: Style, Crisis and Authority in American Television*. New Brunswick: Rutgers University Press.

— 2000. "Introduction: Theorizing the digital landrush," in *Electronic Media and Technoculture*. Ed. John Caldwell. New Brunswick: Rutgers University Press, pp. 1–31.

— 2004. "Convergence television: Aggregating from and repurposing content in the culture of conglomeration," in *Television after TV*. Ed. Lynn Spigel and Jan Olsson. Durham: Duke University Press, pp. 41–74.

— 2006. "Cultural studies of media production: Critical industrial practice," in *Questions of Method in Cultural Studies*. Ed. Mimi White and James Schwoch. London: Wiley-Blackwell, pp. 109–53.

— 2009. *Production Cultures*. Durham: Duke University Press.

Camacho-Hübner, Eduardo, Valérie November, and Bruno Latour. [n.d.]. The territory is the map: Space in the age of digital navigation. Retrieved September 28, 2009 from Bruno Latour's website: <www.bruno-latour.fr>.

Carlsson, Christer and Pirkko Walden. 2007. Mobile TV – to live or die by content. *Proceedings of the 40th Annual Hawaii International Conference on System Sciences*. Retrieved March 11, 2012 from: <www.computer.org/comp/proceedings/hicss/2007/.../27550051b.pdf>.

Castells, Manuel. 1996. *Rise of the Network Society*. Oxford: Blackwell Publishers.

Caves, Richard. 2000. *Creative Industries: Contracts between Art and Commerce*. Cambridge: Harvard University Press.

— 2005. *Switching Channels: Organization and Change in TV Broadcasting*. Cambridge: Harvard University Press.

Cernuschi, Claude. 1992. *Jackson Pollock: Meaning and Significance*. New York: Harper Collins.

Cohendet, Patrick and Laurent Simon. 2007. "Playing across the playground: Paradoxes of knowledge creation in the videogame firm." *Journal of Organizational Behavior* 28: 587–605.

Coleite, Aron (w) and Jason Badower (a). May 21, 2007. The death of Hana Gitelman, part 2. [*Heroes*] #34.

Collins, Max Allan. Writing the CSI novels. Retrieved October 24, 2008 from The International Association of Media website: <www.iamtw.org/art_csi.html>.

Consumers & convergence III: Consumers taking charge. 2009. Retrieved August 26, 2009, from: <www.mf.org/uploads/tx_nemefmarketdata/MEF_and_KPMG_Consumers___Convergence_Report.pdf>.

Costikyan, Greg. 2006 [1994]. "I have no words & I must design," in *The Game Design Reader: A Rules of Play Anthology*. Ed. Katie Salen and Eric Zimmerman. Cambridge: MIT Press, pp. 192–211.

Couldry, Nick. 2000. *The Place of Media Power: Pilgrims and Witnesses of the Media Age*. London: Routledge.

Cox, Greg. 2005a. *The Road Not Taken*. New York: Simon Spotlight Entertainment.

— 2005b. *Two of Kind?* New York: Simon Spotlight Entertainment.

— 2006. *Namesakes*. New York: Simon Spotlight Entertainment.

Creeber, Glen. 2004. *Serial Television*. London: BFI Publishing.

Culler, Jonathan. 1976. "Presupposition and intertextuality." *MLN* 91(6): 1380–96.

Curtin, Michael. 1996. "On edge: Cultural industries in the neo-network era," in *Making and Selling Culture*. Ed. Richard Ohmann. Hanover, NH: Wesleyan University Press, pp. 181–202.

Czarniawska, Barbara and Carmelo Mazza. 2003. "Consulting as a liminal space." *Human Relations* 53(3): 267–90.

D'acci, Julie. 1994. *Defining Women: Television and the Case of Cagney and Lacey*. Chapell Hill: University of North Carolina Press.

Dahlen, Chris. 2007, November 21. MIT: *Heroes*, Narnia panel talks transmedia storytelling. Retrieved February 14, 2010 from Gamasutra website: <www.gamasutra.com/view/news/16294/MIT_Heroes_Narnia_Panel_Talks_Transmedia_Storytelling.php>.

Dawson, Max. [n.d.]. Television's aesthetic of efficiency: Convergence television and the digital short. Retrieved March 16, 2012 from: <bgock.com/maxdawson/...files/Ch_10_Dawson_Revised_DUKE.pdf>.

DeLoura, Mark. 2009, March 16. The engine survey: Technology results. Retrieved February 13, 2010 from Gamasutra website: <www.gamasutra.com/blogs/MarkDeLoura/20090316/903/The_Engine_Survey_Technology_Results.php>.

Deuze, Mark. 2007. *Media Work*. Cambridge: Polity Press.

Deuze, Mark and Chase Bowen Martin. 2007. "The independent production of culture: Digital games case study." *Games and Culture* 4(3): 276–95.

Dick, Philip K. 1981. *Valis*. New York: Bantam Books.

DiMaggio, Paul. 1977. "Market structure, the creative process, and popular culture." *Journal of Popular Culture* 11(2): 436–52.

Dornfeld, Barry. 1998. *Producing Public Television, Producing Public Culture*. Princeton: Princeton University Press.

Douglass, Greg, Robin Murdoch, and Jamyn Edis. 2006. Boiling point: Convergence finally heats up: A primer on convergence. Retrieved August 26, 2009 from: <www.accenture.com/NR/rdonlyres/04EA4AFB-E65C-40E2-A1CF-49A8293A6C25/0/Convergencefinallyheatsup.pdf>.

Doukas, Nick. 2002, October 22. *Buffy the Vampire Slayer: The Collective*. Retrieved February 13, 2010 from Gaming Target website: <www.gamingtarget.com/article.php?artid=1155>.

Durkheim, Émile. 1995 [1915]. *The Elementary Forms of Religious Life*. Trans. Karen E. Fields. New York: Free Press.

Dyer-Witheford, Nick and Greig de Peuter. 'EA spouse and the crisis of video game labor: Enjoyment, exclusion, and exodus. *Canadian Journal of Communication* 31(3). Edis, Jamyn and Gavin Mann. 2006. "Content: Here, there and everywhere: Accenture media content survey 2006." Retrieved January 20, 2010, from: <www.accenture.com/xdoc/en/industries/communications/convergence/landing_convergence.pdf>.

Electronic Arts. 2001, 2002, 2003, 2004, 2005. Form 10-K, commission file number 0–17948. Retrieved February 24, 2010 from the Electronic Arts website: <http://investor.ea.com/sec.cfm>.

Epstein, Michael, Jimmie L. Reeves, and Mark C. Rodgers. 1996. "Rewriting popularity: The cult *Files*," in *Deny all Knowledge: Reading the* X-Files. Ed. Marla Cartwright, Angela Hague, and David Lavery. Syracuse: Syracuse University Press, pp. 22–35.

Ettema, James and D. Charles White. 1982. "Introduction," in *Individuals in Mass Media Organizations*. Ed. James S. Ettema and D. Charles White. Beverly Hills: Sage.

Fabrikant, Geraldine. 1995, August 1. 2 boards approve. *The New York Times*, A1.

Feuer, Jane. 1995. *Seeing through the Eighties: Television and Reaganism*. Durham: Duke University Press.

Feuer, Jane, Paul Kerr, and Tise Vahimagi. 1984, *MTM: "Quality Television."* London: BFI Publishing.

Fitchard, Kevin. 2006, April 3. The making of the mobisode. *Telephony*.

Fritz, Ben. 2006, September 18. Game biz cools on movie tie-ins. *Variety*.

— 2008, March 3. *Lost: Via Domus* [Review]. Retrieved February 13, 2010 from Variety website: <www.variety.com/review/VE1117936377.html>.

Gaborno, Rudy and Chris Hollier. 2005. *Faina*. New York: Simon Spotlight Entertainment.

Gans, Herbert J. 1979. *Deciding What's News: A Study of CBS Nightly News, Newsweek, and* Time. New York: Pantheon Books.

Gaudreault, André and François Jost. 2004. "Enunciation and narration," in *A Companion to Film Theory*. Ed. Toby Miller and Robert Stam. Oxford: Blackwell Publishers, pp. 45–63.

Garfield, Bob. 2007. You tube vs. boob tube. *Wired* 14.12.

Geertz, Clifford. 1976. "From the native's point of view: On the nature of anthropological understanding," in *Meaning in Anthropology*. Ed. Keith H. Basso and Henry A. Selby. Albuquerque: University of New Mexico Press, pp. 221–37.

— 2000 [1973]. *The Interpretation of Cultures*. New York: Basic Books.

Gerrold, David. 1973. *The Trouble with Tribbles*. New York: Ballantine Books.

Getlin, Josh. 2008a, May 30. Troubled book world is going for novel ideas. *Los Angeles Times*, E1.

— 2008b, June 6. HarperCollins shuffles deck. *Los Angeles Times*, E15.

Gibbs, Colin. 2008. Mobile TV suffers from lack of on-demand programming. Retrieved August 26, 2009 from: <www.rcrwireless.com/article/20081119/WIRELESS/811199995/mobile-tv-suffers-from-lack-of-on-demand-programming>.

— 2009. "Executive interview: Paul Palmieri, CEO, Millenial Media." Retrieved August 26, 2009, from: <www.rcrwireless.com/article/20090115/WIRELESS/901149978/executive-interview-paul-palmier i-ceo-millennial-media>.

Gibson, William. 2003. *Pattern Recognition*. New York: G.P. Putnam's Sons.

Giddens, Anthony. 1979. *Central Problems in Social Theory: Action, Structure and Contradiction in Social Analysis*. Berkeley: University of California Press.

— 1986. *The Constitution of Society: Outline of a Theory of Structuration*. Berkeley: University of California Press.

— 1990. *Consequences of Modernity*. Stanford: Stanford University Press.

— 1991. *Modernity and Self-identity: Self and Society in Late Modern Age*. Stanford: Stanford University Press.

Gillan, Jennifer. 2010. *Television and New Media: Must Click TV*. New York: Routledge.

Gitlin, Todd. 1983. *Inside Primetime*. New York: Pantheon Books.

Goffman, Erving. 1961. *Asylums: Essays on the Social Situation of Mental Patients and Other Inmates*. Garden City: Anchor Books.

— 1971. *Relations in Public: Microstudies in Public Order*. New York: Harper Colophon Books.

Gorman, Ed. All tied up: Three writers discuss media tie-in work. Retrieved October 24 2008 from The International Association of the Media Tie-in Writers website: <www.iamtw.org/art_tied.html>.

Gough, Paul J. 2007, January 17. Nielsen sets ad ratings schedule. *Hollywood Reporter*.

Graser, Marc. 2007, August 6. Comics' next H'wood wannabes. *Variety*.

Gray, Jonathan. 2010. *Show Sold Separately*: *Promos, Spoilers and Other Media Paratexts*. New York: New York University.

Grindstaff, Laura. 2002. *The Money Shot: Trash, Class and the Making of TV Talk Shows*. Chicago: University of Chicago Press.

Griswold, Wendy. 1981. "American character and the American novel: An expansion of reflection theory in the sociology of literature." *The American Journal of Sociology* 86(4): 740–65.

— 1987. "A methodological framework for sociology of the culture." *Sociological Methodology* 17: 1–35.

Grossman, Lev. 2006. *Time's* person of the year: You. Retrieved August 26, 2009 from: <www.time.com/time/magazine/article/0,9171,1569514,00.html>.

Gunning, Tom. 1991. "Heard over the phone: *The Lonely Villa* and the de Lorde tradition of the terrors of technology." *Screen* 32(2): 184–96.

Gwellian-Jones, Sara. 2004. "Virtual reality and cult television," in *Cult TV*. Ed. Sara Gwellian-Jones and Roberta E. Pearson. Minneapolis: University of Minnesota Press, pp. 83–98.

Haag, Andrea V. 2003, April. [Interview with Emma Harrison]. Retrieved October 24, 2008 from The Charmed Ones website: <http://thecharmedones.com/emmaharrison.htm>.

— 2004, April. [Interview with Paul Ruditis]. Retrieved October 24, 2008 from The Charmed Ones website: <www.thecharmedones.com/paulruditis.htm>.

Hall, Stuart. "Encoding/decoding," in *Culture, Media, Language*. Ed. Stuart Hall Dorothy Hobson, Andrew Lowe, and Paul Willis. New York: Routledge, pp. 128–38.

Hanna, Steven. 2006. *Old Friends*. New York: Simon Spotlight Entertainment.

Harnick, Chris. 2011. *The Event* heading to SyFy? Retrieved February 24, 2012 from The Huffington Post website: <www.aoltv.com/2011/06/01/the-event-heading-to-syfy/>.

Hatfield, Charles. 2012. *Hand of Fire: The Comics Art of Jack Kirby*. Jackson, MS: University of Mississippi Press.

Havens, Timothy, Amada D. Lotz and Serra Tinic. 2009. "Critical media industry studies: A research approach." *Communication, Culture & Critique* 2: 234–53.

Havok available games. [n.d.] Retrieved February 13, 2010 from Havok website: <www.havok.com/index.php?page=available-games>.

Heath, Stephen. 1981. *Questions of Cinema*. Bloomington: Indiana University Press.

Hills, Matt. 2002. *Fan Cultures*. London: Routledge.

— 2004. "Defining cult TV: Texts, inter-texts and fan audiences," in *The Television Studies Reader*. Ed. Robert Allen and Annette Hill. London: Routledge.

Hirsch, Paul. 1991 [1972]. "Processing fads and fashions: An organization-set analysis of cultural industry systems," in *Re-thinking Popular Culture: Contemporary Perspectives in Cultural Studies*. Ed. Chandra Mukerji and Michael Schudson. Berkeley: University of California Press, pp. 313–34.

Hirschler, Ben. 2007, January 27. Gates: Internet to revolutionize TV in 5 years. Retrieved August 20, 2009 from Reuters website: <www.reuters.com/article/ousiv/idUSL2791097520070128>.

Holson, Laura M. 2006, February 27. Cellphone content, straight from the creators. *The New York Times*.

How consumer conversation will transform business. 2008. [*Pricewaterhouse Coopers*]. Retrieved January 20, 2010, from: <www.pwc.com/en_GX/gx/technology-media-convergence/pdf/consumertransformbusiness.pdf>.

IBISWorld. 2010, January 6. IBISWorld industry report: Video games in the US. Interview: Blackout. [n.d.]. Retrieved April 12, 2010, from: <www.heroeswiki.com/interview:blackout>.

Jameson, Frederic. 1991. *Postmodernism, or the Cultural Logic of Late Capitalism*. Durham: Duke University Press.

Jenkins, Henry. 1992. *Textual Poachers: Television Fans & Participatory Culture*. London: Routledge.

— 2006. *Convergence Culture: Where Old and New Media Collide*. New York: New York University Press.

— 2006 [1998]. "'Complete freedom of movement': Video games as gendered play spaces," in *The Game Design Reader: A Rules of Play Anthology*. Ed. Katie Salen and Eric Zimmerman. Cambridge: MIT Press, pp. 330–63.

Jensen, Jeff. [n.d.]. 'Lost': mind-blowing scoop from its producers. Retrieved January 22, 2009 from Entertainment Weekly website: <www.ew.com/ew/article/0,,20179125,00.html>.

— 2007, November 7. 'Heroes' creator apologizes to fans. Retrieved January 22, 2009 from Entertainment Weekly website: <www.ew.com/ew/article/0,,20158840,00.html>.

Johns, J. 2006. "Video games production networks: Value capture, power relations and embeddedness." *Journal of Economic Geography* 77(4): 639–59.

Johnson, Catherine. 2007. "Telebranding in TVIII: The network as brand and the program as brand." *New Review of Film and Television Studies* 5(1): 5–24.

Johnson, Derek. 2009. Franchising media worlds: Content networks and the collaborative production of culture. UMI microform 3368021.

Johnson, Kenneth. 2008. *V: The Second Generation*. New York: Tor Books.

Johnson, Ted. 2006, October 30. Cost conundrum. Retrieved February 22, 2010 from *Variety* website: <www.variety.com/article/VR1117952819.html>.

Johnston, John. 1998. *Information Multiplicity: American Fiction in the Age of Media Saturation*. Baltimore: Johns Hopkins University Press.

Jones, Jennifer. 2006. "Video games production networks: Value capture, power relations and embeddedness." *Journal of Economic Geography* 6: 151–80.

Kahn, Richard and Tyson Lewis. 2005. "The reptoid hypothesis: Utopian and dystopian representational motifs in David Icke's alien conspiracy theory." *Utopian Studies* 16(1): 45–74.

Kapko, Matt. 2007. Mobile TV state of industry. Retrieved August 26, 2009 from: <www.mattkapko.com/articles/article_2007_03_29_mobileTV.html>.

— 2008. Mobile TV space looks for growth in 2008. Retrieved August 26, 2009 from: <www.mattkapko.com/articles/article_2008_02_01.html>.

Katz, Elihu and Paul F. Lazarsfeld. 1955. *Personal Influence: The Part Played by People in the Flow of Mass Communications*. Glencoe, IL: Free Press.

Kellner, Douglas. 1995. "Media communications vs. cultural studies: Overcoming the divide." *Communication Theory* 5(2): 162–77.

Kerr, Aphra. 2006. *The Business and Culture of Digital Games: Gamework / Gameplay*. London: Sage Publications.

King, Danny. 2008, March 17. TV producers play the video game: Networks test growing market in low-risk effort. *Television Week*, 3.

Kinsella, Sharon. 2000. *Adult Manga: Culture & Power in Contemporary Japanese Society*. Honolulu: University of Hawai'i Press.

Kleinfield, N. R. 1985, March 19. ABC is being sold for $3.5 billion; 1st network sale. *The New York Times*, A1.

Kline, Stephen, Nick Dyer-Witheford, and Greig de Peuter. 2003. *Digital Play: The Interaction of Technology, Culture and Marketing*. Quebec City: McGill-Queen's University Press.

Kryzwinska, Tanya. 2006. "Blood scythes, festivals, quests and backstories: World creation and rhetorics of myth in *World of Warcraft*." *Games and Culture* 1(4): 383–96.

Kushner, David. 2007. Behind the scenes with *Heroes* creator Tim Kring and "Hiro," Masi Oka. *Wired* 15.05.

— April 2008. Rebel alliance. *Fast Company* "Retrieved October 10, 2012 from website: <http://www.fastcompany.com/798975/rebel-alliance>."

Lash, Scott and Celia Lury. 2007. *Global Culure Industry: The Mediation of Things*. Cambridge: Polity.

Lash, Scott and John Urry. 1994. *Economies of Signs and Space*. London: Sage.

Latour, Bruno. 2005. *Reassembling the Social: An Introduction to Actor-network Theory*. Oxford: Oxford University Press.

Le Dour, Corinne Isabelle. 2007, January 10. Localizing brands and licenses. Retrieved February 24, 2010 from the Gamasutra website: <www.gamasutra.com/view/feature/1742/localizing_brands_and_licenses.php>.

Learmonth, Michael. 2006. Nielsen gives it the old college try. Retrieved August 21, 2009 from Variety website: <www.variety.com/article/VR1117938180.html>.

Lewis, Randy. 2009, December 10. Activision fires back at No Doubt in court. Retrieved February 13, 2010 from Los Angeles *Times* website: <http://articles.latimes.com/2009/dec/10/business/la-fi-ct-activision10–2009dec10>.

Lindelof, Damon. 2007, November 11. Mourning TV. *The New York Times*.

Lindelof, Damon and Carlton Cuse. 2006, October 30. *Official "Lost" podcast*. Retrieved October 30, 2006 from website: <http://ll.media.abc.com/podcast/audio/itunes/Lostpodcast_305_abc.mp3>.

Littleton, Cynthia. 2008, November 8. 'Heroes' duo get the ax. Retrieved January 22, 2009 from Variety website: <www.variety.com/VR1117995152.html>.

Logan, Michael. 2010, June 1. Is there power left in *Heroes*? Retrieved February 24, 2012 from TV Guide website: <www.tvguide.com/News/Heroes-Tim-Kring-1019088.aspx>.

Lotz, Amanda. 2007a. *The Television will be Revolutionized*. New York: New York University Press.

— 2007b. "Textual (im)possibilities in the U.S. post-network era: Negotiating production and promotion processes on Lifetime's *Any Day Now*," in

Television: The Critical View, 7th edition. Ed. Horace Newcomb. Oxford: Oxford University Press, pp. 223–44.

Luhmann, Niklas. 1979. *Trust & Power.* New York: Wiley.

Lynch, Jennifer. 1990. *The Secret Diary of Laura Palmer.* New York: Pocket Books.

Maas, John-Michael. 2003a, April 21. Wide angle tie-ins. *Publishers Weekly,* 17.

— 2003b, April 28. Where the fans are. *Publishers Weekly,* 23.

MacBride Allen, Roger. 2005, January 4. Media tie-ins: Why they're nearly impossible for beginners to publish. Retrieved October 24, 2008, from Science Fiction and Fantasy Writers of America, Inc website: <www.sfwa. org/writing/media.htm>.

McMurria, John. 2003. "Long-format TV: Globalization and network branding in a multi-channel environment," in *Quality Popular Television: Cult TV, the Industry and Fans.* Ed. Mark Jancovich and James Lyons. London: BFI Publishing, pp. 65–87.

Manly, Lorne. 2006, October 1. Running the big show: "Lost" inc. *The New York Times.*

— 2006a. For tiny screens, some big dreams. Retrieved August 26, 2010, from *The New York Times* website: <www.nytimes.com/2006/05/21/business/ yourmoney/21mobile.html>.

Martel, Ned. 2005, March 14. Interested to see how it ends? So are the writers. Retrieved January 22, 2009 from *The New York Times* website: <www. nytimes.com/2005/03/14/arts/television/14lost.html>.

Marvel Enterprises, Inc. 2002, 2003, 2004, 2005, 2006, 2007, 2008. Annual report. Retrieved May 16, 2010 from: <http://marvel.com/company/index. htm?sub=annual_current.htm>.

— 2007a, August 7. Marvel Reports Q2 2007 EPS of $0.34 and Six Months 2007 EPS of $0.89. Retrieved January 24, 2010, from: <http://marvel.com/ company/pdfs/MVL_Q2_07_8-7-07.pdf>.

Mason, Fran. 2002. "A poor person's cognitive mapping," in *Conspiracy Nation: The Politics of Paranoia in Postwar America.* Ed. Peter Knight. New York: New York University Press, pp. 40–56.

Mata, Shiai. [n.d.]. Slayer lit interview. Retrieved Octover 24, 2008, from Slayer Lit Website: <www.slayerlit.us/interviews/interview11.htm>.

Media and entertainment: The digital challenge. 2008. Retrieved August 26, 2010, from: <www.ey.com/Publication/vwLUAssets/Industry_Media_ and_Entertainment_The_digital_challenge/$FILE/Industry_Media_and_ Entertainment_The_digital_challenge.pdf>.

Meehan, Eileen. 1990. "Why we don't count: The commodity audience," in *Logics of Television: Essays in Cultural Criticism.* Ed. Patricia Mellencamp. Bloomingon: Indiana University Press, pp. 117–37.

— 1991. "Holy commodity fetish, Batman," in *The Many Lives of Batman: Critical Approaches to a Superhero and His Media.* Ed. Roberta E. Pearson and William Uricchio. London: BFI Publishing, pp. 47–65.

— 2005. "Transindustrialism and synergy: Structural supports for decreasing diversity in commercial culture." *International Journal of Media and Cultural Politics* 1(1): 123–6.

Melley, Timothy. 2002. "Agency panic and the culture of conspiracy," in *Conspiracy Nation: The Politics of Paranoia in Postwar America*. Ed. Peter Knight. New York: New York University Press, pp. 57–84.

Melrose, Kevin. 2011. Brian Fuller offers first look at *Pushing Daisies* comic. Retrieved February 24, 2012 from Comic Book Resources website: <http://robot6.comicbookresources.com/2011/04/bryan-fuller-offers-first-look-at-pushing-daisies-comic/>.

Metzger, Pete. 2008, January 10. Yep, it plays like movie tie in. *Los Angeles Times*, E7.

Milliot, Jim. 1998, June 29. Two new imprints for HarperCollins. *Publishers Weekly*, 10.

Mittell, Jason. 2006. "Narrative complexity in contemporary American television." *The Velvet Light Trap* 58(1): 29–40.

Mobile TV uptake falling short. 2008. Retrieved August 26, 2010, from: <www.rcrwireless.com/article/20081015/WIRELESS/810139975/mobile-tv-uptake-falling-short>.

Morley, David. 1980. *The* Nationwide *Audience: Structure and Decoding*. London: British Film Institute.

Murray, Simone. 2005. "Brand loyalties: Rethinking content within global corporate media." *Media, Culture & Society* 27(3): 415–35.

Nail, Jim, Josh Bernoff, Chris Charron, Jennifer Joseph, and Tenley McHarg. 2005. ABC/iTunes deal cracks open the TV business model. Retrieved January 20, 2010 from: <www.forrester.com/rb/Research/abcitunes_deal_cracks_open_tv_business_model/q/id/38158/t/2>.

Navigating the era of the empowered consumer: A conversation among media, content, distribution and advertising executives. 2008. [*Pricewaterhouse Coopers*]. Retrieved January 20, 2010 from: <www.pwc.com/en_US/us/industry/entertainment-media/assets/empowered-consumer.pdf>.

Ndalianis, Angela. 2005. "Television and the neo-baroque," in *The Contemporary Television Serial*. Ed. Lucy Mazdon and Michael Hammond. Edinburgh: University of Edinburgh, pp. 83–101.

Newcomb, Horace. 1974. *TV: The Most Popular Art*. Garden City, NY: Anchor Press.

— 2007. "The production context," in *Television: The Critical View, 7th edition*. Oxford: Oxford University Press.

Newcomb, Horace and Paul M. Hirsch. 1994. "Television as cultural forum," in *Television: The Critical View, 5th edition*. Ed. Horace Newcomb. Oxford: Oxford University Press, pp. 561–73.

Newman, Michael Z. 2006. "From beats to arcs: Toward a poetics of television narrative." *Velvet Light Trap* 58(1): 16–28.

Nias, Simon. 2008, April 17. Sales models – Will books reach the point of no return. *Printweek*, 23.

Nixon, Scott. 2006. Pros and cons of licensing. Retrieved August 21, 2009 from Gamasutra website: <www.gamasutra.com/view/feature/1766/the_pros_and_cons_of_licensing.php>.

Norcliffe, Glen and Olivero Rendace. 2003. "New geographies of comic book production in North America: The new artisan, distancing and the periodic social economy." *Economic Geography* 79(3): 241–63.

Nordyke, Kimberly. 17 January 2007. Blockbusters are dead, Anderson tells NAPTE. *Hollywood Reporter*.

O'Donnell, Casey. 2008. The work/play of the interactive new economy: Video game development in the United States and India. UMI microform 3329039.

Oi, Walter. 1971. "A Disneyland dilemma: Two-part tariffs for a Mickey Mouse monopoly." *The Quarterly Journal of Economics* 85(1): 77–96.

Oksman, Vipri, Ville Ollikainen, Elina Noppari, Carlos Herrero, and Antti Tammela. 2008. "'Podracing': Experimenting with mobile TV content consumption and delivery methods." *Multimedia Systems* 14: 105–14.

Orgad, Shani. "Mobile TV: Old and new in the construction of an emergent technology." *Convergence: The International Journal of Research into New Media Technologies* 15(2): 197–214

Ott, Brian and Cameron Walter. 2000. "Intertexuality: Interpretive practice and textual strategy." *Critical Studies in Media Communication* 17(4): 429–46.

Pearson, Roberta. 2011. "Cult television as digital television's cutting edge," in *Television as Digital Media*. Ed. James Bennett and Nikki Strange. Durham: Duke University Press, pp. 105–31.

Peckman, Matt. 2008, February 7. "Lost" – The video game: Our exclusive Q&A with its developer. Retrieved February 13, 2010 from *PC World* website: <http://blogs.pcworld.com/gameon/archives/006458.html>.

Perryman, Neil. 2008. "Doctor Who and the convergence of media." *Convergence: The International Journal of Research into New Media Technologies* 41(1): 21–39.

Peterson, Richard A. 1997. *Creating Country Music: Fabricating Authenticity*. Chicago: University of Chicago Press.

Peterson, Richard A. and N. Anand. 2004. "The culture of production perspective." *Annual Review of Sociology* 30: 311–34.

Pink, Daniel H. November 2007. Japan Ink: Inside the Manga Industrial Complex. *Wired*.

Poix, Xavier. 2006, April 1. Ubisoft's Peter Jackson's *King Kong*. *Game Developer*, 28.

Pokaski, Joe (w) and Jason Badower (a). February 12, 2007. Road Kill. [*Heroes*] #20. *The Producers' Medium: Conversations with Creators of American TV*. 1983. Ed. Robert S. Alley and Horace Newcomb. New York: Oxford University Press.

Purdin, Rickey A. 2006, December 20. Joss Whedon sinks his teeth back into the vampire slayer, and you won't believe who he has on tap to help him write it!" *WizardEntertainment.com*

Pynchon, Thomas. 1966. *The Crying of Lot 49*. Philadelphia: Lippincott.

— 1973. *Gravity's Rainbow*. New York: Viking Press.

Quality of life in the games industry: Challenges and best practices. 2004, April 20. Retrieved February 25, 2010 from the IGDA website: <www.igda.org/papers-and-reports>.

Raviv, Dan. 2002. *Comic Wars*. New York: Broadway Books.

Reardon, Marguerite. 2008. Cell phone sales hit 1 billion mark. Retrieved August 25, 2009 from: <http://news.cnet.com/8301-10784_3-9881022-7.html>.

Remo, Chris. 2010, January 15. Ubisoft CEO Guillemot explains what when wrong with *Avatar*. Retrieved from February 13, 2010 from Gamasutra website: <www.gamasutra.com/view/news/26842/Ubisoft_CEO_Guillemot_ Explains_What_Went_Wrong_With_Avatar.php>.

Rich, Motoko. 2006, August 3. HarperCollins stepping up its presence on the internet. *The New York Times*, E3.

— 2007, September 7. President of Simon & Schuster. *The New York Times*, E38.

— 2008a, April 4. New HarperCollins unit to try to cut writer advances and end unsold book returns. *The New York Times*, C3.

— 2008b, June 6. Bosses may have hastened chief's departure at HarperCollins. *New York Times*, C3.

Rise of Middleware 2.0. 2007, July 6. Retrieved February 13, 2010 from Develop website: <www.develop-online.net/features/13/Rise-of-Middleware-20>.

Robischon, Noah. 2005. Thanks to cellphones, TV screens get smaller. Retrieved August 26, 2009, from *The New York Times* website: <www. nytimes.com/2005/02/15/arts/television/15cell.html>.

Rogers, Dan Lee. 2005, June 1. Playing smart with IP: The bottom line on licensing. *Game Developer*, 17.

S&S turns ideas into action. 2006, February 27. *Publishers Weekly*, 4.

Salen, Katie and Eric Zimmerman. 2006. "The game design process," in *The Game Design Reader: A Rules of Play Anthology*. Ed. Katie Salen and Eric Zimmerman. Cambridge: MIT Press, pp. 20–5.

Scherf, Kurt. 2007. Broadband video: A market update. Retrieved August 26, 2009 from: <www.parksassociates.com/free_data/downloads/ parks-BroadbandVideo.pdf>.

Schiller, Herbert. 1969. *Mass Communications and American Empire*. New York: A.M. Kelly.

Schneider, Michael. 2007, January 15. A&E takes whack at mob hit. Retrieved August 26, 2009 from: <www.variety.com/article/VR1117957316. html?categoryid=14&cs=1>.

— 2007, October 29. Nets turn 'niche' shows into hits. *Variety*.

Seabrook, John. 2012, January 16. Streaming dreams: YouTube turns pro. Retrieved February 29, 2012 from New Yorker website: <www.newyorker. com/reporting/2012/01/16/120116fa_fact_seabrook>.

Senior, Antonia. 2008, February 13. Publishers are braced for the slow death of the book. *The Times (London)*, 41.

Sharon Waxman. 2007, June 18. Marvel wants to flex its own heroic muscles. *The New York Times*.

Siklos, Richard. 2006. Seeking executive to tame the digital future. Retrieved August 21, 2009 from *The New York Times* website: <www.nytimes. com/2006/11/26/business/yourmoney/26frenzy.html>.

Singer, Jill. 2004, September 28. *Q&A: Jen Bergstrom*. Retrieved October 24, 2008, from Mediabistro website: <http:///www.mediabistro.com/articles/ cache/a2941.asp>.

Spigel, Lynn. 1992. *Make Room For TV: Television and the Family Ideal in Postwar America*. Chicago: University of Chicago Press.

Spigel, Lynn and Michael Curtin. 1997. "Introduction," in *The Revolution wasn't Televised: Sixties Television and Social Conflict*. Ed. Lynn Spigel and Michael Curtin. London: Routledge, pp. 1–18.

Steinberg, Marc. 2009. "Anytime, anywhere: *Tetsuwan atomu* stickers and the emergence of character merchandising." *Theory, Culture & Society* 26(2–3): 113–38.

Stewart, James B. 2006. *Disney War*. New York: Simon & Schuster.

Stigler, George J. and Gary S. Becker. 1977. "De gustibus non est disputandum." *The American Economics Review* 67(2): 76–90.

Story, Louise. 2008. Nielsen looks beyond TV, and hits roadblocks. Retrieved August 21, 2009 from *The New York Times* website: <www.nytimes.com/2008/02/26/business/media/26nielsen.html>.

Sztompka, Piotr. 1999. *Trust: A Sociological Theory*. Cambridge: Cambridge University Press.

Tabu, Hannibal. 2007, March 16. WWLA: Aspen comics panel. Retrieved January 24, 2010 from the Comic Book Resources website: <www.comicbookresources.com/?page=article&id=9674.>.

Take Two Interactive. 2003, 2004, 2007, 2008. Annual Report. Retrieved February 24, 2010 from Take Two Interactive website: <http://ir.take2games.com/annuals.cfm>.

— 2006, 2007. Form 10-K, commission file number 0–29230. Retrieved February 13, 2010 from Take Two Interactive website: <http://ir.take2games.com/common/download/download.cfm>.

Tapscott, Don and Anthony D. Williams. 2006. *Wikinomics: How Mass Collaboration Changes Everything*. New York: Penguin Books.

Taylor, Alice. 2007, June 27. Hollywood & games: An interview with Jesse Alexander. Retrieved February 13, 2010 from *Wonderland* website: <www.wonderlandblog.com/wonderland/2007/06/hollywood-games.html>.

Television after TV: Essays on a Medium in Transition. 2004. Ed. Lynn Spigel and Jan Olsson. Durham: Duke University Press.

Television as Digital Media. 2011. Ed. James Bennett and Niki Strange. Durham: Duke University Press.

Thomas, Katie. 2009, September 29. Retired N.F.L. player Jim Brown loses. Retrieved February 13, 2010 from *The New York Times* website: <www.nytimes.com/2009/09/30/sports/ncaafootball/30colleges.html>.

Thompson, Robert J. 1996. *Television's Second Golden Age: From* Hill Street Blues *to* ER. Syracuse: Syracuse University Press.

THQ. 2001, 2002, 2003, 2004, 2005, 2006, 2007, 2008, 2009. Form 10-K, commission file number 0–18813. Retrieved February 13, 2010 from THQ website: <http://investor.thq.com/phoenix.zhtml?c=96376&p=irol-sec>.

Three heroes podcast interview with Jason Badower. 2007, June 22. Retrieved April 12, 2010 from: <http://media.podshow.com/media/6154/episodes/67167/3heroes-67167–06–22–2007_pshow_89126.mp3>.

Thrift, Nigel. 2004. "Movement-space: The changing domain of thinking resulting from the development of new kinds of spatial awareness." *Economy and Society* 33(4): 582–604.

Totilo, Stephen. 2008. *Lost* video game preview: Writer taunts me with knowledge of black smoke and four-toed statue. Retrieved February 13, 2010 from Multiplayer website: <http://multiplayerblog.mtv.com/2008/01/17/lost-vi deo-game-preview-writer-taunts-me-with-knowledge-of-black-smoke-and-th ree-toed-statue/>.

Trachtenberg, Jeffrey A. and Martin Peers. 2012, January 6. Barnes & Noble seeks next chapter. Retrieved March 5, 2012 from *Wall Street Journal* website: <http://online.wsj.com/article/SB10001424052970203513604577142 2481239801336.htm>.

Troup, Gary. 2006. *Bad Twin*. New York: Hyperion.

Urry, John. 2006. "Complexity." *Theory Culture Society* 23(2–3): 111–7.

— 2007. *Mobilities*. Cambridge: Polity.

Uzzi, Brian. 1997. "Social structure and competition in interfirm networks: The paradox of embeddedness." *Administrative Science quarterly* 42(1): 35–67.

— 2007. *Mobilities*. Cambridge: Polity.

Van Slyke, Brandon. 2008, July 1. "How a game gets made: A game's journey form concept to store shelves." *Game Developer* 19.

Varlav, W. Alex, April Slayden Mitchell, and Kenton O'Hara. 2007. 'My ipod is my pacifer': An investigation on the everyday practices of mobile video consumption. Proceedings of the eighth IEEE workshop on mobile computing systems and applications.

Venturini, Francesco. 2008. The future of broadcasting: Sustaining share holder value and high performance in a changing industry. Retrieved August 26, 2009, from: <www.accenture.com/NR/rdonlyres/A6E79670–092F-4A41– 93B9–11B63D7A0F0F/0/FutureBroadcastingFinalSingle.pdf>.

Vianello, Robert. 1994. "Rise of the telefilm and the networks' hegemony over the motion picture industry," in *American Television: New Directions in History and Theory*. Ed. Nick Browne. Langhorne, PA: Harwood Academic Pub, pp. 3–22.

Vonnegut, Kurt. 1971 [1968]. *Slaughter-House Five, or the Children's Crusade: A Duty Dance with Death*. New York: Dell.

Wallenstein, Andrew. February 22, 2008. Reilly: TV biz hasn't changed much. *Hollywood Reporter*.

Wasko, Janet. 2001. *Understanding Disney: The Manufacture of Fantasy*. Malden, MA: Blackwell.

Whitney, Daisy. 2007, April 2. Big ads for small packages. *Television week*.

Wild, David. 1999. *The Showrunners: A Season Inside the Billion-dollar, Death-defying, Madcap World of Television's Real Stars*. New York: Harper Collins.

Williams, J. P. 1988. "When you care enough to watch the very best: The mystique of *Moonlighting*." *Journal of Popular Film and Television* 16(3): 90–9.

Williams, Raymond. 1975. *Television: Technology and Cultural Form*. New York: Schocken Books.

Wolf, David. 2007. What is television these days? Retrieved August 21, 2009 from Broadcasting and Cable website: <www.broadcastingcable.com/ article/111262-What_Is_Television_These_Days_.php>.

Writing a Tie-In. [n.d.]. Retrieved October 24, 2008, from International Association of the Media Tie-in Writers website: <www.iamtw.org/art_tie. html>.

Wyatt, Edward. 2005, October 27. Unearthing books embedded in pop culture (watch out Weezer). *The New York Times.*

— 2009, January 18. The man who makes sense of *Lost. The New York Times.*

Wyatt, Justin. 1994. *High Concept: Movies and Marketing in Hollywood.* Austin: University of Texas Press.

York, Christina F. 2006. *Touch of Death.* New York: Simon Spotlight Entertainment.

Index